COMMUNITY, CONFLICT, AND THE EUCHARIST IN ROMAN CORINTH

The Social Setting of Paul's Letter

P. Coutsoumpos

University Press of America,® Inc.
Lanham · Boulder · New York · Toronto · Oxford

Copyright © 2006 by
University Press of America,® Inc.
4501 Forbes Boulevard
Suite 200
Lanham, Maryland 20706
UPA Acquisitions Department (301) 459-3366

PO Box 317
Oxford
OX2 9RU, UK

Library of Congress Control Number: 2005938640
ISBN-13: 978-0-7618-3405-2 (paperback : alk. paper)
ISBN-10: 0-7618-3405-2 (paperback : alk. paper)

CONTENTS

Acknowledgments

The present book is a revised and concise version of my dissertation that was accepted in partial requirement for a Ph.D. in Biblical and New Testament Studies at the University of Sheffield, England. My gratitude is to Professor Ralph P. Martin under whose direction and patience the research was conducted. He not only provided me with the initial idea for this study, but also with invaluable insights in the course of its preparation. I want also to express my appreciation to Professor Herold Weiss and to Dr. Leona G. Running for their special efforts in the proofreading of the study.

I am especially grateful to Mr. M. H. Soper, the director of the library at Andrews University, and Mr. Warren Johns, the Seminary Librarian, for allowing me to use the facilities. I wish to acknowledge the tremendous debt owed to Elder Manuel Vasquez who has encouraged me in more ways than one throughout the preparation of this study. I thank my children, Otis and Alex, for their patience. And my wife, Naomi, who was my typist and without whose help this project, could not have succeeded. Above all, I solely dedicate this study to God: *SOLI DEO GLORIA.*

Abbreviations

AB	Anchor Bible
ABD	Anchor Bible Dictionary
ABR	*Australian Biblical Review*
Affirmation	*Affirmation*
AnBib	Analecta biblica
ANRW	Aufstieg und Niedergang der römischen Welt
BA	Biblical Archaeologist
BAGD	W. Bauer, W. F. Arndt, F. W. Gingrich, and F. W. Danker, *A Greek-Lexicon of New Testament and Other Early Christian Literature*
Bib	*Biblica*
BR	*Biblical Research*
BTB	*Biblical Theology Bulletin*
BZ	*Biblische Zeitschrift*
CBQ	*Catholic Biblical Quarterly*
DPL	R. P. Martin, G. Hawthorne and D. Reid (eds.), *Dictionary of Paul and His Letters*
EDNT	H. Balz and G. Schneider (eds.), *Exegetical Dictionary of the New Testament*
Exp Tim	*Expository Times*
Hesp	*Hesperia*
HibJ	*Hibbert Journal*
Hist. eccl.	*Historia ecclesiastica*
HTR	*Harvard Theological Review*
IBD	J. D. Douglas and N. Hillyer (eds.), *Illustrated Bible Dictionary*
Int	*Interpretation*
JA	*Joseph and Asenath*
JBC	R. E. Brown et al. (eds.), *The Jerome Biblical Commentary*
JBL	*Journal of Biblical Literature*
JHS	*Journal of Hellenic Studies*
JJS	*Journal of Jewish Studies*

JRH	*Journal of Religious History*
JSNT	*Journal for the Study of the New Testament*
JTS	*Journal of Theological Studies*
LCL	Loeb Classical Library
NBD	New Bible Dictionary
NewDocs	G. H. R. Horsley (ed.), *New Documents Illustrating Early Christianity*
NIDNTT	C. Brown (ed.), *The New International Dictionary of New Testament Theology*
NovT	*Novum Testamentum*
NT	New Testament
NTS	*New Testament Studies*
OCD	Oxford Classical Dictionary
OT	Old Testament
RB	*Revue Biblique*
RelSRev	*Religious Studies Review*
RevExp	*Review and Expositor*
RevistB	*Revista Bíblica*
RevQ	*Revue de Qumrân*
SBLDS	Society of Biblical Literature Dissertation Series
SBLSP	Society of Biblical Literature Seminar Papers
SCHNT	Studia ad Corpus Hellenisticum Novi Testamenti
SE	*Studia Evangelica*
SJT	*Scottish Journal of Theology* Str-B (H. Strack and) P. Billerbeck, *Kommentar zum Neuen Testament aus Talmud und Midrasch*
TDNT	G. Kittel and G. Friedrich (eds.), *Theological Dictionary of the New Testament*
ThRu	*Theologische Rundschau*
TJ	*Trinity Journal*
TS	*Theological Studies*
TynBul	*Tyndale Bulletin*
TZ	*Theologische Zeitschrift*
ZNW	*Zeitschrift für die Neutestamentliche Wissenschaft*

Chapter 1

Introduction

It is recognized by the majority of scholars that the city of Corinth was established as a Roman colony in 44 B.C.E. Roman Corinth made use of the Roman way of government and architecture. On the other hand, the city of Corinth had Hellenistic social way of life and its influence all around it.[1] The apostle Paul established a Christian Church in Roman Corinth (1 Cor. 3:6,10; 4:15; Acts 18) during the second missionary journey to Greece (Acts 18:11,18). As leader and founder, Paul kept a continuing association with the church community there and wrote at least four letters to the Corinthians. Paul's epistles were written to solve problems and to encourage the church members in their faith.[2] In 1 Corinthians, Paul refers to a specific form of idolatry that he apparently had discussed in a previous letter. Another issue was the conflict caused by gluttony and drunkenness. As chapter three of this study suggests, gluttony was characteristic of the *symposia*, especially at the *eranos* dinner party. In Paul's view, these gluttony and drunkenness were the main causes of factions and the social problems in the church at Roman Corinth.

Furthermore, Paul addresses a wide range of social issues in the life of the church, such as factions, litigation, sexual morality, food offered to idols, and son on. This letter in particular (1 Corinthians) thus gives an exclusive window onto the social life of an early Christian congregation. It is clear that the Corinthians congregation faced various kinds of division and tensions, and a range of problematic issues, but the nature and causes of these problems are, as we will see, topic to much debate.

The divisions at the Lord's Supper (Eucharist in 1 Corinthians 11:17-34) were basically divisions along social groups, with the well-to-do receiving higher quality and quantity of food, and the poor members going without. This practice was common in the Greco-Roman world. Paul was concern with the well being of the church and their behavior. However, the Eucharist embarrassment (the behavior of the well-to-do) of 1 Corinthians 11: 17-34 increases the suspicious of the false theology on the sacrament in line with the false theology stress on baptism as well.[3] Therefore, the behavior of the rich was condemned by Paul because it went against of the principle of decorum and of the church's practices, especially the Lord's Supper.

The apostle probably had two groups in mind, those who had their own meal and those who had nothing. In other words, as in the common practice of the *eranos*, or "potluck dinner" (a social custom instituted in classical Greece through the Roman Empire), the participants brought their own food-basket. The ones who arrived late often had neither time nor money to prepare sufficiently for them. This conduct was not a problem for the wealthy Gentile Christians at Roman Corinth. In the Gentile social context, this was common behavior.

In addition, there were the problems of temple banquets and food sold in the marketplace (*macellum*). These practices were a regular part of life in the Greco-Roman world and the city of Roman Corinth.[4] The eating of meat offered to idols (cultic meals) was evidently so common; no one gave it a second thought. Thus, the problem in chapter 8 to show the background of the Gentile Christians in Roman Corinth who had been participating in such banquets and buying meat sacrificed to idols. Paul deals with this problem directly in chapters 8 and 10, and indirectly in chapter 9. Related to the above issues are the following questions: (a) what was the Corinthian attitude towards participation in table fellowship with pagans and the use of meat offered to idols? (b) Did Paul approve or disapprove of such attitudes? (c) What was Paul's answer to their question regarding εἰδωλόθυτα?

Another piece of information can be obtained from Paul's explanation of the unique situation of the church at Roman Corinth. His first epistle indicates that the practice of the Lord's Supper, together with the worship activities, corresponds to the same practice of sacred meals, especially the *eranos* normally held in Greco-Roman societies.[5] Further, the existence of αἱρέσει and σχίσματα among the church members (1 Cor. 1:10; 11:18) was only one cause of the many problems Paul had with the Corinthians. It is possible; therefore, that some of the divisions in Roman Corinth arose from divisions among household gatherings.

This study addresses the problem that arose from their not having been adequately resocialized into the traditions of their newly adopted Christian religion. It seems clear that some members still participated in religious meals in the pagan temples (1 Cor. 8:10; 10:20-21). Many were invited to meals where the food served had been offered to the idols (1 Cor. 10: 27-32). Consequently, it is no surprise that Greco-Roman social practices with regard to Greek *eranos,*[6] within the context of religious societies, had a considerable impact on the structure, customs, and decorum of the Lord's meal eaten at Roman Corinth. It may be significant to put forward the thesis that these conflicts have a social background.[7] Consequently, understanding social distinctions and practices is an essential part of understanding the Corinthian letter.

The apostle evidently regarded the eating of idol food and participating in a banquet in a pagan temple as a much more serious problem than he had dealt with before. This matter strikes at the heart of both the Lord's Supper and the gospel tradition handed down to the Corinthian Church by Paul. These issues, as well as additional ones, will be studied as part of the whole picture of the Lord's Supper in 1 Corinthians 11.

The Significance of the Problem

This study is significant, first of all, as a contribution to the understanding of several specific conflicts that arose in Paul's church community at Roman Corinth. It also explores the internal social dynamics and the relationship between Paul and the church members as they dealt with those problems. This research has to consider both the character of this particular congregation and the socio-theological issue involved in the Lord's Supper. 1 Corinthians 8, 10, and 11 clearly show that there was disagreement and factiousness (σχίσμα) among the church members because of gluttony, drunkenness, and the lack of tolerance in understanding one another's social and religious differences. These difficulties within the Corinthian congregation had led to animosity among church members, especially in regard to participation in the Lord's Supper. Thus, this investigation is significant as a study of the social, theological, and cultural conflict within the Christian Church and of Paul's way of dealing with such difficulties.

This research is significant for understanding the apostle's particular approach to socio-ethical problems, and especially Paul's response to the Corinthian dilemma regarding the Lord's Supper. The discussion is basically about interpersonal behavior between the church members. It is important for this study to know the way Paul deals with those specific problems at Roman Corinth.

General Introduction to this Study

The problem of the influence of sacred and social meals in the Greco-Roman world on the Lord's Supper has not been the focus of an in-depth study.

Furthermore, some of the social customs and problems (discussed in chapters 2 and 5) in the Corinthian assembly were quite similar to the ones in Greco-Roman culture. For example, in the Corinthian Church there were problems of divisions and factions, similar to those of the ancient *symposia* and the *eranos*. These factions stemmed from competition over status issues such as place of honor, and portion or quality of food and wine.

Additionally, as well as the differences in food, location, and posture, the length of time one had to eat were important. The wealthy Corinthians, after a series of exercises at the bath, arrived first at the meal, while the poor working class came later. This would explain Paul's suggestion to wait for one another (1 Cor. 11: 33, 34). Another important point typical of the *eranos* meal is the conduct of the host and sometimes the guests. The wealthy ones did not have any problem with their consciences when they began eating before the others arrived. Nobody at a Greco-Roman dinner party would ask the latecomers whether they had already eaten. Thus, the way the Gentile Christians behaved at Roman Corinth did not correspond to the spirit of selflessness exemplified in Christ.

According to the Greco-Roman "potluck" custom, each member brought his or her own food, but some came early and began to eat before the others arrived. This corresponds to the pattern found in the Christian *eranos* meal at Roman Corinth. The Corinthian Gentile Christians simply continued to behave as a part of the Greco-Roman society.

In his monograph, *The Social Setting of Christianity*, Theissen studies the "Social World of Early Christianity." In four essays he considers Paul's exchange of letters with the Corinthians. These essays contain a coherent exegetical study and give a point-by-point exposition of Theissen's innovative, yet generally accepted, way of interpreting the social context of the New Testament. He adds, "Exegetical attention has largely concentrated on the theological dimensions of the dissension in Corinth."[8] But more than merely a theological controversy, this conflict has a social background and becomes clearer when we connect its social conditions with the theological issues in 1 Cor. 11:17ff.

The next section of this study tackles the problem of meat sacrificed to idols. Barrett rightly points out that "The subject is one that raises several of the most pressing problems in the literary study of 1 Corinthians and the historical study of the life of Paul, to say nothing of important theological issues."[9] The problem of eating εἰδωλόθυτα occupied part of a letter written to Paul by the Christian Church at Roman Corinth.

The question is whether Paul is consistent in what he says when he rebukes the church for eating food sacrificed to idols and participating in the Lord's Supper at the same time. It seems contradictory since Paul is against eating εἰδωλόθυτα, yet in vv. 25ff. he tells the congregation that they are free to eat anything sold in the *macellum*. Much of the study and exegetical work on 1 Cor. 11: 17-26 that has been done just focuses on the theological dimension rather than the social aspect of it (especially vv.23-25). We will attempt, however, to link an exegesis of the theological and sociological issues. The social and theological issues are intrinsically connected in Paul's view to the factions problems over which the Corinthian congregation is divided (1 Cor. 12:12-31), an issue that some scholars do not address.

Very little attention has been devoted to the sociological problems involved in the practice of the Lord's Supper in the Hellenistic Corinthian Church. Even the commentaries on the epistle (such as Barrett, Conzelmann, and Fee), because of their larger interests, have not thoroughly explored the important role of the social background.

G. Wainwright has commented that most books on Eucharistic theology treat only three main aspects: The presence of the Lord at the sacrament, the cross in relation to the sacrificial nature of the sacrament, and the effects on the individual of participating in the communion.[10] Furthermore, he is concerned with an element that has been neglected in previous works: "The eschatological nature of the Lord's Supper."

Notes

[1] John Fotopoulos, *Food Offered to Idols in Roman Corinth.* (Tübingen: J. C. B. Mohr (Paul Siebeck), 2003), 158.

[2] A. Chapple, "Local Leadership in the Pauline Churches: Theological and Social Factors in Its Development." (Ph. D. diss., Durham University, 1984), 1ff.

[3] Michael D. Goulder. *Paul and the Competing Mission in Corinth.* (Peabody: Hendrickson Publishers, 2001), 31.

[4] P. Coutsoumpos. "The Social Implication of Idolatry in Revelation 2:12: Christ or Caesar?" *Biblical Theology Bulletin* 27 (1997): 25.

[5] Frequently, the patterns of Jewish religious associations are assumed to have had the greatest influence on early Christian socio-religious structures. However, a warning must be considered against the tendency to find single socio-cultural explanations for the various organizations of Christian groups throughout the Greco-Roman world.

[6] Peter Lampe, "The Corinthians Eucharistic Dinner Party: Exegesis of a Cultural Context (1 Cor. 11:17-34)," *Affirmation* 4 (1991): 1-3. "*Eranos* can be translated as 'potluck dinner,' although "potluck" has a narrow definition as a meal where all the food brought by the participants is shared on a common table." Further discussion regarding the *eranos* meal will appear in chapters 2 and 5 of this thesis.

[7] Especially significant here is the information we can obtain from 1 Cor. 11 on the conflict at the Lord's Supper. In this chapter, Paul is silent regarding theological issues. It seems clear that the problem is of a social nature.

[8] Ibid. 18f.

[9] C. K. Barrett, *Essays on Paul* (London: SPCK, 1982), 35-40. Barrett says that Dr. Ehrhardt accepts Hans Lietzmann's argument that all or almost all the meat that was sold in the macellum was εἰδωλόθυτον, sacrificed to idols in nearby temples. This argument is not completely acceptable because H. J. Cadbury, in his article published in the *Journal of Biblical Literature,* "The Macellum of Corinth," shows that "the meat may have been sold on the hoof or slaughtered in the macellum as well as sold already butchered or sacrificed in a temple."

[10] G. Wainwright, *Eucharist and Eschatology* (London: Epworth Press, 1978), 64-68.

Chapter 2

Social Meals in the Greco-Roman World

The purpose of this chapter is to set the background for the chapters which follow, especially for the examination of 1 Corinthians in chapters 4 and 5. In this section of the study my dependence on the work of others, especially D. E. Smith, will be clear. Most meals follow a similar pattern in the Greco-Roman social world. The next step is to study the social meal and its different customs in the Greco-Roman world.

Introduction

We have mentioned some aspects of the social Greco-Roman meal custom which throw light on parts of Paul's discussion of the Lord's Supper.[1] The practices of the meals in the entire Mediterranean world seem to have become standardized in some details during the Greco-Roman times and beyond (ca. 200 B.C.E. to 200 C. E.).[2] Although some differences occurred, all these meals essentially adapted the same standard practices to suit specific functions. Certainly, the influence of these cultures had an impact on the practices of the meal at Roman Corinth. Generally, in the Greco-Roman society a formal meal indicated an assembly of a group of friends and family for a celebration that meant more than to satisfy the appetite. It was a social occasion, and the social meal was understood in the Greco-Roman period as "Communal meal."[3]

Four types of communal or formal meals in the Greco-Roman society are particularly significant to this study: (1) the Greek meal: *Deipnon/symposium*; (2) the Roman meal: *Cena/Convivium*; (3) the Greco-Roman *Eranos* meal, and

(4) the Christian *Eranos* meal. Also important is the social stratification and rank in the Greco-Roman society.

The Greek Meal: *Deipnon Symposium*

The symposium custom became very popular and was considered in classical times a social event, particularly in the Greco-Roman time. The fundamental structure of the symposium appears to be unchanged from the time of Homer. The symposium was both a private and public celebration. Generally, the symposium was set in the context of the big meal of the day, the Greek δεῖπνον (or as we will discuss later, the Roman *cena*), which normally began around the ninth or tenth hour of the day.[4]

It is interesting to notice that in Homer's time, it was often eaten about the middle of the day. The other two meals of the day would be the αἴριστον, morning meal (probably breakfast), and the δόρποι, or the meal of the night.[5] These and other changes in the structure of the meal in the classical time showed a fundamental change in the total aspect of the different meals. If a man reclined at a meal, he took the posture of the social high class, a posture commonly taken by the aristocratic class.[6] The Greek δεῖπνον normally took place shortly before sundown, or sometimes even after sundown. In the Greek symposium (δεῖπνον), 36 or more guests attended the meal, while in the Roman *convivium* 6, 9, or sometimes 12 guests participated in the meal. Plutarch also mentioned that couches were shared, and some rich people built large dinning-rooms that had the capacity to hold thirty couches or probably even more.[7] It was a common practice not to serve wine with the meal, but to save it for the πότος after the δεῖπνον proper.[8] Clearly, in both the tradition and the practice, the symposium was considered as a social expression of Greek religion.

It was the normal custom to issue invitations to the banquets. To get together with friends or business or religious associates, one would invite them to his home for a meal.[9] Banquets were also held on significant family occasions, such as birthdays, weddings, and funerals. Invitations to the banquet usually specified the hour, but the most probable time was a little before sunset.

The host expected the guests to arrive on time, but latecomers were quite common. Similar situations happened at Corinth, where some members came earlier and others arrived late for the Lord's Supper. Plato commented that Agathon, the host of the banquet, started the banquet without one of his guests, who arrived late, though the latecomer was warmly welcomed when the meal was almost finished.[10]

As the guests arrived, certain customs often were observed before the banquet started. A servant met the participant at the door and led him to the dining room. Then, other servants would remove his shoes and wash his feet, after which he would be ready to take his place on the couch.[11] Normally, the guest took his place according to his social status. "These positions became especially well defined in the Roman period."[12]

Thus, the use of this practice, promoted a consciousness of the social rank of the guest invited into the banquet. Lucian describes a banquet at which women were invited, and a latecomer guest was welcomed to sit, since all the reclining positions were taken by the other guests. He refused, on the ground that sitting at a banquet was 'womanish and weak' (γυναικεῖον καί μαλθακόν). Rather he decided to recline on the floor as a sign of his high social status.[13]

However, for the classical Greek era, the correlation of positions and status is more difficult. The position most honored was the first place (πρῶτος), apparently to the right of the host. The positions around the room to the right were given to the guests according to their rank, with the last position being the lowest. These places were commonly assigned by the owner of the house to the guests according to their social status.[14] There were some instances where two or three people shared the same couch.[15] While the social status of the guests was assumed, there was also a sense of social equality among the participants. Smith points out that it is not always clear what is meant by the term "equal," since it did not indispensably rule out the traditional pre-requisites of one's status.[16]

Plutarch's observation is especially instructive. He pointed out that, "in the accompanying conversation, such equality at the meal is argued for as an inherent aspect of banquet 'friendship'." According to this line of argument, the diners should leave behind the divisive social rankings of outer society and in effect form a new society with new social rules when they entered the door of the dining chamber."[17] Plutarch suggested that when the members participated in the meal, they should agree to sit wherever they wished, without worrying about their social rank.

In addition to differences in food, location, and posture, Smith observes that another division is mentioned in 1 Corinthians: Distinctions in the length of time one had to eat. The well-to-do were the main offenders in eating a private meal, because they could begin earlier than the others. They had more time in the evening, whereas the working class would arrive late to the meeting.[18]

Paul admonished the Corinthians to wait for one another (1 Cor. 11:33). It is interesting to notice that in one matter Pliny's suggested solution can be compared with Paul's: In the communal meal, one of the social high classes should adjust his eating habits to those appropriate to one of a lower social class. Martial's criticism is with the idea to elevate those of the lower class to the same level as the ones in the high social class:

Since I am asked to dinner, no longer, as before, a purchased guest, why is
not the same dinner served to me as to you? You take oysters fattened in the
Lucrine lake, I suck a mussel through a hole in the shell; you get mushrooms,
I take hog funguses; you tackle turbot, but I brill. Golden with fat, a
turtledove gorges you with bloated rump; there is set before me a magpie that
has died in its cage. Why do I dine without you although, Ponticus, I am
dining with you? The dole has gone: let us have the benefit of that; let us eat
the same fare.[19]

In another passage, Martial expressed himself more bitterly, even cursing
his host who flaunted before all the other guests his social superiority.
Differences in honor according to the place the person should sit naturally
caused further social offenses.[20]

It was customary for the household slaves to serve the food on the table.
Trays were also placed on the tables. Tables were arranged one to a couch or
group of couches, so as Lucian mentioned in many cases, diners might partake
from the same table.

A characteristic arrangement is the one provided by the dining room of the
Asklepeion at Roman Corinth, which dates from the 4th century B. C. E.[21] For
instance, there were nine couches of stone arranged along the wall with an
opening for the doorway. It seems that the couches were of a size to
accommodate one person at a time. Obviously the portable tables were more
practical for cleaning the floor between the courses and after the completion of
the meal.[22]

Another characteristic element was the menu of the meals. It consisted of
bread, a variety of vegetables, and fish or meat if the meal was especially
luxurious. There was a variety of bread since it was considered part of the main
course. The vegetables might be lettuce, beans, onions, leeks, herbs, or olives.
Fish might be prepared in a variety of ways. Meat was generally available to the
public only at special celebrations whenever sacrifices were made.[23] In fact, all
the meat for the Greek table came from the temple where meat was sacrificed to
the idols. Frequently, according to Athenaeus, meat from sacrificial animals
seems to have been preferred for the δεῖπνον proper.[24]

An elaborate series of events marked the end of the main meal (the
δεῖπνον) and the beginning of the second part of the meal (the symposium).
The tables were removed (αἴρειν τὰς τραπέζας) and one of the servant swept
the floor. Hand washing before and after the meals was a common part of
Greco-Roman meal customs. This is an allusion that Athenaeus also mentioned,
"water over the hand, tables brought in."[25] The bringing of the tables to the
meals refers to the serving of the food. After the meal was finished the tables
were removed, and the πότος or symposium itself began.

There was a libation of unmixed wine offered to "the good demon" ($\dot{\alpha}\gamma\alpha\theta o\hat{\upsilon}$ $\delta\alpha\dot{\iota}\mu o\nu o\varsigma$) and a paean was sung ($\pi\alpha\iota\alpha\nu\dot{\iota}\zeta\epsilon\iota\nu$).[26] According to Smith, the order of these events probably was different.[27] It is understandable that the libation and the removal of the tables usually distinguished the transition from the eating to the drinking part of the meal.

The wine ceremonies were different from place to place. However, the first libation was given with unmixed wine and was dedicated to the "Good gods." But most of the time this libation took place immediately after the main meal rather than during the meal.[28] The symposium was begun with three libations to: (1) the Olympian gods generally, (2) the heroes, and (3) Zeus Soter; after the first libation a song was sung in honor of Dionysos (the god of wine and intoxication).[29]

Furthermore, the main cup from the bowl of mixed wine was offered to Zeus- Savior. Another common practice called for three bowls to be mixed at once. The first cup from each of these bowls was then offered to the Olympians, the second to the Heroes, and the last one to Zeus-Savior.[30] When the wine was poured into the cup, the name of the god was mentioned ($\dot{\alpha}\gamma\alpha\theta o\hat{\upsilon}$ $\delta\alpha\dot{\iota}\mu o\nu o\varsigma$, $\Delta\iota\dot{o}\varsigma$ $\sigma\omega\tau\hat{\eta}\rho o\varsigma$). The symposiarch would then pronounce the name of the god once again and pour a portion of wine into the fire or onto the floor. He would drink from it and pass the cup around for each participant to drink from the cup, mentioning the name of the god in the genitive as all of them did likewise.[31]

Next, a song of victory was sung. The specific nature of the hymn at the end of the meal is not known, but the religious element is clear. Plato also pointed out that the guests sang a hymn of victory to the god: "after this, it seems, when Socrates had taken his place and had dined with the rest, they made libation and sang a chant to the god and so forth, as custom bids, till they betook them to drinking"[32] It is interesting to see here a close parallel with the Jewish and Christian benediction. In its basic nature, the custom is quite similar to the Greco-Roman custom which, of course, involved a different god and a different motive.

The second or final event of the meal was the serving of the dessert ($\tau\rho\alpha\gamma\dot{\eta}\mu\alpha\tau\alpha$). A variety of fruits and salty nuts were served, which made the people thirsty and prepared them for the enjoyment of the drinking section. This part of the meal was known as the *symposium or potos* (the drinking party). It was the time left aside for serious consumption of wine.[33]

The entertainment might include music, art, dance, and philosophical conversation. In the classical Greek period it was difficult to imagine a meal without drinking. Normally, the Greeks finished their meal with some drinking and conversation which was the basic element of a symposium. The philosophical tradition of the symposium was contained in a motif in which one of the main diversions of the meal was the philosophical conversation appropriate to an assembly of philosophers. The meals in the philosophical schools often were accompanied by philosophical conversation.[34]

In the symposia a philosopher was considered a poor guest if he did not speak in a rhetorical way.[35] Those who thought themselves as sophists were normally invited to banquets. Athenaeus called this kind of person a "dinner-chasing sophist."[36] This philosophical tradition was developed on the precedent constituted in Plato's Symposium:

> Since it has been resolved, then, said Eryximachus, that we are to drink only so as each desires, with no constraint on any, I next propose that the flute-girl who came in just now be dismissed: let her pipe to herself or, if she likes, to the women-folk within, but let us seek our entertainment today in conversation.[37]

This philosophical tradition became one of the most important elements of the symposium and was also used in Jewish and Christian communities. Early Christianity took in the conversation form fairly quickly, but was very slow in adopting the symposium as a literary genre.[38] In fact, in the Early Christian literature, there are no examples of the literary genre of the symposium. This made Early Christianity independent of such influence.

Besides the philosophical conversation, party games and dramatic presentation became also part of the banquet. However, the overstatement of the vase painters and satirists should not be taken as the norm for the symposium.[39] Plato and other writers emphasized that the purpose of a symposium was not just for eating and drinking without control, but where decency and refinement was the ideal norm.[40]

The Roman Meal: *Cena or Convivium*

In general, the meal practices of the Romans were quite similar to those of the Greeks. Both commonly ate three times a day. Normally, however, the majority of the people would eat their main meal of the day in the evening.[41] The first meal of the morning was called *ientaculum* which was regularly taken at the early hours of the morning or the third or fourth hour of the day. It was considered a very light meal, but not as light than the Greek meal called ἀκράτισμα.[42]

A characteristic morning breakfast might have bread with salt and a variety of dried fruit, olives, cheese, or eggs.[43] The common drink of the morning meal could be a glass of milk or *mulsum*, a drink which was made of wine mixed with pure honey.[44]

The meal of the middle of the day was called *prandium* which was eaten around the sixth hour. Like the Greeks, the Roman considered this midday meal the most important meal of the day and it was called the *cena*. The custom was changed and this meal became the evening meal, taking the place of the *vesperna*, and the meal at the middle of the day was called the *prandium*.[45] Subsequently, the *cena* followed this midday meal just three hours later, so the *prandium* meal was considered a light meal. This meal normally consisted of what they called *reliquies* or leftovers from the meal eaten the day before.[46]

The example from Seneca could be considered illustrative of one of the most sober meals, and might be characterized by: "dry bread," and no "need of a table, no need to wash my hands afterwards."[47] Guests might be invited too, but this was not the common practice. It was a familiar type of meal.

During the summer time, the *prandium* was succeeded by the siesta or *meridiatio* which was taken around the seventh hour of the day. In winter the days were cooler, and shorter, so no siesta was taken after the *prandium* meal.[48] The *merenda* was a less common term; it seems synonymous with the *prandium* meal. Isidorus commented that there was not time for the *merenda* between the *prandium* meal and the *cena*.[49]

It was very common for the Roman aristocrats to exercise and take a bath after the siesta. This was to stimulate the appetite for the *cena*, the main meal of the day. Regularly, it started around the ninth hour and finished at dark, lasting two or three hours. In the summertime, the ninth hour began around 2:31 to 3:46 and the sunset was not until about 7:30. The ninth hour in winter was around 1:20 to 2:13, since the days were shorter, and a meal could also last until dark at about 4:30.[50] A typical meal in the evening would commonly finish with a time of relaxation, including a drink and conversation. The Greeks, according to Pliny, have a distinction between the familiar meal at home and the formal meal taken with a friend or one's club or special celebration. When the family ate together, they might use a special family room for the meal at home.

However, a formal supper would be taken in the dining room of the house. On this special occasion the host invited the guests for the enjoyment of fine food and good wine. The invitations to such meal would usually be extended in advance because the host family paid a *quota* for the participants and bought enough food for everybody.[51]

The banquet size varied from three to nine guests according to the occasion. The ideal size of the room was large enough in order to accommodate all the guests comfortably. Plutarch's opinion was the same.[52] If the available space was too small for the guests, it was considered an insult to the participants of the banquet. The proper custom was that even if the host had plenty of space, the meeting should be kept to the smallest size possible.[53] Plutarch commented on the matter and concluded:

If both space and the provisions are ample, we must still avoid great number, because they in themselves interfere with sociability and conversation. It is worse to take away the pleasure of conversation at table than to run out of wine. . . . People who bring together too many guests to one place do prevent general conversation; they allow only a few to enjoy each other's society, for the guests separate into groups of two or three in order to meet and converse, completely unconscious of those whose place on the couches is remote and not looking their way because they are separated from them by practically the length of a race course. . . . So it is a mistake for the wealthy to build showy dining rooms that hold thirty couches or more. Such magnificence makes for unsociable and unfriendly banquets (ἄμικτον καὶ ἄφιλον δεῖπνον) where the manager of a fair is needed more than a toastmaster.[54]

Obviously, the solution was to entertain regularly a small company of guests, so the banquet would not lose its ideal purpose. Thus, it was preferable to invite a group of three or four guests to the meal. Martial observed that the Roman *cena* consisted of three different main meals. The *gustatio* or *promulsis* consisted of dishes that were intended to whet the appetite. This meal normally included eggs as well as certain vegetables which were thought to help the digestion.[55] The drink used on this occasion was what they called *mulsum*, a wine mixed with honey.

The main Roman meal was called the *fercula* or courses. It was divided in three parts: The *prima, altera,* and *tertia cena.* Specifically, the *altera cena* was customarily the main meal or what they called the *caput cenae.*[56] The third meal was the dessert or *mensae secundae* (second tables). It consisted of different kinds of nuts, fruits, and sweet cakes or *bellaria* which had become popular during the Roman time. Similar to the Greek symposium, this part of the meal was named the *comissatio* or *convivium*, which was considered as the time for drinking and amusement.

Moreover, the Roman meal might have drinking and entertainment during the banquet, while the *convivium* was reserved especially for the dialogue.[57] The Roman aristocrats became notorious for their intemperance. There were laws against drunkenness and gluttony.[58] Though these excesses were common in the Roman period, they were not considered proper behaviour at the table.

The Greco-Roman *Eranos* Meal

The fundamental pattern of the fellowship meal in ancient times was widely followed in different settings and cultural backgrounds. Thus Greeks, Romans, Jews, and probably Christians, followed the same pattern for a formal meal whether it was a family meal, philosophical gathering, club meeting or a sacred meal.[59]

Private meals were of two major kinds, those for which the cost was shared among the participants (*eranos*), and those free to the guests.[60] The family and invitational meals belong to the latter group while the religious meals of different clubs or association belong to the former group. The symposium as well as the *eranos* meal was very popular social customs in classical times, especially among the Greeks, and Romans.[61] The main practices and rules of etiquette in the Corinthian Church appear to be similar to the customs of the surrounding Greco-Roman culture. However, there is one important aspect of the meal at Roman Corinth that has not adequately been treated, the Greco-Roman *eranos* meal.[62] Therefore, a study of the *eranos* meal is in order. It will provide the proper background for the interpretation of the social meal in the church at Corinth.

The Greek term *eranos* can be translated as "potluck dinner" or "picnic," although the meaning of the term can be understood in a more ample sense. H. G. Liddell's Greek English Lexicon defined the term as: "meal to which each contributed his share, picnic."[63] The *eranos* practice can be traced back to Homer's days. The visitors either contributed with money or food in baskets.[64] According to Aristophanes, the invitation was to "Come at once to dinner, and bring your pitcher and your supper chest."[65] The entertainer normally provided wreaths, perfumes, and sweets, while the visitors, especially the wealthy, sometimes contributed their own meal, which was prepared in the home of the host. Packed fish, several kinds of meat, and cooked goods were prepared for the *eranos* meal. For instance, Xenophon describes how the partakers at a potluck dinner brought *opson:*

> Whenever some of those who came together for dinner brought more meat and fish (*opson*) than others, Socrates would tell the waiter either to put the small contributions into the common stock or to portion them out equally among the diners. So the ones who brought a lot felt obliged not only to take their share of the pool, but to pool their own supplies in return; and so they put their own food also into the common stock. Thus they got no more that those who brought little with them.[66]

Xenophon's description of the *eranos* ("potluck dinner") shows a problem similar to the problem in the Corinthian Church. Paul as well as Socrates tried to protect the *eranos* meal from such abuses; it was not allowed that some should eat a lot while others remained hungry. Greco-Roman clubs of all types often had potluck dinners, and sometimes seem too had been organized almost specially with the idea of providing banquets for their members from a common purpose. Literary and archeological sources contain the records of their official business and often describe rules for their *eranos* meals.[67]

In order to understand the social-cultural context of the Gentile Christian meal at Roman Corinth, it is necessary to know what happened in a typical Greco-Roman *eranos*. Habitually, a bath was taken in the afternoon at the eighth hour of the day.[68] Commonly, at the ninth hour the participants met for the meal in the host's house.[69] Participants reclined at the so-called "First Tables" and various servings were given. Next was the *symposium* at the "Second Tables."[70] The following chart outlines a typical Greco-Roman *eranos* meal.

The Greco-Roman Dinner Party
(Dinner + Symposium/*Eranos*)

- Dinner at "First Tables"
Break
Start of the **"Second Tables"**
- a sacrifice, invocation of the house
  gods and of the geniuses of
  the host and of the emperor

-Second Tables
(often with guests who had newly arrived)
- a toast for the good spirit of
the house, the tables are removed
- the first wine jug is mixed,
libation, singing

- drinking, conversation
music, singing, entertainment
in a loose sequence

The significance of the *eranos* meal is described by Athenaeus. Together with the dinners (δεῖπνα), in private and social associations such as the *orgeones* and *thiasoi*, the participants gather together and share the food basket brought by the diners:

καλεῖτας δ᾽ ὁ αὐτος καὶ ἔρανος καὶ θίασος καί οἱ συνίοντες ἐρανισταί καὶ θιασῶται (and the same dinner may be called *eranos* or *thiasos*, and the members who come together *eranistai* or *thiasotai*).[71]

Greco-Roman clubs normally provided or assigned their members to bring food to the *eranos* meals. Similar to the symposium, the *eranos* meal was a drinking party and often resulted in intoxication.[72] According to Aune, this was the reason *eranos* was prohibited in Sparta and Crete; elsewhere the person in charge tried to stop the meal on time in order to avoid such behavior.[73] To an educated person such as Plutarch, the danger of disorder (ἀταξία) was a constant threat to the *eranos* meal (*qu. conv.* 615E, 618C). Gluttony (as it happened in many symposia) was also another form of self-gratification peculiar to the *eranos* meal.[74] Plutarch also described a meal at which guests brought food for them and complains that this resulted in a disorganized *eranos* meal and the destruction of the real fellowship. He adds that "where each guest has his own private portion, fellowship perishes."[75] It seems clear that according to this data, some of the participants brought their own meal and ate it on their own schedule. Another common practice in the Greco-Roman meals was to serve different types of food to different guests according to their social status. This difference in food was not so much intended to save money, but to reinforce the social distinction.[76] Juvenal describes an *eranos* meal where a patron practices such unfair serving:

> You're given a wine that even a poultice would not take. . . but your host drinks vintage wine, bottled when consuls wore long hair and beards. You're served bread you can scarley break, a hard lump of dough already spread with mold, impervious to teeth and sure to crack your jaws. But a loaf made out of fine flour, snow-white and soft as gauze, is served your host.

> Look at that mammoth lobster, with garnish of asparagus, being served your host . . . For you a shrimp is served in state--one shrimp afloat on one half of one egg on a tiny plate.

> Look, that half-eaten hare he'll give us now, or from the haunch of boar some bits; we'll get what's left of the capon soon. So all of you sit in silence, ready, with bread held tight, untasted, and wait.[77]

Given such practice, it would have been common behavior for the wealthier to have for themselves the best food without considering the welfare of the poor. Regardless of the arrangement, there was a ranking assigned to the position and social status of the guests.[78] Often Plutarch stresses the point that there should be equality among the visitors: σὴ ἰσότης τοῖς ἀνδράσι.[79] Some thought that the participants at an *eranos* meal should change in age and outlook. Exclusiveness should not exist when the idea of real fellowship is in mind. There was a time when both slaves and masters found themselves at the same *eranos* meal.

Plutarch's ethical meal discussions are relevant to the study of the *eranos* meal, for he follows second century C. E. philosophical and popular ethics, and also he gives a rich discussion of meals. He shows people from different social status sharing a meal in a friendly atmosphere. The friendship terminology is common in the language of social ethics among the Greek. He mentions that when a guest comes to a meal "ὁ γὰρ σύνδειπνος οὐκ ὄψου καί οἴνου καί τραγημάτων μόνον, αλλά καί λόγων κοινωνο;" ἤκει καί παιδιας καί φιλοφροσύνης εἰ εὐνοιαν τελευτώσης.[80] When a guest just eats his meal and does not share it in a friendly manner, he just eats the meal with his stomach, not with the mind. If the meal is conducted according to the principle of friendship, the real concept of the *eranos* meal (to make of the participants friends rather than enemies)[81] is demonstrated. The *eranos* meal is understood to create a special relationship among meal participants.

The Greek *eranos* meals of the Greco-Roman era, while having a basic formal structure, were characterized by a numerous of elements that were the same or standard in most of the cultures and groups in the Mediterranean world. The symposia of religious θίασοι and especially the ἔρανοι meal appear to be the closest one to the practice of the early Christian cultic associations which held religious and social meals as part of their worship. This same model lies behind Paul's ethical instruction in 1 Cor. 8-11.

The Christian *Eranos* Meal at Roman Corinth

The Christian assemblies of the Corinthians were not different from the other social groups in their world. They got together to eat an *eranos meal* and when they held their meals, they normally followed the examples and rules of the Greco-Roman society. These meals were mostly celebrated in private houses,[82] and this was the case of the *eranos* meal at Roman Corinth. Furthermore, in the ancient world, the custom was that a person would host a meal in his house for friends, associates, and also the family. On a special occasion the banquets were celebrated in public buildings which were connected to the temple complexes.[83] For this reason, Paul advised the Corinthians to be careful about the way they exercised their freedom while eating in an idol's temple or any public building related to a pagan temple (1 Corinthian 8: 9, 10).

Another serious situation the Christians at Roman Corinth confronted was that eating idol meat was socially and culturally accepted in the Greco-Roman world. So, it was common that in any gathering such as in the Greek *eranos* meal, the meat sacrificed to an idol was the main course of the banquet.[84] The participants to the banquets also attended social events (such as weddings, birthdays, and funerals) in the temple. Paul's reference is in regard to an invitation from an unbeliever (1 Cor. 10: 27-28). But, some of them did participate in public banquets and private social meals with their friends and associates. Some of them held membership in pagan clubs, probably because still had some business with their previous partners (1 Cor. 8-10).

Their behavior is understandable once we remember the Greco-Roman social distinction and what happened in the *eranos* meal. Some clubs had specific rules of behavior at the meals:

> (1) injunctions against quarreling and fighting, (2) injunctions against taking the assigned place of another, (3) injunctions against speaking out of turn or without permission, (4) injunctions against fomenting factions, (5) injunctions against accusing a fellow member before a public court, (6) specifications for trials within the club for inter-club disputes, (7) specifications for worship activities.[85]

Also remarkable in these rules is that they refer to secular (social) conduct in the meals, although the last point is related to worship services, possibly at the temple. All the above factors, plus the ones mentioned in the other sections, such as quality and portion of food, leisurely versus late dining, and seating positions, worked together to reflect and reinforce social status. Consequently, people with ambition were constantly competing to be perceived as *asteios, urbanus,* or *sophos*, and the main environment for such competition was the *eranos* meal or *symposion.*

Pogoloff points out that "this is strongly reflected in *symposia* literature, prolifically produced after the model provided by Plato's and Xenophon's *Symposia*."[86] It is highly probable that the social problems Paul confronted in the *eranos* meal at Roman Corinth were a distinctive sign of a community with typical problems found in the Greco-Roman society.

It is clear that rivalries, quarrels, and abusive behavior were not allowed at any club meeting or banquet. However, many conflicts arose because of the individualist behavior of some of the hosts and the guests as well. It is possible that rich Christians did not suffer from a guilty conscience in this whole matter. It is highly probable also that some Gentile Christians thought of themselves as helping the poorer members by providing food for the banquet.[87] As it was normal in the Greek *eranos* meal, the host provided most of the food and the house for the meal, while wealthy guests contributed to the potluck dinners. For this reason some of the hosts felt justified in their behavior.

Consequently, Paul's goal in 1 Cor. 11: 17ff was to settle the problem of the "private meal" by restricting the eating to private homes. At their own homes they could eat and behave the way they wanted. At the Lord's Supper they should behave according to the rules of the congregation. Paul also criticised the "early beginning" (προλαμβάνει) of any *eranos* meal. No "potluck dinner" should take place before the Eucharist meal (1 Cor. 11:21), which began with the blessing of the bread. The wealthy Corinthian had to wait for the other (1 Cor. 11:33) before participating in their *eranos* meal. Thus Paul suggested that the *eranos* meal should follow this order:

-Waiting for one another
-Blessing of the bread
-A Eucharist potluck dinner that nourishes everybody (*Eranos*)
-Drinking followed by the worship activities of 1 Cor. 14:26-32.[88]

It seems logical that the earliest celebrations of the Christian meal consisted of a complete *eranos* meal or one which normally started with the breaking of bread and finished with the sharing of the cup. However, some scholars such as Schweizer and Conzelmann argue that by Paul's time the act of breaking the bread may have been moved to the end of the meal and linked with the sharing of the cup.[89] In other words, the Christian meal had two parts: A fellowship *eranos* meal followed by the sacramental actions. It is highly probable also that such a change had already been in effect.[90]

Nevertheless, Theissen and Fee argue that there is not enough proof to demonstrate whether the breaking of the bread had been moved to the end of the Christian meal, and that the only thing we can be sure of is that commemorative acts were practiced in accordance with the *eranos* communal meal.[91] According to v. 17 Paul did not criticize the sequence of the *eranos* meal, but he is very critical of the manner in which they celebrated it.

On the one hand, G. Theissen and H. J. Klauck[92] commented that Paul wanted just bread and wine to be served at the Lord's Supper. Further the apostle did not want the Christians at Corinth to have an *eranos* complete meal, a nourishing dinner between the breaking of bread and the blessing of the cup. On the other hand, Paul would be antisocial if he just wanted the hungry to have bread and wine during the *eranos* meal; meanwhile the wealthy Christian at Roman Corinth would have their own meal at home, and not share with the hungry ones.[93] But Paul wanted (according to 1 Cor. 11: 33) the Corinthians to have an *eranos* meal. He just did not want them to eat at home, but also during the Eucharist meal at the church. It is interesting to notice that the Greek term "dinner" (δεῖπνον, 1 Cor. 11:20, 25) that Paul used to identify the Eucharist meal not only means a piece of dry bread, but it also included several kinds of food eaten along with the bread: "fish or meat, sometimes also vegetables (opson)."[94] Obviously, Paul in verse 33 exhorted the Christians at Corinth to wait for one another, in order to partake in the *eranos* meal.

Therefore, if all the Christians members waited before they participated in the *eranos* meal, then this means that all their food for the potluck would be shared in a common plate. Otherwise, the waiting for the *eranos* meal would be meaningless for those who remained hungry. Paul's pastoral and practical advice aimed to solve the selfish behavior of the *eranos* meal at Roman Corinth. According to Xenophon, an *eranos* meal only is a communal meal once the food brought by the members is shared with all in community of believers.[95] Consequently, only when they shared the food did they enter into real fellowship with one another.

Social Stratification and Rank in Greco-Roman Society

In the Greco-Roman world, those who partook in a meal were conscious of their differing social position. For instance, in a formal meal, as it has been discussed before, the act of reclining indicated the social status. It was a common tradition to recline at a meal attended by free citizens with no women, children, and slaves.[96] The beginning of the practice of reclining, which was not original from the Greeks or the Romans, has been ascribed mainly with the posture as the common rule in any banquet of ancient times.[97] The reclining custom was adopted as a symbol of high social class among the Greeks and the Romans as well.

The use of the reclining custom was promoted as an awareness of social ranking, although some of the aspects of this practice changed in the first century C.E. Women were not permitted to recline, the disgrace of social position was still linked with the reclining custom. We have mentioned the incident of Lucian's explanation of a banquet, when a guest arrived late and did not find a place to recline, he refused to sit, because he considered sitting as "womanish and weak." (*Symposion*,13). The symbol found in early Greek iconography[98] showed that whenever an aristocrat was with his wife or children the whole family were shown sitting rather than reclining.

According to Jerome Murphy-O'Connor, it was essential for the host to distribute his guests into two groups: The first group was invited into the *triclinium* while the others stayed outside in the *atrium*. Obviously, the ones who went to the *triclinium* were his closest friends, and probably were members of the same social class. The other group took their places in the *atrium* where conditions were inferior.[99] So, those in the first group went to the *triclinium* where they were able to recline according to the social custom. In the last period of the Roman republic, the custom of reclining for a meal appears to have changed. The early practice was for wealthy women to be seated at a formal meal; by the first century C.E., they seemed to have been reclining. In a significant book, K. E. Corley explains the evidences as follows:

> Just as women were moving into public roles and gaining rights previously
> denied them under a more restrictive Greek social code, Roman women were

attending public meals. From Hellenistic sources of the second century BCE through second century CE we can conveniently chart these fluctuations in Greco-Roman society by analyzing changes in the meal etiquette of the Greco-Roman women. The presence of women in public meals during the Roman period has been identified as a sign of the shift in the status of women during the Roman period.[100]

Petronius also described the Roman cultural superiority over the Greek custom regarding the admission of women to a dinner party:

> On the other hand, many actions are seemly according to our code which the Greeks look upon as shameful. For instance, what Roman would hesitate to take his wife to a dinner party? What matron does not frequent the front rooms of her dwelling and show herself in public? But it is very different in Greece; for there a woman is not admitted to a dinner party, unless relatives only are present, and she keeps to the more retired part of the house called "the woman's apartment."[101]

At the turn of the second century C.E. the incorporation of women into the banquets had been more acceptable at Greek dinner parties. The question of whether women were allowed to recline is not clear.[102] However, Lucian comments that women were present at both a wedding feast and in the philosophical meal, though seated in the lowest couch at the table.[103] Whenever this fundamental Greco-Roman social custom was adopted in a different context, the normal ethical ideas accompanied it.[104]

The guest invited for a meal was expected to be served. The host was supposed to provide good service. The wealthy people normally had servants who did all the work for them. This was a sign of high social status. Plato mentioned that in Agathon's banquet whenever a guest arrived for the meal, he ordered his servants to take care of his needs.[105] Commonly the host provided all of the servants for the banquet. Even among the high class who reclined, there were distinctions of rank. It was seen by the seating order, that the rich were seated in different couches around the tables. The Greeks and Romans[106] assigned the guests to their couches according to their high social status.

In addition, the issue of social status became a problem that had to be resolved at almost every banquet by the host assigning the positions on the table according to the social rank in order to avoid jealousies and inconvenience.[107] The subsequent problem was that some would be insulted if they did not receive the recognition they felt they deserved. Similarly, the church at Roman Corinth confronted almost the same predicament and this was why the apostle asked, "Who distinguished you?" (τίς σε διάκρινει). He may have been responding to their demands to "regularly distinguish in this way."[108] In 1 Cor. 11:29 Paul used the same Corinthian claims and language to stress the fact that it is the whole body, the body of Jesus Christ, not the social exaltation of the person. Paul's main concern is as elsewhere in the letter to remove obstacles to unity among the members of the Corinthian congregation.

Besides the assignment of a good place at the table, there were other means to indicate the social position of a guest. It was customary that a special guest would receive the best food. For instance, a big portion was assigned to an honored guest of the community. So, Smith and Taussig's observation is relevant when they say that, "to honor a person's social rank was considered appropriate and was defended according to the ethical argument that it was a sign of the 'good order' that should characterize a banquet."[109] But when a guest received a lower portion of food by the host, this was a sign that the host considered that guest to be of a lower social status. This practice seems to have been commonly accepted in the Roman society; but it was also condemned by many of the conscientious people of the time.[110]

Paul also condemned such practice too. Take for example what happened in the early Christian community, especially the Gentile Christian Church at Roman Corinth. Some of the Corinthian Christians were eating without taking cognizance of their brothers and sisters.[111] Many of the problems faced by the Greco-Roman people had parallels in the Corinthian community.

Summary

The study of the different social settings in which the Greco-Roman meal occurred demonstrates a consistent model of the social context connected with it. This same model lies behind Paul's social-ethical instruction to the Christians at Roman Corinth (1 Cor. 10-14). Some complex banquet and social traditions in the Greco-Roman society explain why different early Christian groups, especially the Christian community at Roman Corinth got together for the *eranos* or *symposia* meal. The similarity of some customs in this pagan society influenced early Christianity through the new converts. As it has been discussed, they usually ate a meal together. The basic models were present whether the meal was considered "sacred" or "social."

The Greek δεῖπνον or *symposium* was a communal meal which had religious and social meaning as well. As we pointed out before, it started with the offering of food to a god and finished with libations and the singing of a hymn. In this Greek meal, sacrificial meat was preferred for the δεῖπνον. The κυριακὸν δεῖπνον mentioned by Paul in 1 Cor. 11:20; 10:14-22, in all probability had the same characteristics as that of the Greeks but to a different god.[112] However, we believe that according to the information presented in this study (see further details in chapter six of this thesis), in many aspects the

Christian meal is closer to the Greek *eranos* meal than to the Greek *deipnon* or *symposium*.

Like the Greek host and some guests in the *symposia*, the Roman aristocrats were quite individualistic and anxious to be recognized at the banquets. The Romans' attitude to the meal was common practice in the society of the time. They usually ate their meals first without waiting for the latecomers. They got drunk and made the host and guests sometimes feel embarrassed because of their uncontrolled behavior. A similar situation happened at Roman Corinth. Paul was offended by the excessive individualism and lack of decorum in the *eranos* meal. There was no respect for the sacred meaning of the Lord's meal. Aune rightly observes that "the disorder at Corinth seems fairly representative of the real nature of such occasions."[113] However, for this reason Paul advised them to go home and forbade them to continue humiliating people (1 Cor. 11:20-22).

The whole structure of the Christian gathering appears to have been influenced by the Greek *eranos* meal. The wealthy Corinthians ate early; the same happened in the Greek *eranos* meal. The dinner at the first table (see chart in chapter six of this study) concluded with the blessing of the cup; they finished with a ceremony involving wine. In essence we cannot deny the close resemblance of the Greek *eranos* meal to the Christian *eranos* meal, though the Greeks made sacrifice to a different god.

The Christian *eranos* meal was not just a nourishing meal but its main purpose was to unite the whole body of the believers. Paul's social and ethical concern was to lead them to understand the eschatological purpose of the meal. But for some of the Corinthians the social aspect of the meal was more important to them than caring and sharing for others. This practice was common in the Greco-Roman society. But by sharing the meal with one another, Christians are led to care for others, and in this way they proclaimed Christ's death.

Notes

[1] In this chapter and the previous one, several particular objectives which correspond to the various aspects of the problem have been set forth. The first objective was to understand the influence of the sacred meals (especially the mystery religion meals discussed already in chapter two) in the Greco-Roman world. Another objective of the study is to consider the social meals in order to understand the social-cultural context of the Gentile Christian meal at Corinth. Thus, it is necessary to know what happened in a typical Greco-Roman dinner party.

[2] D. E. Smith, "Meal Custom," *ABD* vol. 4 (New York: Doubleday, 1992), 648-655.

[3] D. E. Smith, "Social Obligation in the Context of Communal Meals: A Study of the Christian Meal in 1 Corinthians in Comparison with Greco-Roman Meals," (Th.D. diss., Harvard, 1980), 3.

[4] D. E. Aune, "Septem Sapientium Convivium," ed. Hans Dieter Betz *SCHNT* 4 (Leiden: E. J. Brill, 1978), 71.

[5] Homer, *Ody.* 9.311, 15. 76, 19. 321. In some instances, the dei'pnon meal was considered as the morning meal.

[6] Plutarch, *Quaest. conv.* 8.6. See also the discussion of reclining below in part 3.3 of this chapter.

[7] Ibid, 5.6.

[8] Lucian, *Symp.* 14f.

[9] D. E. Smith and Hal E. Taussing, *Many Tables: The Eucharist in the New Testament and Liturgy Today* (Philadelphia: Trinity Press International, 1990), 28. "Various kinds of organized clubs also met for communal meals, and sometimes seem to have been organized almost exclusively for the purpose of providing banquets for their members from a common purse. We know of various kinds of such clubs, especially from inscriptions which provide records of their official business and often define the rules for their banquets. One type of club could be called a trade guild, since it was made up of individuals who had the same occupation. Their purpose, however, was to provide a social outlet rather than a political lobby."

[10] Plato, *Symp.* 175C-D.

[11] Ibib, 175A.

[12] Smith, *Social Obligation*, 8.

[13] Lucian, *Symp.* 13.

[14] Plato, *Symp.* 177D-E. Generally, the host assigned the places. Phaedrus occupied first place at the table (πρῶτος κατακεῖσθαι), others followed to the right (ἐπί δεξια/), and Socrates spoke as one who occupied the lower position at the end of the table (ὁ ὕστατος κατακεῖσθαι).

[15] W. S. Ferguson, "The Attic Orgeones," *HTR* 37 (1944): 80. He mentions, especially, the reference to cases of 3, 4, or even 5 sharing a couch on some vase paintings.

[16] Smith and Taussing, 34.

[17] Plutarch, *Table Talk* 616C-F.

[18] Smith, *Social Obligation*, 189. Smith describes the typical afternoon schedule for a member of the upper class: Exercise, bathing, perfuming, and attiring oneself for dinner. In the summer, the Romans preceded this regimen with a siesta.

[19] Martial, *Epigrammata*, III, 60.

[20] Ibid, I, 20. See also Gerd Theissen, *The Social Setting of Pauline Christianity*, trans. J. H. Schütz (Philadelphia: Fortress Press, 1982), 162.

[21] Carl Roebuck, *Corinth XIV: The Asklepieion and Lerna* (Princeton: The American School of Classical Studies at Athens, 1951), 51-57.

[22] Ibid, 54.

[23] Athenaeus 7. 281-330. On the different kinds of fish, it was generally considered the o[fon (relish) *par excellence*.

[24] Athenaeus, *Deipn.* 4. 140, 173; II. 459; 12.534.

[25] Ibid, 14. 641d.
[26] H. Blümmer, *The Home Life of the Ancient Greeks* (New York: Harper & Row, 1966), 212-213. While the basic structure of the symposion remained the same through Plutarch's time, the many specific gods invoked and honored exhibits wide variety in the sources. Dionysos, however, was commonly honored at symposia because of the intimate association with wine, intoxication, and ecstasy. See also W. F. Otto, *Dionysus: Myth and Cult* (Bloomington, 1965), 143ff.
[27] Smith, *Social Obligation*, 13.
[28] Karl Bircher, *Die sacral Bedwetting des Wines* (RVV 9.2; Geese: A. Töpelmann, 1910), 16-17. He mentioned two different customs; the cup to Hygieia was not considered a libation.
[29] Blümmer, *The Home Life*, 213ff.
[30] Schol. Pind, *Isthm* 6.10. Τὸν μὲν γὰρ πρῶτον κρατῆρα Διὸς Ὀλυμπίου ἐκίρνασαν, τὸν δὲ δεύτερον ἡρώων, τὸν δὲ τρίτον Διὸς σωτῆρος.
[31] W. W. Tarn, "The Hellenistic Ruler-Cult and the Daemon," *JHS* 48 (1928): 210-213.
[32] Plato, *Symposium* 176A.
[33] W. A. Becker, *Charicles: Illustrating of the Private Life of the Ancient Greeks*, 8th ed. (London: Longman Press, 1889), 333-347.
[34] Dennis E. Smith, "Meals and Morality in Paul and His World," *SBLSP* (1981), 321. "Plato mentioned the story that the δειπνον portion is passed over briefly, while the philosophical dialogue which takes place during the symposium is described in detail. This discussion takes place, as noted above, as the substitute for the scheduled entertainment. The subject discussed is ἔρως or 'Love,' and the discussion proceeds jovially, with asides and other references to the setting interspersed within. Thus Plato provided a literary form in which a certain type of topic and a certain type of discussion were considered more appropriate to the symposium setting."
[35] Stephen M. Pogoloff, *Logos and Sophia: The Rhetorical Situation of 1 Corinthians* (Atlanta: Scholars Press, 1992), 267ff.
[36] Athenaeus, *Deipnon* 1.4.
[37] Plato, *Symp* 176E.
[38] Aune, "Septem Sapientium," 69.
[39] Smith, *Social Obligation*, 22.
[40] Athenaeus, *Deipnon* 5. 186a.
[41] Jerome Carcopino, *Daily Life in Ancient Rome* (New Haven: Yale University, 1940), 263-276; J. P. V. D. Balsdon, *Life and Leisure in Ancient Rome* (New York: Mcgraw-Hill, 1969), 19-54.
[42] Pliny, *Ep.* 3.5.10.
[43] Seneca, *Ep.* 82.
[44] W. A. Becker, *Gallus* (London: Longman's, Green, 1915), 451-504.
[45] Martial, *Epig.* 4. 8. 4.
[46] Becker, *Gallus*, 454-455.
[47] Seneca, *Ep.* 83.6.
[48] J. P. V. D. Balsdon, *Life and Leisure in Ancient Rome* (New York: McGraw-Hill, 1969), 25-26. Exceptionally busy men may have not taken the siesta after the *prandium*

meal; for instance, Cicero claimed never to have taken a siesta as long as he was actively engaged in politics or at the bar with the friends.

[49] Isidorus, *Orig.* XX. 2, 12.

[50] Balsdon, *Life and Leisure,* 19, 33-34.

[51] Pliny, *Ep.* 1. 15.1., see also Martial, *Epig.* 11.52.2. This is an example of Martial's informal invitation: "If you have no better appointment, come."

[52] Plutarch, *Quaest. conv.* 5.5.

[53] Ibid, 678E-F. Plutarch pointed out that: "For the size of a party also is right, so long as it easily remains one party. If it gets too large, so that the guests can no longer talk to each other or enjoy the hospitality together or even know one another, then it ceases to be a party at all (καὶ γὰρ συμποσίου μέγεθος ἱκανόν ἐστιν, ἄχρι οὐ συμπόσιον ἐθέλει μένειν. ἐάν δ᾽ ὑπερβάλη διὰ πλῆτος, ὡς μηκετι προσήγορον ἑαυτῷ μηδὲ συμπάθες εἶναι ταῖς φιλοφροσύναις μηδέ γνώριμον οὐδὲ συμπόσιόν ἐστι)."

[54] Ibid, 679BOC. A piece of advice was also given by him: "the rest of us can protect ourselves against the risk of gathering too large a crowd by entertaining frequently in small groups. . . of three or four guests at a time."

[55] Martial, *Epig.* 13.14.

[56] Ibid, 10.31.

[57] Becker, *Gallus,* 485-504.

[58] Pliny, *Ep.* 3.5.13. He mentioned that "in summer he rose from dinner while it was still light, in winter as soon as darkness fell, as if some law compelled him." In winter the meal could last until dark, up to 2 to 3 hours. See the further discussion by J. P. Balsdon, 19.

[59] Smith, "Meals and Morality," 319.

[60] Aune, "Septem Sapientium," 72.

[61] Plutarch *Sept, sap. conv* 150 D.

[62] Peter Lampe, "Das Korinthische Herrenmahl im Schnittpunkt hellenistisch-römischer Mahlpraxis und Paulinischer Theologia (1 Kor 11:17-34)," *ZNW* 82 (1991): 192. See also Lampe, "The Eucharist: Identifying with Christ on the Cross," *Int* 48 (1994): 36-49.

[63] H. G. Liddell and R. S. Scott, *A Greek-English Lexicon,* 9th edition, revised by H.S. Jones (Oxford: At the Clarendon Press, 1940), 680.

[64] Homer, *Odyssey* 1. 226-27. See also Lampe, "Das Korinthische Herrenmahl," 192-203.

[65] Aristophanes, *Acharnenses* 1085-1149.

[66] Xenophon, *Memorabilia* 3.14.1.

[67] Franz Poland, *Geschichte des griechischen Vereinsenswesens* (Leipzig: Teubner, 1909), 156-166.

[68] Martial *Epigrammata* 11.52, 10.48; Plato *Symposium* 174 A.

[69] Cicero *Ad Familiares* 9.26.1. The eighth or ninth hour is mentioned also in: *Oxyrhynchus Papyri* 110, 2678 (3rd century C.E.), 2791 (2nd century C.E.).

[70] For more details on Graeco-Roman dinner party (*eranos*), see D. E. Smith, *Social Obligation* 5-32; Peter Lampe, *Affirmation* 4 (1991): 1-15; S. M. Pogoloff, *Logos and Sophia* 237ff; D. E. Aune, "Septem sapientium convivium," in *Plutarch's Ethical*

Writings And Early Christian Literature, ed. Hans Dieter Betz, *SCHNT* 4 (Leiden: E. J. Brill, 1978), 51-105.

[71] Athenaeus, *Attic Orgeones* 362E. The standard article on the subject is W. S. Ferguson, " The Attic Orgeones", *HTR* (1944): 62-146.

[72] Lucian *Symp*, 17 and Athenaeus *Deipn.* 2. 36.

[73] Aune, "Septem Sapientium," 73.

[74] Lucian *Par.* 5 and Athenaeus *Deipn* 5. 178; 12. 527.

[75] Plutarch *Table Talk* 644C.

[76] Juvenal *Satires* 5. 156-170. "You may perhaps suppose that Virro grudges the expense; not a bit of it! His object is to give you pain. For what comedy, what mime, is so amusing as a disappointed belly? His one object, let me tell you, is to compel you to pour out your wrath in tears, and to keep gnashing your molars against each other. . . . In treating you thus, the great man shows his wisdom."

[77] Juvenal *Satires* 5.152-155, and *Epigrams* 3.60; 4.85.

[78] Lucian *Symp.* 9.

[79] Plutarch *qu. conv.* 613F.

[80] Ibid, 660B.

[81] Plato *Leg* 2.671C-72A.

[82] Jerome Murphy-O'Connor, *St. Paul's Corinth* (Wilmington: Michael Glazier, Inc, 1983), 153ff. "Christianity in the 1st cent. A.D., and long afterwards, did not have he status of a recognized religion, so there was no question of a public meeting-place, such as the Jewish synagogue. Hence, use had to be made of the only facilities available, namely, the dwellings of families that had become Christian."

[83] Smith and Taussig, 23.

[84] Peter Lampe, "The Corinthian Eucharistic Dinner Party: Exegesis of a Cultural Context (1 Cor. 11: 17-34)," *Affirmation* 4 (1991): 6.

[85] Smith, *Meals and Morality*, 323.

[86] Pogoloff, *Logos and Sophia*, 257.

[87] Theissen, *The Social Setting*, 162ff.

[88] Lampe, "The Corinthian," 7ff.

[89] E. Schweizer, *The Lord's Supper according to the New Testament* (Philadelphia: Fortress Press, 1982), 5. Hans Conzelmann, *1 Corinthians* (Philadelphia: Fortress Press, 1875), 194 n.18.

[90] Nigel Watson, *The First Epistle to the Corinthians* (London: Epworth Press, 1992), 116. "One can imagine such a change being made to enable those members of the community who could not count on getting to its gathering on time, the slaves and poor freedmen and women, to participate in the most significant part of the occasion. Something that favors this reconstruction is the fact that when he describes the way in which latecomers are being deprived (if that is indeed the problem...)" mentioned by Paul in 1 Cor. 11:21.

[91] Theissen, *The Social Setting*, 152f and Fee, 541 n.52.

[92] Ibid., 145-168 and Hans-Josef Klauck, *Herrenmahl und Hellenistischer kult* (Münster: Aschendorffsche Verlagsbuchandlung GmbH & Co., 1986), 294, 371.

[93] Lampe, "The Corinthian," 8.

[94] Ibid, 9.

[95] Xenophon, *Symposium* 2.1.

[96] Smith and Taussig, 32f.

[97] Jean-Marie Dentzer, "Aux origines de l'iconographie du banquet couché," *RA* (1971): 215-258.

[98] Ibid, 246.

[99] Murphy-O'Connor, *St. Paul*, 158-159.

[100] Kathleen E. Corley, *Private Women Public Meals* (Peabody: Hendrickson, 1993), 24-79. "As Roman matrons would have been free to accompany their husbands to public banquets, and in particular would have been allowed in religious meal settings, the inclusion of women in Christian meals would have been noteworthy but not unique."

[101] Petronius, *Satyricon* 67-69.

[102] Corley, *Private Women*, 25ff. She rightly points out that, "Women, if matrons, were expected to be present for certain portions of the meal, such as the δεῖπνον, but they were also to be somewhat circumscribed by those with more idealistic views. Such social criticism attempted to limit women's practice and restrict their dining companions. Therefore, women dining or reclining with those outside of their immediate family would still elicit a degree of social criticism even during the Roman period." See also K. E. Corley, "Were the Women around Jesus Really Prostitutes? Women in the Context of Greco-Roman Meals," *SBL* (Atlanta: Scholars Press, 1989), 487-521.

[103] Lucian, *Symp.* 8. "On the right as you enter, the women occupied the whole couch, as there were a good many of them, with the bride among them, very scrupulously veiled and hedged in by the women. Toward the back door comes the rest of the company according to the esteem in which each was held. Opposite the women, the first was Eucritus. . . ."

[104] Smith, *Meals and Morality*, 323.

[105] Plato, *Symp* 175A, 213B.

[106] Plutarch, *Quaest. conv.* 1.3.

[107] Ibid, 1. 2.

[108] Pogoloff, *Logos and Sophia*, 246ff.

[109] Smith and Taussig, 33. "Various clubs and social organizations utilized this custom to designate rank within the group. Thus club officers would be designated places at table and special portions in the distribution of the meal."

[110] Pliny, *Ep.* 2.6.

[111] R. MacMullen, *Roman Social Relations 50 B. C. to A. D. 248* (New Haven: Yale University, 1974), 73. "Probably some people saw Christian gatherings as meetings of some sort of association or *collegium*, especially in view of the fact that early Christianity had no temples, no priests, and no sacrifices. Furthermore, just like a Christian meeting, an association meeting could involve a variety of people from up and down the social strata. It could involve a wealthy patron, male or female, a group of artisans both freeborn and freed, and even some slaves, who perhaps had taken up a trade or started a business using their *peculium*, money of their own."

[112] Pogoloff, *Logos and Sophia*, 238.

[113] Aune, "Septum Sapientium," 75-78.

Chapter 3

The Social Setting in the Corinthian Church

After looking into the social meals in the Greco-Roman world, the study of the social setting of the city and the early Christian Church at Roman Corinth is in order. To set the context for our examination of 1 Cor. 8, 10, and 11, we must begin with several matters of prolegomena. To be specific, we must answer two questions: (1) Why is the social setting of the Corinthian Church so important? (2) How does the social setting of the church at Roman Corinth contribute to our understanding of the complex social issues in the Lord's Supper?

Introduction to Sociology and the Study of Early Christianity

Interest in the social stratification of ancient societies, especially in early Christianity, is not new. The topic was widely considered at the beginning of the twentieth century, but abandoned in the period between the first and second World Wars. Lohmeyer and the so-called Chicago School were the exceptions because they kept working with the topic. In 1921, Lohmeyer published a little book in German (*Soziale Fragen im Urchristentum*) that surveys the economic and social conditions of the Greco-Roman world and the early church. S. Jackson Case and S. Matthews, both of Chicago, were the main exponents of the socio-historical approach that became the mark of distinction of the Chicago School.[1] Case clarified the ideas, values, and common practices of the early Christians simply as responses to "needs" that were manifest in the society of those days.

In contrast, not everyone welcomes the renewed attempts to describe the social history of early Christianity. Most scholars, especially theologians, have warned that the sociological explanation of religious phenomena is inevitably reductionist.[2] Sociology of early Christianity is not interested in reductionistically confining the true being of Christianity to a social dynamic. Instead, it should be seen as an attempt to protect against a reductionism from the other extreme, a limitation of the true being of Christianity to an "inner spiritual" or "objective-cognitive" logical order.[3]

W. A. Meeks takes up the challenge and argues that those who limit legitimate interpretation of theological readings of the canonical text are practising an example of another kind of reductionism. The assertion that all texts are really about theological ideals hides much confusion, including the following: (1) It fails to distinguish the differences among distinct contexts of meaning and among different uses of the text in question. (2) Theological reductionism hides what religion is, prohibiting clarity and preventing criticism. (3) The theological critics seem frequently to refer to a reduction of language's meaning to its "ostensive, locutionary force, its manifest intention."[4]

However, as with any other scholarly field and method of interpretation of the text, there are benefits to be obtained and pitfalls to be avoided.[5] The use of these sociological principles and methodologies in the interpretation of the early Christian church will help us to distinguish their social environment. Consequently, contrary to the worries of many, one may use sociological methods today without endorsing the scientism which typified, for instance, the early psychologist who reduced the apostle Paul to the completion of his own incompetence often on the basis of virtually fundamentalist interpretation of the NT texts.[6] Sociology, then, helps to explain certain typical features and not particular examples.[7]

Furthermore, today the interest in studying the social reality of early Christianity is alive again. This is not to say that all is easy for sociologists of the New Testament. There are serious problems that they must deal with: The problem of methodology, the problem of the data, and the problem of reductionism.[8] This study does not address these issues, but considers the common life of the ordinary Christians of the first century (especially the Corinthian congregation). To establish the social level of any community there are some measurable criteria: Economic class, status, and power.[9]

Social Status of the Early Christians

The Apostle Paul sent several letters to the church at Roman Corinth in the early 50s of the first century C.E. In one epistle he provided a general view of what constituted the social background of the Corinthian congregation. Paul says, "Now remember what you were, my brothers, when God called you. From the human point of view few of you were wise or powerful or of high social standing. God purposely chose what the world considers nonsense in order to shame the wise, and he chose what the world considers weak in order to shame the powerful. He chose what the world looks down on and despises and thinks is nothing, in order to destroy what the world thinks is important" (1 Cor. 1:26-28).

Some scholars interpret Paul's statement to the Corinthians as a description of the social constituency of earliest Christianity and, therefore, some use it to support their argument that Christians in the early church belonged to a lower social class. This questionable assumption has not been accepted by the majority of scholars.

A century later, the Christian writer and apologist Minucius Felix said: "That many of us are called poor is not our disgrace, but our glory."[10] Contemporary with Minucius was the pagan Celsus who described Christians as follows: "Their injunctions are like this: 'Let no one educated, no one wise, no one sensible draw near. For these abilities are thought by us to be evils. By the fact that they themselves admit that these people are worthy of their God, they show that they want and are able to convince only the foolish, dishonourable, and stupid, and only slaves, women and little children."[11] Even in Celsus's remarks and exaggerated tone, he is recognising that the apostle Paul implies that there were at least some Christians of wisdom, power, and high social standing in the early Christian church. This issue will be considered further in the next main section.

The Older Viewpoint Regarding the Christian Social Status

Several opinions have been expressed on the problem of the social level of primitive Christianity. According to Deissmann, early Christians belonged to a movement within the lower class. Meeks reminds us that Deissmann found that hundreds of newly discovered documents written on papyrus or ostraca letters, contracts, school lessons, bills of sale, magical spells had revolutionary implications for understanding not only the vocabulary and grammar, but also the social setting of the New Testament.[12] The language of the New Testament and the *Koine* language found in the papyri from Egypt have some similarities. In other words, the two groups of texts appeared to him to belong to the same vulgar literary level, and in consequence this is what constitutes evidence for the "folk" (*volkstümlich*) character of the early Christians' lower social status.[13] So, his justification for this view rests in the vulgar level of literary culture and the language the writers used (*Koine*). But Bengt Holmberg says that this feeling of agreement was general, but not homogeneous.[14]

At the other end we have Ernst Troeltsch's description of the social class of the early Christians.[15] Using Harnack's argument, Troeltsch considers the social standing of the early Christians to have been fairly low. Most of them belonged to the urban areas, but from the lowest class of society. Part of these groups would have been artisans, house slaves, freedmen and free workers, but not belonging to any real social class.[16] J. G. Gager rightly points out that even such classicists as A. D. Nock, A. H. M. Jones and E. R. Dodds agree that the social subdivision of early Christianity has again come into focus.

Among this limited circle, something approaching a consensus has emerged on two aspects of the social question: (1) that for more than two hundred years, Christianity was fundamentally a movement among the poor groups in the Empire; and (2), that its appeal among these groups depended on social as much as ideological considerations.[17]

A contemporary variant of the old consensus is presented by Gager in his pioneering book on sociological interpretation of the New Testament, *Kingdom and Community* (1975). Gager posits that the early Christians did not actually exist at the absolute bottom level of the social class, nor did they come exclusively from the aristocratic group or the middle classes. Inside these social stratifications, the early Christians belonged to a group that fell far from their relative expectations.[18]

Holmberg criticizes Gager's use of terms like "disinherited, deprived, disadvantaged, outsiders, disprivileged, and dispossessed" as if they were all exchangeable terms. They are not. Being an "outsider" and being "dispossessed" refer to two different kinds of alienation, one social and the other economic. According to Holmberg, through this lack of precision in his analytical language, Gager is able to mix two sets of ideas when describing the first Christians, although they need not have anything to do with each other.[19]

It seems that Gager places the early believers in sociological world outside the normal standards of society. They were not at the bottom of the social level, nor high nor middle class, but deprived of their expectations. This criterion used by Gager is useless because it does not measure the social level of the individual or group in the church. The next section will deal with a more up-to-date view that has shown that the social class of early Christians may be higher than some scholars, especially Deissmann, had supposed.

The Newer Viewpoint Regarding the Christian Social Status

More than thirty years ago, E. A. Judge, in his small book *The Social Pattern of the Christian Group in the First Century,* challenged the consensus. Judge observes that the common notion is that the Christian groups were constituted from the lower orders of society; if this meant to imply that they did not draw upon the upper orders of the Roman ranking system, the observation is correct, and pointless. Although the original Christians came from the Aramaic community in Palestine, they flourished and their writings spread among Jewish and Gentile believers living under the influence of the urban Greco-Roman society and institutions.[20]

Judge's studies not only represent a new interpretation of the evidence, but also show an improvement in methodology. Judge differentiated between separate times and milieus of early Christianity. The Aramaic-speaking, rural movement around Jesus is not simply the same thing as Jewish Christianity in Jerusalem, not to mention the groups we encounter ten years later in Syria or twenty-five years later in Corinth or Rome.[21]   The impact of Judge's reinterpretation has hardly been noticed among New Testament scholars, although his book was translated and published in Germany in 1964.

His view about the socially combined character of the early Christian church has received some support from scholars, such as Heinz Kreissig, Clarence L. Lee and especially Martin Hengel, who points out that,

> What Pliny the Younger, as governor of Bithynia in Asia Minor, wrote to the emperor Trajan, also applied to the communities founded during the mission of the apostle to the Gentiles: "many . . . of every class . . . are endangered now and will be endangered in the future" (by the new "superstition": *multi enim . . . omnis ordinis . . . vocantur in periculum et vocabuntur)*. That is, there were members of Christian communities in all strata of the populace, from slaves and freedmen to the local aristocracy, the decurions, and in some circumstances even to the local nobility of the Senate. . . . "The majority of early Christians will have belonged to the 'middle class' of antiquity from which the 'godfearers' of the Jewish mission were recruited (cf. Acts 13:43, 50; 16:14; 17:4, 17; 18:7)."[22]

Evidence for this expansion is abundant in the second half of the second century, especially as more educated people became members of the early church. Hengel stresses the fact that new members of the "upper class" frequently came into contact with the church. In Acts, Luke mentioned a list of prominent people who joined the early Christian church.   The list of people included Joanna the wife of Chusa, who was the financial administrator of Herod Antipas; the centurion Cornelius; the Athenian assessor, Dionysius; Menahem, the friend of Herod Antipas; Sergius Paulus, governor of Cyprus.

To this list can be added the group of "God-fearers" on whom the Gentile-Christian mission concentrated its attention; maybe Luke himself came from this high-class society. According to Eusebius (*Hist. eccl.* 5, 21,1), in the time of Commodus (180-192), "Large numbers even of those at Rome, highly distinguished for wealth and birth, were advancing towards their own salvation with all their households and kindred."[23]   Christianity moved rapidly in all segments of society, and even some senators were persuaded to become Christians. The church's move toward social universalism in fact had already been initiated by Paul.

The negative opinion given by a critic like Celsus that Christians belonged to the lower and uneducated segment of society should not be taken at face value. Obviously, this is a part of Celsus' anti-Christian propaganda to set people of high social rank against the new religion from the East. Celsus alleged that the church "deliberately excluded educated people because the religion was attractive only to the foolish, dishonourable and stupid, and only slaves, women, and little children."[24] However, during the past twenty years, several scholars have looked at the data afresh and some of them have come to very different conclusions than Celsus and Deissmann about the social stratification of the early Christianity.

The diverse viewpoints have led Malherbe to suggest that "a new consensus may be emerging."[25] A similar view was expressed more than forty years ago by Floyd V. Filson when he said: "The apostolic church was more nearly a cross section of society than we emphasized."[26] The evidence from the second through the fourth centuries is clear, and the triumph of Christianity in a hierarchically organised society necessarily took place from the top down.[27] Early Christianity should be viewed not as a proletarian group movement, but as a relatively small community, largely composed of people of middle-class origin.

R. M. Grant's explanation is not far from Heinz Kreissig's conclusion that the early Christian church spread in the first century of our era not so much among "proletarians" or solitary handworkers of the smallest scale or small peasants, but rather in the urban circles of well-situated artisans, merchants, and members of the liberal professions.[28]

Malherbe's contribution to the new consensus, in his book *Social Aspects of Early Christianity,* is contrary to Deissmann's presuppositions, especially in what he believes was the relationship between social rank and literary culture.[29]

Of course there are differences regarding the New Testament Greek language literature level. The fact is that even at its simple level it is not as vulgar as many of the nonliterary papyri were on which Deissmann based his argument. Holmberg says that another point to be considered is that the association between the literary level of a document and the social level of its author (not to speak of its readers) is not straight forward.[30]

If the high educational level in ancient times is somehow connected with wealth and social rank, one could surmise that a very high literary level of a document is an indirect proof of a higher social rank of the social community in which it belonged.[31] It is obvious that Paul's own literary style very well indicates that his personal educational level is higher than the one found, for instance, in the Gospel of John and others. In summarizing the new viewpoint, we cannot measure social level along an individual scale. A person has to be located along several different variables like power, wealth, occupation, ethnic background, education, and family connections.[32]

Gager's criticism of the new consensus is found in a couple of articles in which he reviewed the work of several scholars like Robert Grant, A. J. Malherbe, and Gerd Theissen. Gager disagrees with the picture drawn by Malherbe's focus on the letter and the person of the apostle Paul alone, and believes that no weighty conclusions could be taken from this as to the social stratification of early Christianity as a whole. Gager distances himself a little bit from his own position and the old viewpoint. He pointed out of the "presentations of early Christianity as exclusively proletarian, a movement of slaves, labourers, and outcasts of various sorts . . . that it may be seriously doubted that such a view ever existed apart from a few romantics and early Marxists. . . ."[33] It is fair to say that the new consensus has not really been shaken by Gager's own criticism, although he reluctantly has to acknowledge the evidence presented by the scholars.

Besides Gager, Georg Schöllgen has expressed a sharp critique of Meeks' book. Schöllgen's basic argument is that we know almost nothing about the social realities of the ancient cities and of the Christian church on which to base any strong conclusions. He concludes that,

> So berechtigt die Frage nach der Sozialstruktur der frühchristlichen Gemeinden exegetisch wie theologisch ist, so notwendig scheint mir das Eingeständnis, dass sie angesichts der Unergiebigkeit des Materials nach dem gegenwärtigen Stand der Exegese nicht zureichend beantwortet werden kann. Dies gilt im übrigen für die gesamte vorkonstantinische Zeit. Selbst die Gemeinden von Karthago, Rom und Alexandrien in der ersten Hälfte des 3. Jh., die für die wesentlich ergiebigere Quellen zur Verfügung stehen, bleiben, was ihre soziale Schichtung angeht, weitgehend im Dunkeln.[34]

Schöllgen also finds fault with Meeks' conclusion that it is very unlikely that all church members of Paul's time had the same social status.[35] This criticism is untenable, and the available data indicate that there existed socio-economic differences among Paul's churches. For instance, there was a difference between the poor church members of Macedonia and some well-to-do Christians at Roman Corinth. Furthermore, Corinth (perhaps Philippi, too) is the only Pauline congregation about which we know enough details to draw any conclusions regarding its social stratification.[36] In an article published in 1982, Meeks clearly states his view and says that when we look at single members and groups who joined the Pauline churches, then we should not right away classify them to some general level. To put them into "the middle class," for example, would be vague and misleading--vague, because it ignores the multi-dimensionality of stratification, and misleading, because it assumes that there was something in the ancient Greek city corresponding to the middle class in modern industrial society.[37]

In conclusion, it could be said that neither the older consensus nor the new consensus has produced sufficient evidence to prove that the early Christians were poor, middle-class, or high-class. The evidence is too inadequate to allow a full description of the social history or full description of the social level of the first Christians. The romantic picture of the proletarian origins has been rejected because early Christianity is seen to be spread throughout more social levels than are classifiable into a single social rank. Each Christian congregation has to be studied in the context of its contemporary society. Both groups of scholars attempt to show how the New Testament social world and its message related to the reality of everyday social life of the early Christian church and its community.[38]

Social Stratification of the Corinthian Community and Church

The knowledge of the social level of the first Christians is interesting not only in itself, but it usually holds the clue to understanding problems in the primitive church. It appears that no other church in the early days of Christianity experiences as many difficulties, both moral and social, as the church at Roman Corinth. This is evident because the sources focus on the Corinthian Church to the exclusion of other Christian groups. In order to understand some of these problems, we will deal with the social structure of the city of Roman Corinth, the evidence of the social status of the Corinthian congregation, and finally the mission and social status of Paul.

Social Structure of the City of Roman Corinth

The city of Roman Corinth was one of the more important cities of Greece from the eighth to the second centuries B.C.E. Its strategic location at the isthmus connecting the Peloponnesus to mainland Greece gave it tremendous political and commercial power. After its total destruction in 146 B.C.E., Julius Caesar refounded Corinth as a Roman colony in 44 B.C.E. It was the capital of Achaia which included all of southern Greece. Paul visited Corinth around 50 C.E. and by that time it was a major city once again.[39] Caesar settled mostly freedmen, but not exclusively ἐποίχους πέμψαντος τοῦ ἀπελευθερικοῦ γένους πλείστους, "sending people for the most part who belonged to the freedmen class." Veterans were probably also among the colonists. In any event, the settlers were Roman citizens, from any of the Roman colonies.[40]

The style of government was that of a typical Roman colony, with annually elected *duoviri* and *aediles*. The depth of this "romanization," however, should not be exaggerated.[41] It is especially important to notice that the refounded city of Corinth--its constitution, buildings, families or cults--was not an old city. During this time, many families were moving up socially; it may be that their grandfathers and great-grandfathers were slaves. Such a city was very receptive to new ideas. Paul's choice of Roman Corinth as a testing ground for the new religion proved to be a happy one.

Being a relatively new city it could be expected to be more receptive to novel religious beliefs than a place like Athens with her unbroken cultural history of many hundreds of years. Perhaps even more important are the many visitors who came to this great cosmopolitan city on the isthmus. Some of Paul's most faithful followers in missionary work were, like the apostle himself, foreigners in the city.[42]   Therefore, it is not by chance that he had little success in the tradition-conscious Athens; but according to Acts 18, he won many people to the Christian faith in Roman Corinth. In a relatively new city the desire for a new cultural and social identity is more likely to be expected than in an already established cultural centre.

Among the archaeological records of gods worshipped at Roman Corinth, the goddess Aphrodite was worshipped with great devotion. There are also indications that members of many religious groups, here as elsewhere, met to eat a common cultic meal. Note Paul's argument with the local Christians (1 Corinthians 8 -11). Devotees of Dionysus met in subterranean dining rooms, with six couches cut into the rock around a rock-hewn table. Comparable dining rooms, found in the rock at the sanctuary of Asclepius, could accommodate eleven persons with small tables in front of them.

Outdoor meals served in tents were major elements of the ritual at the sanctuary offering to Demeter and Core.[43] Not only were the citizens of Corinth on the rise socially, but also the city had experienced a rapid economic revival. The resumption by Corinth of the Isthmian games was an indicator of this economic upturn. The games involved the participation of many people. Dio Chrysostom says that the θεωρόν is the pilgrim festival second to the merchant celebration, signifying the close association between the games and commercial activity.[44]

There are four basic factors in Roman Corinth's prosperity: (1) Corinth had the reputation of being a great wealthy city and its wealth was based mainly on trade; Strabo writes: ὁ δὲ Κόρινθος ἀφνειὸς μὲν λέγεται διὰ τὸ ἐμπόριον (Corinth is said to be "wealthy" on account of its commerce) (VIII, 6, 20). (2) A second factor is its banking system. (3) A third factor is the production of the artisans. Strabo calls special attention to Corinthian τέχνας τὰς δημιούργικα" (arts of the craftsman). Metalwork production had declined in several cities, but Corinthian bronze, a special bronze alloy, was coveted. (4) Finally, governmental administration must be mentioned.[45] The senatorial province of Achaia had its capital at Corinth.[46]

This was a factor that brought many people to the city. It is understandable that in such an aspiring city as Corinth there were more opportunities to become wealthy. It thus appears that the Christian believers in Roman Corinth came from several social classes, and in all probability faced special difficulties of integration because of the church's inner social structure

Evidence of the Social Status of the Corinthian Church

The conversion to Christianity made an important impact on many individuals both in terms of the individual's self-perception and the social context of the new religion. The Christian movement experienced certain transitions in the generation following Jesus' death and resurrection. The most important transition was from a Jewish community of believers to a Gentile one and from a rural setting to an urban context. The record of Acts shows the transition from a Jewish community to a Gentile movement. We can see also the early opposition between the Greek-speaking Jews and more traditional ones (Acts 6:1). In general, the gospel made a notable advance in the urban cities, a fact that included a great change in the cultural social status of Christianity from a reform movement inside Palestinian Judaism to becoming a Hellenistic movement based in the urban cities of the Greco-Roman world.[47]

In Acts 18:17 some Jewish leaders were very receptive to the Christian message, and were wealthy such as Priscilla and Aquila. The most influential church members, especially the missionaries like Paul and his companions and main patrons, came from a high social class of Hellenistic Judaism. Gentile Christians also came from the high levels of their societies. Wealthy men and women served as partners, and in many instances the whole household followed its master and mistress into Christianity. Christianity was a multicultural and socio-economic phenomenon which indeed attracted also the slaves and poor people of the first-century society (Acts 11:14ff; 16:15; 18:18).

C. S. Hill comments that the Christian church at Roman Corinth gave Paul more problems than any other group or community with which he was closely associated. Hill further adds that in spite of the scant record in Acts 18:1-7, we possibly know more about the social composition of the Christian community in Corinth than in any other city of this period.[48] This information is based on the two epistles from the Apostle Paul to Roman Corinth. Paul described the social status of the Corinthian congregation when he wrote that there were not "many" of the wise, the noble, or the powerful in the church at Roman Corinth (1 Cor. 1:26), suggesting that there were not many Corinthian Church members who belonged to high socio-economic levels. Yet the congregation included the city treasurer of Roman Corinth and a certain person by the name of Gaius whose wealth and house were sufficient to provide hospitality for Paul and the whole church.[49]

Paul's assertion has been taken at face value by many, who refuse to permit any qualification of his rhetorical debate at the beginning of his epistle to the Corinthians, and who hold to the general presupposition that early Christianity was a lower-class movement. Derek Tidball mentions two well-known classic Marxists like Frederick Engels and Karl Kautsky.[50]

The expressions "wise" and "powerful" are linked to previously stated ideas about wisdom and foolishness, power and weakness. But noble birth (εὐγενεῖς) brings into play something entirely new, a specific sociological category which Paul especially emphasizes. When repeating the idea in vv. 27-28 he not only contrasts "noble birth" with "lower born," but sharpens the contrast between εὐγενεῖς and ἀγενῆ by two further designations: τὰ ἐξουθενημένα ("despised") and τὰ μὴ ὄντα ("things that are not").[51] It may be that Paul has a social factor in mind and probably wants the first two categories to be understood sociologically as well. The term δυνατός makes clear the political aspect, but εὐγενής emphasizes the social. In the group are the educated, the influential, and people of distinguished family social background. Indeed, it is interesting that the apostle did not support an ideal of poverty. The wealthy are not exempted as such.[52]

Along the same line, Philo mentions references to the strong, powerful, and understanding in a similar way when he writes:

> Are not private citizens continually becoming officials, and officials private citizens, rich men becoming poor men and poor men, men of ample means, nobodies becoming celebrated, obscure people becoming distinguished, weak men (ἀσθενεῖς) strong (ἰσχυροί), insignificant men powerful (δυνατοί), foolish men wise men of understanding (συνετοί), witless men sound reasoners?[53]

It is the contention that this statement by Philo, especially the language in 1 Cor.1:26-29 is sociologically significant. The causes for the sociological interpretation associated with 1 Cor. 1:26 since Patristic times are now apparent. In addition, W. Wuellner argues that the grammatical considerations are presented in two further arguments which confirmed the grammatical revision and the elimination of any sociological implications of 1 Cor. 1:26-29. But in verses 26-28 there not even a trace of any indication that the Corinthian Christians form part of the proletarian circles.[54]

The evidence from the New Testament and the Patristic sources is the basic source of information about the social level of early Christianity. If Wuellner's argument is correct, why did Paul devote a substantial part of this epistle to an exchange with the wisdom group? For instance, in 1 Cor. 4:10, Paul says that "for Christ's sake we are fools; but you are wise in union with Christ! We are weak, but you are strong! We are despised, but you are honored!" In a modified way, we once again find the three groups: The wise, the powerful, and the honoured. Once again we have terms of sociological importance. In 1 Cor. 1:26ff. Paul does not seek to diminish the social level of some of his church members, but simply objects to their wealthy self-perception. Perhaps those wealthy members represented a minority within the congregation, but they apparently were a dominant minority.[55]

Another point worthy of mention are the four criteria used by some of the scholars to identify the social status of the early church: (1) To have a civil or religious office in the city, (2) to have a "house," (3) to have been of service to the church or Paul, and (4) to travel (for the church). The last two criteria are not sufficient in themselves to indicate high status.[56] This prosopographical description shows that a large section of the most active and influential members of the Corinthian congregation, which we consider typical of the Hellenistic churches in general, most likely belonged to the small portion of Christians at Roman Corinth with high social standing. In addition, a closer analysis of the problem of the Lord's Supper (1 Corinthians 11) and the relationship between the "strong" and the "weak" clarifies the picture.

The issue of the social divisions is evident when Paul comments on the Corinthians' behaviour. An examination of divisions within the membership of the Corinthian church confirms the supposition of an internal problem between social classes. It is obvious that the Lord's Supper revealed social differences, a split between the "haves" and the "have-nots."[57] The exact situation of the meal is not entirely clear, but it may be that the owner of the house would invite all the Christian church members of whatever social strata to share in a simple meal of bread and wine. The main difficulty came when, in addition to that, the hosts would invite their own social equals to a superior meal before the poorer class members came to participate in the meal. Paul's objection is directed to those groups whose members were presumably of the high social strata.[58]

The Corinthian church was not homogeneous, but included a fairly wealthy and high-class minority in its membership. The wealthy and more educated of the members were perhaps the leaders and hosts for their fellow believers. As part of the different factions within the church, they were clearly a dominant minority.[59]

In spite of being a dominant minority, they represent the high social class in the church who appear to be very active. For this reason we need not cast doubt on Paul's statement that "not many" at the Corinthian church belonged to a high social level. We may conclude that it is probable that the most active and important members of the church belonged to the οὐ πολλοὶ σοφοὶ δυνατοί and εὐγενεῖς.

Social Context of Paul's Ministry and Mission

The social status of the apostle Paul, like that of the early Christian church, has been more recently under review. Deissmann is especially interested in "the traces which hint at the social class to which Paul belonged." Deissmann identifies three: Paul's trade, his citizenship, and his education or cultural background. On the basis of Paul's citizenship and language, one would have to assign Paul to the high social class. Deissmann's viewpoint is not new. Many centuries earlier, church fathers like John Chrysostom, Gregory of Nyssa, and Theodoret had expressed an identical view concerning Paul's social class.[60] Nevertheless, Deissmann's argument has influenced few scholars; many of them still hold different views.

For instance, W. Ramsay did not look to Paul's trade, but to his Roman citizenship (cf. Acts 16:37; 22:25-29). He said that Paul's citizenship would have "placed Paul amid the aristocracy of any provincial town. Paul's Roman citizenship, Ramsay explained, was proof that his family was one of distinction and at least moderate wealth."[61] Paul's *civitas Romana* has been challenged by W. Stegemann who says that this was a Lucan fiction or misunderstanding.[62] But on the contrary, it is quite clear that Paul was by birth a Roman citizen. On the available data, this was still an unusual distinction in the 30s-50s C.E.[63] Paul's citizenship was like a passport in the Roman Empire which gave him the entrance to almost all the segments of social elites of his time.[64]

The subject of Paul's Roman citizenship is troublesome, though not quite such an inaccessible as Stegemann suggests. The topic is discussed at some length by Sherwin-White, who comments that the dilemma of establishing citizenship was probably not nearly as hard for the first-century Roman as we think since the majority of the people stayed in the same place from one generation to the next and family origins would be public knowledge. The exceptions were soldiers, who were issued with a small metal certificate, a diploma, and merchants who probably carried a small wooden diptych. The general belief is that most Romans citizens carried some kind of document showing the registration of their place of birth.[65]

Among the fundamental evidences about Paul's life belongs his own testimony. Paul's own remark: Ἐγὼ δὲ καὶ γεγέννημαις (*civis Romanus*) is probably no more than a straightforward answer to Claudius Lysias' statement," Ἐγώ πολλοῦ κεφαλαίου τὴν πολιτείαν ταύτην ἐκτησάμηνς (Acts 16:37; 22:25-28)." So, according to Acts 22:3, Paul is reported to have said that he was born in Tarsus. The city of Tarsus was the capital of the Roman province of Cilicia. It is most likely that his birth in Tarsus and his Roman citizenship (*civitas Romana*), which presupposes a relatively high social level, may have given him an appreciation of the Roman Empire.[66] The question of the origin and social status of Paul's relatives is closely linked with his. The assumption for Paul's father being granted Roman citizenship is not very clear. It may be that his father or grandfather had performed some special service for the emperor or other high official, perhaps in relationship with their tent-making business.

There are some apparent difficulties in assuming that the apostle was a citizen of the city in which he was born. Paul describes himself as a Jew and "from Tarsus in Cilicia. . . a citizen of no ordinary city" (Acts 21:37-39). The question is how we are to understand the terms *Tarseus* and *polites*. It was very difficult for foreigners to obtain Roman citizenship. It seems most likely that from his birth Paul was a member of the Jewish community in Tarsus, which as in other places had certain privileges, but not full citizenship,[67] and that in this case as in the Septuagint, *polites* and *Tarseus* refer only to Paul's place of birth; but of course, it is difficult to obtain real clarity in this inquiry.

Therefore, such views could be mere speculation. What is clear is that Paul's status as a *civis Romanus* gives him certain rights and privileges that the common citizens of the empire might expect. Primarily, the social status had been granted to only free-born citizens of the city of Rome, but its privileges were made more widely available as the borders of the empire extended.[68] It seems quite logical that Paul would appeal to people whose social status was similar to his. It gives him the privilege of being among the higher classes of the empire. Perhaps this is the reason why Paul gave a proud answer to his opponents, the arrogant aristocrats in the Christian community at Roman Corinth, when he said: Ἐλεύθερος γὰρ ὢν ἐκ πάντων πᾶσιν ἐμαυτὸν ἐδούλωσας (1 Cor. 9:19). This testimony from Paul's lips is one of the clearest evidences we have concerning his personal social status.

The argument among scholars regarding the nature of Paul's trade has usually also raised the related question of when Paul learned the skills of tent-making. Scholars answer this question by saying that the apostle Paul learned it as part of his Jewish background and some say that Paul learned the trade from his father. Some scholars, however, say that Paul did not learn a trade until later, until he was a student of Gamaliel (Acts 22:3), providing as their warrant the later rabbinic ideal of combining study and teaching of Torah with the practice of a trade: "Excellent is the study of Torah together with worldly occupation."[69]

This is the *communis opinio* of several scholars. G. Bornkamm says that "with Paul, theological training in Judaism was combined with the learning and practice of an occupation."[70] F. F. Bruce states that "many rabbis practiced a trade. . . Paul scrupulously maintained this tradition as a Christian preacher."[71] On the other hand, the idea that Paul's father trained him, thereby following Jewish practice, should not be taken to mean that the practice was followed only in Jewish tradition. In the Graeco-Roman society, the custom was also that the father taught his son a manual trade, as can be seen from the generalizations of Plato and other writers.[72]

The Acts of the Apostles tells us that Paul's mission started with the Jews and then the Gentiles. More exactly, he went to the "God-fearers." They were Gentiles (the σεβόμενοι or φοβούμενοι τὸν θεόν) who sympathized with Jewish beliefs and the moral practices of Judaism. They did not fully convert to Judaism or become circumcised. Luke says that, during Paul's mission at Corinth, he was rejected by the local synagogue rulers and members and declared, "From now on I will go to the Gentiles" (Acts 18:6). Between Paul's first and second missionary journeys, he consciously changed his strategy. On the first trip he used the Jewish synagogue as a platform for his mission, and as a result, he encountered opposition. On his second and third journeys he created an alternative platform for his preaching ministry. He used his social status as a *civis Romanus* and often got sufficient help from wealthy patrons to support his mission.[73]

Paul's ministries (preaching and teaching) took place in the Greco-Roman society where itinerant preachers were many, including the Cynic "beggar philosophers" and their close relatives, the sophisticated Stoic rhetoricians. These professional speakers, for whom rhetorical abilities were often an art, strongly promoted religious ideas and values, particularly in the realm of moral and social ethics.[74] Paul's method of teaching and form of disputation were or seem to be very similar to those of the philosophers of the Greco-Roman philosophical schools of the time.[75]

These similarities between Paul and the popular philosophers of his day have been stressed to the point that some see him as a type of Hellenistic philosopher. Stowers have challenged Judge's categorizing of Paul as a professional "sophist," who belonged to the social class of touring lecturers. He stresses the fact that Judge went so far in comparing Paul with the Cynics as to compare him with the eminent ones as Aelius Aristides and Dio Chrysostom. However, he points out that even if there are some similarities between a Cynic outlook and Paul's preaching and teaching, the Cynic marketplace approach was not well suited to someone who has in mind the formation of permanent community.[76]

On the other hand, Malherbe agrees with the view that there are some similarities, but he wants to stress the function in which Paul adapted what he had learned from the moral philosophers. That function, he says, is mainly pastoral, and Paul's adoption and adaptation of the philosophical tradition show his awareness and understanding of the philosophical pastoral system of his day.[77]

A further indication of Paul's high-class status is the way he moved freely in the highest social circles in the provinces of the empire. His ability to speak

Aramaic and Greek enabled him to be an effective evangelist in both the Jewish and the Greco-Roman worlds. His fluency with the Hebrew language sometimes caused the hostility of the leaders in Jerusalem, according to Acts. At the same time his knowledge of Greek helped him to gain a hearing among the philosophers of Athens as in Acts 17. Paul would hardly have been invited to speak in the council of the Areopagus if he had been ignorant of the Greek language and its culture. A final aspect of Paul's life and social status is to be found by looking at his social attitudes. Paul's position regarding secular authority and the powers vested in the state and other established institutions is highly conservative, but very common of a typical member of the social high class. He believed that all existing authorities, whether good or bad, were instituted by God (Rom. 13:1-7).[78]

Paul did not make any attempt to change the existing social structure of his society (1 Cor. 7:17-23). For Paul, the slaves were to give complete obedience to their earthly masters (Col. 3:22), while the masters had to do their own duty and be just and fair to their slaves (Col. 4:1). Therefore, Paul took a typical attitude of a high-class person, but also was willing to condescend to the lower social classes for the sake of the gospel. Having examined the social context of Paul's ministry, we can now examine the social significance of the house churches where some of these houses served as the base of his ministry.

Social Significance of the House Churches

The study of the significance of the household concept in the New Testament is a relevant one. A misunderstanding of this concept would mean that a good deal of the New Testament socio-historical and theological problems would remain obscured, and especially the household issue in the Corinthian church. Filson is among the first to give attention to the subject. The New Testament church would be better understood if more attention were paid to the actual physical environment under which the first Christians lived, in particular, the significance and function of the house church.[79] Most of the early Christians met in Greco-Roman households. The record of the book of Acts gives the house church a prominent place in the narrative of early Christianity. Voluntary and apologetic sermons were preached in public, but the life of the church was in houses.[80]

Since the beginning of the church, Christian gatherings in homes served as the base of the movement. The first centres of Christian worship were houses owned by church members. In the first century C.E. and for a long time afterwards, Christianity was not recognised as a religion, so there was no such thing as a public meeting place, like the synagogue. Therefore, the early Christians had to use the only facilities available, namely, the houses of some of the believers.[81] The gathering of Christians in homes goes back to the very beginning of the church. Luke's record in Acts mentions such gatherings in the early church (Acts 1:13; 2:46; 5:42; 12:12; etc.). As the church moved outside Palestine, the same pattern is found in other cities.[82]

Other passages refer to the conversion of complete households (Acts 11:14; 16:15, 31-34; 18:8). In the majority of the cases the entire households were converted, including the husband, wives, and the slaves; in some instances, the conversion of the head of the family did not mean the conversion of the slaves (cf. Onesimus in Philemon 10), although it could usually be assumed that when the head of the household became a Christian, the slaves were converted as well.[83] It is not chance that slaves and servants are named οἰκέται (Rom 14:4; 1 Peter 2:18; Luke 16:13). Nor is it accidental that they are referred to beside wives and children in the so-called *Haustafeln*, while other relatives play no role in such lists.[84] Wives, children, and slaves are clearly mentioned in passages such as Col. 3:18ff; Eph. 5.22ff. It is also appears that in 1 Tim. 3:12 the mention of the households could include the slaves as part of the entire *Haustafeln*.

The Lucan and Pauline terms are especially significant in this study. Luke mentions the word "houses" five times. In these references are mentioned the houses of the centurion (Acts 10:2; 11:14); of Lydia the merchant of purple in Philippi (Acts 16:15); of the jailer in Philippi (Acts 16:31); and of Crispus the ruler of the synagogue in Corinth (1 Cor. 18:18). A special connection exists with Paul and the household. He mentions in 1 Cor. 1:16 that ἐβάπτισα δὲ καὶ τὸν Στεφανᾶ οἶκον . . . as the firstfruits of Achaia, who have dedicated themselves to the service of the church.[85]

Some of these people mentioned had slaves, operated businesses, or were normally well-traveled, and in all likelihood were of high social background and lived in the genteel surroundings exemplified by the homes in Pompeii and Ephesus. They were the ones who provided the congregation with a place for worship, but also, like the patrons of the clubs (brotherhoods), became the benefactors (προστάται) and leaders (συνεργοί, διάκονοι, οἱ ἀδελφοί) in the local house churches.[86]

According to Paul, Priscilla and Aquila made their home a centre of Christian fellowship and teaching (1 Cor. 16:19; Rom. 16:5). Romans 16 indicate that each Christian congregation or group had its own place of worship. Paul's comment in Romans 16 indicates that there were various Christian congregations in the capital city. Banks says that there is no reference, (probably due to the size of the city), that Christians ever met as a whole in one place.[87] The church at Rome met in private residences, assuming that chapter 16 was part of the letter to that city.[88] However, some scholars (such as P. Lampe, K. P. Donfried, C. E. B. Cranfield) argue that Romans 16 was added to a copy of the letter that was addressed to Ephesus.

Furthermore, there were some congregations or groups formed in households where their leaders were not Christians, such as the ones mentioned in Rom. 16:10, 11, 14, 15, not to mention the *familia Caesaris*.[89] It seems that Paul knew of at least three such house churches in Rome (Rom. 16:5, 14, 15), and there may have been more than one congregation in Thessalonica (1 Thess. 5:27) and also in Laodicea (Col. 4:15). Despite the fact that they may have formed separate house churches, such congregations were not viewed as being separate churches.[90] As it was mentioned previously in 1 Corinthians 11, they do not have separate communion services.

The house churches as places of worship helped the congregation to a certain extent to have some privacy, a degree of intimacy and stability of place. However, it also created the potential environment for factions among the members. The house church context also set the stage for some conflicts in the allocation of authority among the church members. It is not surprising, then, that in many instances ethical and moral exhortation is addressed to households. This especially applied in the Corinthian congregation where many problems arose because of the internal socio-theological tensions and divisions among the members. Christians of a certain doctrinal tendency clustered together.

Christians from the same social background would also tend to group together. In each of these groups were found feelings of pride and prestige. Such a divided church inevitably became an open setting for any kind of doctrinal and social differences.[91] It is probable that here we could discover the sources of the tensions that are found in Paul's account of the Eucharistic liturgy in the Corinthian church (1 Cor. 11:17-34).

Paul censures the wealthy members for not eating the Lord's Supper in reality. He says that "when you meet together, it is not the Lord's Supper (κυριακὸν δεῖπνον) that you eat. For in eating, each one goes ahead with his own meal (ἴδιον δεῖπνον), and one is hungry and another is drunk. What! Do you not have houses to eat and drink in? Or do you despise the church of God and humiliate those who have nothing?" (1Cor. 11:20ff). It thus appears that an excessive gluttony and other social problems caused the divisions (σιχίσματα, 1Cor. 11:18) and factions (αἱρέσεις, 1Cor. 11:19) mentioned by Paul. Furthermore, it is in this a context that we could find the dilemma among the "strong" and the "weak" arguing over the question of eating meat offered to idols (1 Cor. 8, 10).

The Social Dilemma of the "Strong" and the "Weak" at Roman Corinth

Several of the social difficulties within the Corinthian church can be understood in the light of evidence that people from different social backgrounds had difficulty relating to each other even after they became Christians. They realized that as far as God was concerned, such differences were not important (1 Cor. 7:22; Col. 3:4), but in practice their mutual acceptance still had to be learned the hard way. A closer look at 1 Corinthians shows how these social differences exhibited themselves in the church in Roman Corinth. The problems and divisions in the First Epistle may well have been due to an interpretation of socio-cultural distinctions among the Corinthian congregation.[92]

The different social ranks of the church members in Roman Corinth, were partly responsible for the conflicts between the "strong" and the "weak" Christians over the question of εἰδωλόθυτα, food sacrificed to idols (1 Cor. 8:10).[93] To question the legitimacy of seeking for the theological grounds of the conflict does not exclude the sociological analysis. Furthermore, such an analysis does not reduce a theological conflict to social factors.[94] In his analysis of the strong and the weak in Roman Corinth, Theissen does not identify the weak as either Jews or Gentiles. Paul saw the dilemma as a general one, and the socio-economic factors help us to grasp the whole picture of the conflict. Paul makes a contrast between the strong and the weak in 1 Cor. 1:26ff and relates that contrast to the social stratification of the Christian church at Roman Corinth.[95]

It seems probable; therefore, that the weak Christians could be found on the lower social level rather than in a particular national group, and the apostle appears to identify himself with them in his dialogue over their difficulties. It is noteworthy to mention that the diet of the majority of the people (including the church members in Corinth) did not include meat. It is likely, then, that the problem of eating meat sold in the market place (1 Cor. 10:25ff) "was to them purely theoretical" because they did not have enough money to afford what the wealthy members of the community and church could afford on an almost daily basis.

Nevertheless, that is not the main problem, for Paul's concern was mostly with the eating of meat sacrificed to idols in the pagan temples.[96] It has been argued that all, or very nearly all, of the meat sold in the macellum was εἰδωλόθυτον, meat offered presumably in nearby temples.[97]

On the contrary, it seems that the argument that the meat sold in the macellum was εἰδωλόθυτον is not wholly convincing, but the observation that the macella and temples "most of the time have been contiguous is not on account of any religious connection but because public buildings are almost inevitably grouped together in the middle of a city."[98] The presence also in one shop [in Pompeii] of entire skeletons of sheep suggests that the meat may have been sold on the hoof or slaughtered in the macellum as well as sold already butchered or sacrificed in a temple.[99] Thus, it appears that the contention that in Paul's day practically all meat came from the macellum cannot be accepted in toto because the data show the contrary.[100] However, as a matter of fact, the data show that there was in pagan ceremony an open immolation.

The animal was again divided into three parts: A token part to be burned, a share for the priest, and a substantial amount left to the magistrates. What they did not use, they sold to the shops and markets for resale to the public. Such meat was eagerly bought by pagans. Aesop bought tongues of sacrificial pigs in the butcher shop. Pliny indicates the purchaser knew what she or he was buying.[101]

In addition, it is also known that the only time that meat came on the market was after pagan festivals where it had been part of the victims sacrificed to the gods.[102]   Nevertheless, some members of the Corinthian church (the "strong") argued that eating meat sacrificed in the pagan temples did not pose a social-ethical problem, whereas for others (the "weak"), it certainly did cause some problems.

It was the custom that in public festivals all citizens, regardless of their social status, could eat meat. However, Theissen questions whether the citizens from the low social class were able to attend those meals that contained meat offered to idols. But the main questions of some of the new converts from the lower class were whether to eat meat sacrificed in pagan temples and how to deal with their consciences (1 Cor. 8:7). For the Jews converted to Christianity, it was also difficult to deal with the public distribution of such meat sacrificed to idols (1 Cor. 8:10).[103]   However, the strong from the upper social level were used to eating meat almost every day and therefore did not associate it with a cult because they did not believe in the existence of idols (1 Corinthians 8). On the other hand, we find the weak Christians (1 Cor. 8:10f; 9:22) described as having weak συνείδησιν (1 Cor. 8:7, 12), lacking this γνῶσις, and because of their former pagan customs regarding εἰδωλόθυτα as a dangerous matter.

Many scholars have attempted to define these positions in terms of their theological views or beliefs.[104]   Nevertheless, Theissen does not at all reject these positions, but tries to show that there is also a social dimension to the problem, to which the ideological factors would have to be connected.[105]   In his interpretation of 1 Cor. 1:26ff, the strong are the socially powerful, who accept invitations to dinner where εἰδωλόθυτα would be served (1 Cor. 10:27) in a pagan temple, and have had some social or business responsibilities with the community and the church.[106]   Furthermore, an invitation to a social gathering presented a dilemma to the weak, who didn't want to appear impolite to the host family and his family as well.[107]

The strong justified their behaviour by appealing to their "γνῶσις," because idols do not exist, as Paul states. Some have found parallels between the "strong" Christians and later Christians Gnostics, who also had a liberal attitude toward eating meat sacrificed to idols.[108] However Pétrement makes this observation: "Gnosticism does not consist merely of the use of the word 'gnosis'; it is a teaching that is concerned with the relations of God, man, and the world, and this teaching is nowhere found, it seems, before Christianity."[109]   On the other hand, Wilson points out that "the problem remains that for the earliest stages we have no clear knowledge of it, no documentation that would allow us to trace its development.

In regard to the beginnings of this movement we are still in the main reduced to hypothesis."[110]   Furthermore, there is not a sequence between the Corinthian "γνῶσις" and the Christian Gnosticism of the second century, but neither can some similarities between the two be ignored.

In conclusion, the connections between the "gnosis" problem in Roman Corinth and Christian Gnosticism of the second century are a matter of debate, and with good reason. There is scarcely a direct association.[111] However, among the "strong" Christians who did not see anything wrong in eating meat sacrificed to idols, the only analogies within Christianity come from Gnostic groups, as may be seen in the following examples:[112]

> Justin on Gnostics in general: "But know that there are many who profess their faith in Jesus and are considered Christians, yet claim there is no harm in their eating meat sacrificed to idols" (*Dialogus cum Tryphone* 35, 1). ". . .Of these some are called Marcionites, some Valentinians, some Basilidians and some Saturnilians" (*Dial.* 35, 6).

> Irenaeus on the Valentinians: "For this reason the most perfect among them freely practice everything which is forbidden. . . . For they eat food that was offered to idols with indifference, and they are the first to arrive at any festival party of the gentiles that takes place in honor of the idols, while some of them do not even avoid the murderous spectacle of fights with beasts and single combats, which are hateful to God and man.   And some, who immoderately indulge the desires of the flesh, say that they are repaying to the flesh what belongs to the flesh and to the spirit what belongs to the spirit" (*Adversus haereses* I,6,3).

> Irenaeus on the followers of Basilides: "They despise things sacrificed to idols and think nothing of them, but enjoy them without any anxiety at all. They also enjoy the other (pagan) festivals and all that can be called appetite" (*Adv.haer.*I,24,5; cf. Eusebius, *Historia ecclesiastica* IV,7,7).

> Origen on the Simonians: "Nowhere in the world are Simonians now to be found, although Simon, in order to win a larger following, freed his disciples from the peril of death, which the Christians are taught to prefer, by instructing them to regard pagan worship as a matter of indifference" (*Contra Celsum* VI,11).

> Epiphanius on libertine Gnostics of a much later period: "And whatever we eat, be it meat, vegetables, bread or anything else, we are doing a

kindness to created things by collecting the soul from all things   and transmitting it with ourselves to the heavenly world. For this reason they eat every kind of meat and say they do so that we may show mercy to our kind" (*Panarion* XXXVI,9,2).

It cannot be argued on the assumption of these examples that eating meat offered to idols was the normal custom in all the Gnostic groups. There were some of these Gnostics who practised asceticism. To eat meat sacrificed to idols was not the typical habit, but one of the customs of the Gnostics.[113] It seems most likely that there was a Gnostic element in the Corinthian church which appealed to and believed in the intellectual level, soteriology based on knowledge and self-consciousness and social power within the church and the community and their openness to the pagan world.[114] However, these examples do not prove that some of the Corinthians practised what the Gnostics of the second or even third century practised.

Paul was informed of the conflict between the strong and the weak Christians in a letter that appeared obviously written from the viewpoint of the strong (1 Cor. 8:1), but he also received oral information (1 Cor. 1:11; 11:18). The strong and the weak Christians together ate the Lord's Supper, and at those fellowship meals their different social status was responsible for conflicts. It is interesting to note that Paul addresses his response exclusively to the strong Christians,[115] and appeals to them to be careful to regulate their behaviour by "the obligation of love" (*Liebespflicht*).[116]

On the whole case, the conflict between the weak and the strong reveals the presence among the church members at Roman Corinth of persons of significantly different social strata.[117] It seems also that the conflict appears to be caused by "excessive individualism" on the part of some members (the "strong"), but in view of the divisions (σχίσματα, 1 Cor. 11:18) and factions (αἱρέσεις, 1 Cor. 11:19) noted by Paul, Theissen observes that probably Paul has two groups in mind, those who could provide their own meal and those who had nothing.[118]

The fellowship meal that the wealthy ate is contrasted with the Lord's Supper (ἴδιον δεῖπνον' σ. κυριακὸν δεῖπνον). The misunderstanding, as Paul sees it, is that the wealthy Christians continued to consider it as their own meal. Therefore, Paul repeats to them once again the words of institution (1 Cor. 11:23ff) to confirm that it should be considered as the Lord's Supper, to be shared by the entire congregation. Although the fellowship meal was not a private meal, the participants were guests in Gaius's house; and it is understandable that the custom, if not the specific rationale for it, appears to have created the tension within the congregation.[119]

The wealthy members may have acted without any wrong motives. They probably thought that they were doing a social service for the poor members of the church. Malherbe says, however, the conflict was rooted in the fact that the social structure and the attendant behaviour that it brought into the church collided with the traditional Christian concept of the nature of community.[120] Paul does not, however, adopt a practical approach in addressing himself to these conflicts. He advises the wealthy members to eat at home, but their conduct in the table fellowship, his main concern, is seen from a theological viewpoint. Paul does not consistently agree with the "strong's" position, even though he is in basic agreement with their ideas about idolatry.[121]

Paul's recommendation, based on *Liebespflicht*, that the members from the high social levels accommodate their conduct to the low classes, is designed to reduce the tension between them and keep the unity of the church. It seems clear that an exclusively mental compromise to unity is not practical.[122]   In 1 Corinthians 9 Paul introduces himself as an example of the necessity to be willing to give up one's own rights for the sake of others. He has the right to earn his living through the preaching of the good news, but he gives up that right for the sake of the church members in Roman Corinth to whom he ministers.

Paul's view is that the gospel is a life-and-death matter, and he is willing to give up his right rather than become an obstacle in the way of a person's acceptance of the gospel. Paul's desire is to become all things to all people in order to win them for Christ.[123]   The behaviour of the well-to-do is not just offensive to the others' feelings, but it also involves judgment (1 Cor. 11:29-32).[124] This type of recommendation from Paul is given with the desire that a greater social unity may come about whenever the church members at Roman Corinth celebrate together the Lord's Supper.

Summary

The social setting of early Christianity, especially the Hellenistic Corinthian Church, was neither a proletarian movement among the poorer social classes nor a movement among the aristocrats of the Roman Empire, although some of the latter were converted by Paul to Christianity. Nevertheless, early Christianity was a movement which spread rapidly and grew in all segments of the society of the Graeco-Roman world. Therefore, Paul's statement in 1 Cor. 1: 26-28 cannot be used to support the assumption that early Christianity was a lower-class phenomenon. Though the apostle Paul worked with his hands (1 Cor 4:12), yet this does not put him in a lower social class. The social-status terms that Paul uses to describe his idea about work express the proper language of a person of the upper class.

The similarities between Paul and the philosophers of his day have been stressed. Some see Paul as a type of "sophist" or Hellenistic philosopher. This view has been challenged, since Paul's ministry of preaching and teaching was different from the Cynic's approach in the marketplace, an approach not well suited to someone who had in mind to build and nurture a permanent community. Paul's style befits a pastor more than a moral philosopher. His example reveals that he wanted to show a Christ-like pattern for cultural and religious contact with the outside society. Paul's apostolic ministry serves as an example, for he instructed the Corinthian Church members that his *modus operandi* was an *imitatio Christi.*[125]

It seems clear that Paul adopted and adapted some traditions of the philosopher and applied them to his pastoral system. One indication of Paul's social status is the way he moved freely in the high circles in the Roman society. His ability to speak Hebrew and Greek enabled him to be an effective preacher in both the Jewish and Greco-Roman worlds.

Paul's attitude toward the secular society and institutions and power vested in the state was typical of a member of the high social class. Paul was at home in the Greek society and was fluent in several languages, but he was also at home as a *civis Romanus* in the Roman Empire. These aspects of his inheritance and background, combined with his training in Judaism, made him a gifted preacher and teacher to the Gentiles on behalf of Christ's gospel.

The study of the importance of the house churches has become one of the fascinating subjects in the investigation of early Christianity. As mentioned above, to fail to understand the house church in the New Testament times is to close a window through which students may see more clearly how the early church functioned at the beginning (Acts 1:13; 2:46; 5:42; 12:12). The house church has a prominent place in the formation of early Christianity as the life of the church takes place in houses.[126] It is in this context that we find the apostle Paul exhorting and addressing the house churches, especially the Corinthian congregation where many problems arose because of the social and theological conflicts among the members.

Consequently, it is also in this social setting that the strong and the weak argue over the question of the legitimacy of eating meat sacrificed to idols (1Cor. 8,10). It has been argued that the main motive which caused the conflicts between the two parties (besides the socio-theological differences) was an "excessive individualism" on the part of the strong Christians who take advantage of their high social status over the poor weak members.[127]

It thus appears that the main problem in the tension between the strong and the weak is not εἰδωλόθυτα *per se*, but the problem of the conscience of the weak in a pluralistic society.[128] It is well known that the meat came from the *macellum*, where it was offered to the pagan gods and afterwards sold in the shop.[129] It seems quite clear, then, that the weak Christians were worried about participating in the pagan festivals eating such meat.

Paul knows about the conflicts between the strong and the weak through a letter that he received written supposedly from the standpoint of the strong Christians. It seems that the conflicts happened not when they participated together in the Lord's Supper, but during the preceding fellowship meal. Again, the main issue is not that the poor were complaining because they could not eat meat, but because of the way they were treated, because the strong Christians used to bring the best portion of the food, whether it was meat or not, for those who belonged to the same social level; and obviously when the poor Christians arrived, almost all the food was gone. Paul's desire is that the unity of the church be kept, no matter what is the participant's social background in the Lord's Supper.

Notes

[1] Abraham J. Malherbe, *Social Aspects of Early Christianity* (Philadelphia: Fortress Press, 1983), 1-28. See also further details in W. G. Kümmel's article. He says that "Interesse in der sozialen Wirklichkeit des frühen Christentums ist natürlich nichts Neues, stellt R. Scroggs zu Beginn eines Berichts über die gegenwärtige Lage der soziologischen Erforschung des Neuen Testaments mit Recht fest und verweist auf die Arbeiten von A. Deissmann, E. Lohmeyer, C. J. Cadoux und der sog. Chicago-Schule; aber ebenso kann G. Theissen mit Recht die Feststellung, dass man in meinem Forschungsbericht über die neutestamentliche Wissenschaft im 20. Jh. von 1970, vergeblich nach dem Stichwort Soziologie oder Sozialgeschichte suchen wird, als zweifellos zeittreffend bezeichnen." W. G. Kümmel, "Das Urchristentum," *TRu* 50 (1985), 327. D. J. Harrington, "Sociological Concepts and the Early Church: A Decade of Research," *Theological Studies* 41 (1980), 181.

[2] W. A. Meeks, *The First Urban Christians* (New Haven: Yale University Press, 1983), 2.

[3] Robin Scroggs, "The Sociological Interpretation of the New Testament: The Present State of Research," *New Testament Studies* 26 (1980): 164.

[4] Meeks, 4-5. The truth of the matter is that there are tensions on both sides, and both claim that they have the right methods to interpret the text. Tidball rightly comments that "the root of the tensions which exist between a sociological interpretation of behaviour and a theological interpretation of the same behaviour usually lies in the imperialist claims which each discipline makes. That is, a sociologist is being imperial when he claims that his explanation of behaviour is the total explanation of that behaviour. Or to put it in another way, he is a reductionist in that he says that his version of reality is the only valid explanation and ultimately all explanations are reduced or boil down to nothing but his own. Similarly Christians may claim that the problems in society are caused by sin and that is all there is to it. Such a claim, however, would be equally imperialist or reductionist." Derek Tidball, *An Introduction to the Sociology of the New Testament* (Exeter: The Paternoster Press, 1983), 17.

[5] David A. Black & David S. Dockery, *New Testament Criticism & Interpretation* (Grand Rapids: Zondervan Publishing House, 1991). "Sociological Criticism," by M. Robert Mulholland, Jr., 304-306. There are several weaknesses and strengths in the field of

Sociological Criticism: (1) One of the primary weaknesses of any behavioural methology applied to the Scriptures is the almost overpowering tendency to view the realities of spiritual experience from within a human-centered frame of reference. (2) Another potential weakness in Sociological Criticism is to apply to the world of the New Testament sociological paradigms developed in the present world whose social, political, economic, and cultural dynamics are radically, if not totally alien to the Roman world of the first century. (3) Another weakness, as noted above in reference to the work of Malina, is to employ sociological models and/or methods in a Procrustian manner that trims the evidence to fit the parameters of the model/method, often casting aside evidence whose presence is crucial for an accurate understanding of the text. (4) Perhaps the most subtle weakness in Sociological Criticism, implicit in all that has been said, is the tendency toward sociological reductionism. "However, there are several good points that can be considered as strengths of Sociological Criticism: (1) "One strength of Sociological Criticism is its ability to help us distinguish between our own sociological matrix and that of the New Testament. (2) Another important strength is Sociological Criticism's insights into the essentially sociological dimension of language. (3) Perhaps the greatest strength of Sociological Criticism is its focus upon the incarnational reality of human life. (4) Sociological Criticism can be an effective means of radical encounter with God by enabling us to enter into the life-matrix of the community of faith, understand the reality of God's incarnation in that particular sociological milieu, and open ourselves and our community of faith to the same kind of relationship with God in our own life-matrix."

[6] Thomas F. Best, "The Sociological Study of the New Testament: Promise and Peril of a New Discipline," *Scottish Journal of Theology* 36 (1983): 190.

[7] Gerd Theissen, *Sociology of Early Palestinian Christianity,* trans. J. Bowden (Philadelphia: Fortress Press, 1978), 97. He says that "we can explain why there was widespread social rootlessness in Palestine at that time, but not why one man became a criminal, another holy man, the third an emigrant and the fourth an ascetic. Sociological explanations only apply to typical features and not to individual instances."

[8] Scroggs, "The Sociological Interpretation," 166.

[9] P. F. Esler, *Community and Gospel in Luke-Acts: The Social and Political Motivations of Lucan Theology* (Cambridge: Cambridge University Press, 1987), 172.

[10] *Octavius* 36. See also J. G. Gager, *Kingdom and Community: The Social World of Early Christianity* (Englewood: Prentice-Hall, 1975), 94.

[11] Origen, *Contra Celsum,* trans. H. Chadwick (Cambridge: The University Press, 1965), 158.

[12] Meeks, *The First Urban,* 51-73. He adds, "He had a genius for popularizing the results of his own and others' research, and two extended trips through the Middle East enabled him to reconstruct 'the world of St. Paul' in terms of a vivid, thoroughly romantic travelogue. In general his identification of the language of the New Testament with the vulgar Koine of the nonliterary papyri supported the view that the writers had belonged to the lower classes, but Deissmann had some difficulty in situating Paul himself."

[13] "Ohne sie [die Volkstümlichkeit des Urchristentums] zu kennen und stark zu unterstreichen, können wir den Erfolg der Werbekraft des Evangeliums historisch nicht

verstehen. Die Mission des Paulus war Handwerkermission, nicht Mission eines Studierten." "Was Kautsky instinkiv gesehen hat, ist richtig: der enge Zusammenhang des Urchristentums mit den volkstümlichen Schichten." A. Deissmann, *Licht vom Osten. Das Neue Testament und die neu entdeckten Texte der Hellenistisch-Römischen Welt* (4. Aufl., Tübingen, 1923), 329, 405. English version, A. Deissmann, *Light from the Ancient East* (London: Hodder & Stoughton, 1927).

[14] Bengt Holmberg, *Sociology and The New Testament* (Minneapolis: Fortress Press, 1990), 29. He further adds: "At one extreme one could find a Marxist like Karl Kautsky, describing the first Christians as originally a proletarian and revolutionary movement among the lower classes, characterized by wild class hate, intense egalitarianism, contempt for work, and destruction of family life. The leading elite were radically poor, spirit filled 'apostles and prophets.' Only gradually and as a consequence of spreading into a non-Jewish environment, the new movement received a few educated and socially higher placed converts."

[15] Ernst Troeltsch, *Die Soziallehren der Christlichen Kirchen und Gruppen* (in Gesammelte Schriften I, Tübingen, 1912), 15-17. E. Troeltsch, *The Social Teaching of the Christian Churches*, trans. O. Wyon, 2 vols., 1931 (New York, 1960), says that "For the understanding of the whole fundamental direction of Christianity in relation to the social problem, it is decisive to realize that the preaching of Jesus and the creation of the new religious community was not the creation of a social movement, which means that it did not evolve from or adapt to any class struggle, and actually never relates directly to the social upheavals of ancient society."

[16] Ibid., 22-25.

[17] Gager, *Kingdom and Community*, 96.

[18] Ibid., 106-108.

[19] Holmberg, *Sociology*, 35. "One refers to economic level ("class," "dispossessed"), the other refers to interior feelings of alienation from established society. He aligns himself with and quotes from scholars who have only the first set of criteria in mind, but guards himself by constant reference to a 'relative deprivation,' which is experienced especially by people of some means. Relative deprivation can actually be experienced by any person, at whatever level of society. Consequently it is useless as a criterion for indicating any social level."

[20] E. A. Judge, *The Social Pattern of the Christian Groups in the First Century* (London: The Tyndale Press, 1960), 52-54.

[21] Holmberg, *Sociology*, 39-42. He also comments: "Judge relates the data concerning social level to social structures of the surrounding society, Palestinian, Greek, and Roman (class system, patrons, and their clientele). He also evidences a clearer grasp of the complexity of the issue as such: data are generally scarce, there exists no statistical material, and some of our information only permits of indirect, vague conclusions. Furthermore, he points out that the data that are more directly relevant, namely prosopographical information may not have any high degree of representation."

[22] Martin Hengel, *Property and Riches in the Early Church*, trans. J. Bowden (London: SCM Press, 1974), 36-39. The old dispute concerning whether the nephew of the emperor Domitian, "Flavius Clemens and his wife, Flavia Domitilla, because of their Judaizing tendencies--thus Dio Cassius 67, 14. Flavius Clemens' niece of the same name,

because of her conversion to Christianity--thus Eusebius, HE 3, 18, 4--were executed or exiled by the emperor, is still unresolved. It shows that we must at least reckon with the possibility that in individual cases the new faith quickly penetrated to the heights of society. The evidence for these increases it is found in the second half of the second century."

[23] Ibid. 64-65.

[24] Holmberg, *Sociology*, 41.

[25] Malherbe, *Social Aspects*, 31.

[26] Floyd V. Filson, "The Significance of the Early House Churches," *Journal of Biblical Literature* 39 (1939): 105-107.

[27] Robert M. Grant, *Early Christianity and Society* (London: W. Collins, 1978), 11.

[28] Heinz Kreissig, "Zur Sozialen Zusammensetzung der frühchristlichen Gemeinden im ersten Jahrhundert U.Z.," *Eirene, Studia Graeca et Latina* 6 (1967): 91-100.

[29] Malherbe, *Social Aspects*, 13. Furthermore, we must be aware of the different relationships that "were possible between the literature and the communities to which it was addressed. We must, for instance, resist the temptation to see so much of early Christian literature either as a community product or as reflecting the actual circumstances of the communities with which the writings are associated. We too frequently read of communities that virtually produced one or another of the Gospels or for which they were produced. It is at least possible that some documents were rescued from obscurity, not because they represented the viewpoint of communities, but precisely because they challenged them."

[30] olmberg, *Sociology*, 55.

[31] Loveday Alexander, "Luke's Preface in the Context of Greek Preface-Writing," *Novum Testamentum* 18 (1986): 49.

[32] Meeks, *The First Urban*, 55.

[33] John G. Gager, "Social Description and Sociological Explanation," *Religious Study Review* 5, (1979): 174-180. Holmberg comments, "In his 1982 article, however, Gager seems to draw nearer to his original position again. The early Christians may not have been poverty-stricken slaves, but they were among the disinherited of the Roman social order." Holmberg, p. 61: "Recent times have seen a rather lively debate about the social status of the early Christians and about what it meant to be among the disinherited in the Roman world. One side of the debate, represented by Theissen and myself, holds that most of the members of Christian communities came from the lower classes. The other side, represented by E. A. Judge, Abraham Malherbe, Robert Grant, holds that 'the triumph of Christianity took place from the top down."

[34] Georg Schöllgen, "Was wissen wir über die Sozialstruktur der paulinischen Gemeinden?" *New Testament Studies* 34 (1988): 78.

[35] Ibid., 72-74.

[36] Holmberg, *Sociology*, 67-69.

[37] W. A. Meeks, "The Social Context of Pauline Theology," *Interpretation* 37 (1982): 266-277. He adds, "we should ask rather what clues we have that would indicate ranking in the several hierarchies that were relevant in that time and place. We would want to know about ethnic origins, citizenship, personal liberty, wealth, occupation, age, sex, and

public offices or honours. We musk ask, too, about the context within which each of these rankings is valid; for example, to be a freedman in the early years of Roman Corinth, a colony whose first settlers were mostly freedmen, would be less of a social liability than in Rome or in Antioch."

[38] Meeks,*The First Urban*, 269-271.

[39] J. E. Stambaugh andD. L. Balch, *The New Testament in Its Social Environment.* Philadelphia: The Westminster Press, 157.

[40] Strabo, VIII, 6, 23. See also Gerd Theissen, *The Social Setting of Pauline Christianity*, trans. J. H. Schütz (Edinburgh: T. & T. Clark, 1982), 99. Under these circumstances, the Roman element was powerful, even if we can find there some Greek slaves, for instance, among the freedmen. He says: "Thus it is certainly no accident that eight of the seventeen surviving names of Corinthian Christians are Latin: Aquila, Fortunatus, Gaius, Lucius, Priscilla, Quartus, Titius Justus, and Tertius," even though some of them have Jewish background (Aquila and Priscilla, for instance).

[41] Meeks, *The First Urban*, 47.

[42] Oscar Broneer, "Corinth: Centre of St. Paul's Missionary Work," *Biblical Archaeologist* 14 (1951): 78-96.

[43] Stambaugh and Balch, *The New Testament*, 158-159.

[44] Dio *Orationes* 37, 8.

[45] Strabo, VIII, 6, 20. See also G. Theissen, 101.

[46] Meeks, *The First Urban*. 47.

[47] Stambaugh, and Balch, *The New Testament*, 52-55.

[48] C. S. Hill, "The Sociology of the New Testament Church to A.D. 62: An Examination of the Early New Testament Church in Relation to Its Contemporary Social Setting" (unpublished Ph.D. diss., Nottingham University, 1972), 175.

[49] Howard C. Kee, *Christian Origins in Sociological Perspective* (London: SCM Press, 1980), 97.

[50] Derek Tidball, *An Introduction to the Sociology of the New Testament* (Exeter: The Paternoster Press, 1983), 91. This position was further developed by other influential Marxist writers, most notably Karl Kautsky. "He cites as evidence for his views both 1 Cor. 1:26 and Jerome who said that Christianity recruited not from the Lyceum or the Academy but from the lowest rabble. In fact, Kautsky claims, it was a common joke in the Roman Empire that Christians could convert only the simple minded" and also adds that "the history of early Christianity has notable points of resemblance with the modern working class movement. Like the latter, Christianity was originally a movement of oppressed people; it first appeared as the religion of slaves and emancipated slaves, of poor people deprived of all rights, of people subjugated or dispersed by Rome."

[51] Theissen, *The Social Setting*, 70, 71.

[52] Hans Conzelmann, *1 Corinthians*, trans. J. W. Leitch (Philadelphia: Fortress Press, 1975), 50.

[53] Philo, *De somniis* 155.

[54] W. Wuellner, "The Sociological Implications of 1 Corinthians 1:26-28 Reconsidered," *Studia Evangelica* 43 (1973): 666-672.

[55] Theissen, *The Social Setting*, 73.

---

[56] Holmberg, *Sociology*, 45.   See also Gerd Theissen's detailed study of his four criteria on pages 73-96.

[57] Theissen, *The Social Setting*, 96.

[58] Tidball, *An Introduction*, 101. Meeks also observes that "there is a good reason to suspect that the 'strong' in Corinth belong to the wealthier and socially better placed minority of the Christian group (compare 1 Cor. 1:26). Perhaps, as many modern scholars have argued, 'the strong' Christians had developed some complex ideology, an early form of Gnosticism, for example, or some mystical interpretation of baptism and spirit-possession, but we do not have to imagine anything so elaborate in order to understand the argument of these three chapters." Wayne Meeks, *The Moral World of the First Christians* (London: SPCK, 1987), 133.

[59] Holmberg, *Sociology*, 45-47.

[60] Ronald F. Hock, "Paul's Tent Making and the Problem of His Social Class," *Journal of Biblical Literature* 97 (1978): 555-564.

[61] W. Ramsay, *St. Paul the Traveler and the Roman Citizen* (New York: Putman's Sons, 1896), 31.

[62] Wolfgang Stegemann, "War der Apostel Paulus ein römischer Bürger?" *ZNW* 78 (1987): 200.

[63] Gillian Clark, "The Social Status of Paul," *Expository Times* 96 (1984-85): 110-111.

[64] Tidball, *An Introduction*, 92.

[65] Hill, 195.

[66] Seyoon Kim, *The Origin of Paul's Gospel* (Grand Rapids: Eerdmans, 1981), 38.

[67] Martin Hengel, "The Pre-Christian Paul" in *The Jews Among Pagans and Christians*, edited by Judith Lieu, John North, and Tessa Rajak, (New York: Routledge, Chapman and Hall, Inc., 1992), 30. He further comments that "there is no reason for doubting Luke's information that the apostle had Roman citizenship. The reasons brought forward against this are not convincing. Thus Paul may have been flogged three times (2 Corinthians 11:25) because he deliberately kept quiet about his citizenship in order to follow Christ in his suffering. We must also take into account the possibility that the city magistrates may not have felt themselves constrained by his claim to privilege. That Paul never mentions it does not mean anything, since he keeps quiet about almost all private matters. Had he been a mere *peregrinus* Paul would have been condemned in Judaea without much fuss and would not have been sent to the imperial court in Rome." Nor does the statement that Paul never mentions his full three-part Roman name mean anything, "since this usage was not always customary in Greek-speaking circles and went against the custom of Judaism and of early Christianity."

[68] Tidball, *An Introduction*, 93.

[69] Ronald F. Hock, *The Social Context of Paul's Ministry* (Philadelphia: Fortress Press, 1980), 22. He adds that "however widely and confidently expressed this view, it is open to question at three points. First, the history of Paul being educated by Gamaliel, known only from Acts 22:3, is open to question for a variety of reasons, chief among them the incongruity of a persecuting Paul having been the student of so tolerant a teacher as Gamaliel (cf.5:34). Second, even if we grant Paul's education under Gamaliel, this fact does not require that Paul's education was done with a professional goal in mind, which

the rabbinic ideal of combining trade and Torah has in view. Third, even if Paul were a professional student, the ideal of combining Torah and trade is difficult to establish much earlier than the middle of the second century A.D., that is, long after Paul."

[70] G. Bornkamm, *Paul* (New York: Harper & Row, 1971), 12.

[71] F. F. Bruce, *Paul: Apostle of the Heart Set Free* (Grand Rapids: Eerdmans, 1977), 108.

[72] Plato *Protag* 328A. For the early empire: Dio *Orat* 4.47; 7.111; 71.4, and Lucian *Abd* 22. See also R. F. Hock, 23. Among the latter we may note the well-known case of Socrates learning the trade from his father Sophroniscus and the lesser-known case of Tryphon, a weaver from Oxyrhynchus and a contemporary of Paul, who also learned the trade from his father and in turn taught one of his sons.

[73] E. A. Judge, "Early Christians as a Scholastic Community," *Journal of Religious History* 1 (1960-61): 127. In this article Judge tries to compare Paul with other contemporaries. Although the detailed research is helpful, the attempt to present the early Christians as a scholastic community is not altogether convincing.

[74] E. E. Ellis, *Pauline Theology: Ministry and Society* (Grand Rapids: Eerdmans, 1989), 147.

[75] Abraham J. Malherbe, *Paul and the Popular Philosophers* (Minneapolis: Fortress Press, 1989), 68. During the last hundred years, New Testament scholars have shown that many aspects of Paul's life and letters are illuminated when they are examined in the light of Graeco-Roman culture. "There can no longer be any doubt that Paul was familiar with the teaching, methods of operation, and style of argumentation of the philosophers of the period, all of which he adopted and adapted to his own purposes. This is not to argue that he was a technical philosopher; neither were his philosophical contemporaries. The philosophers with whom Paul should be compared were not metaphysicians who specialized in systematizing abstractions, but, like Paul, were preachers and teachers who saw their main goal to be the reformation of the lives of people encountered in a variety of contexts, ranging from the imperial court and the salons of the rich to the street corners."

[76] Stanley K. Stowers, "Social Status, Public Speaking and Private Teaching: The Circumstances of Paul's Preaching Activity," *Novum Testamentum* 24 (1984): 69.

[77] Malherbe, *Paul* 68.

[78] ill, 198.

[79] Filson, "Early House Churches," 105-106.

[80] Stambaugh, and Balch. *The New Testament,,*39.

[81] J. Murphy-O'Connor, *St. Paul's Corinth* (Wilmington: Michael Glazier, Inc., 1982), 153-155. The archaeological excavation at Corinth has brought to light relevant information regarding the size and style of some houses of the Roman period. One of the mosaic floors discovered is dated to the late 1st century C.E. Some of the houses discovered reveal that their owners were upper-class wealthy people.

[82] Filson, 106, finds that "outside of Jerusalem, no temple served as a partial centre of attention for the Christians. Whenever the synagogue was closed to Christian propaganda--and this seems to have occurred early in the development of Paul's work in the cities he visited--the house church dominated the situation. Only rarely could a public assembly hall be obtained (Acts 19:9). With the exception of such limited use as

could be made of the market place and other public areas of the city, the regular setting for both Christian meetings and evangelistic preaching was found in the homes of believers."

[83] Stambaugh,, and Balch. *The New Testament,* 139.

[84] Theissen, 86. He mentions also that "the centurion is εὐσεβὴς. . . σὺν παντὶ τῷ οἴκῳ αὐτοῦ (Acts 10:2). He relates his vision to "two of his slaves and a devout soldier from among those that waited on him" (Acts 10:7). Luke surely doesn't want to say that the slaves were not themselves devout, although the soldier belongs to the God-fearers--as if the centurion would entrust his vision to slaves who were unbelievers. Rather, the predicate εὐσεβὴς is needed only for the soldier, since the slaves were already characterized in 10:2 as God-fearing."

[85] Meeks, *The First Urban,* 75.

[86] Ellis, *Pauline Theology* 142.

[87] Robert Banks, *Paul's Idea of Community* (Exeter: The Paternoster Press, 1980), 39.

[88] Ibid., 146. "In that chapter four or five Christian congregations may be distinguished. The assembly in the home of Priscilla and Aquila and 'the saints' with Philologus and Julia were probably congregations meeting in those residences. The 'brothers' with Hermas may refer to a house used both for Christian workers and for congregational meetings. Those from Aristobulus and from Narcissus were, like the believers from Caesar's house (Phil. 4:22) and the Roman synagogues of the Augustesians and the Agrippesians, probably congregations centering on the freedmen and slaves of those two households and meeting there."

[89] Meeks, *The First Urban,* 76.

[90] Malherbe, *Social Aspects,* 70.

[91] Filson, "Early House Churches," 110. Another situation which probably had developed in the house church is the problem of the four-sided party strife at Corinth. "The only reasonable supposition is that the Apollos partisans, for example, found each other's company and ideas congenial, and therefore met together, and that the other groups likewise had not only their own party slogans, but also their separate places of assembly."

[92] Tidball, *An Introduction,* 99-100. "Paul was not arguing that the social distinctions should be completely abandoned by Christians any more than the biological differences between the sexes disappeared when people became Christians. But he was arguing that the church was an alternative society which operated on different principles from the normal society and enjoyed entirely new relationships. Within the church there must be acceptance and respect for people whatever their class background and the acknowledgement that God may use some prominently within the church who would not normally have risen to positions of leadership. In a word, the prominent members of the Church at Corinth needed to repent of their snobbery and treat the ordinary members with more seriousness."

[93] Theissen, *The Social Setting,* 121.

[94] Malherbe, *Social Aspects,* 78. He insists, however, that as a rule, "theological convictions   become operative only when social groups bestow on them the power to govern their conduct."

[95] Theissen, *The Social Setting,* 122-124.

[96] Malherbe, *Social Aspects,* 79.

[97] Ehrhardt, 280-282.

[98] Barrett, 47-48. "That meat was to be had that was not ἱερόθυτον is confirmed by Plutarch, *Sympos.* VIII 8, 3, where it is said that the Pythagoreans ὡς μάλιστα μὲν ἐγεύοντο τῶν ἱεροθύτων ἀπαρχόμενοι τοῖς θεοῖς, which seems to mean that the Pythagoreans, who took flesh very sparingly, ate it only in the form of ἱερόθυτα. It is implied that others, who did not share the vegetarian principles of the Pythagoreans, would eat it when it had not been sacrificed--that is, that non-sacrificed meat was available."

[99] H. J. Cadbury, "The Macellum in Corinth," *Journal of Biblical Literature* 53 (1934): 134-141.

[100] Conzelmann, 176.

[101] Aesop, *Life of Aesop* 51 and Pliny, *Letter to Trajan* 10.96.10. See also Charles H. Talbert, *Reading Corinthians: A Literary and Theological Commentary on 1 and 2 Corinthians* (New York: Crossroad, 1987), 56-58. This food was prohibited to Jews because it was connected with idolatry, it was not slaughtered in the proper way, and tithe had not been paid on it. "So, instead of calling this meat 'sacrificed for sacred purposes' (ἱεροθυτόν), Jews termed it 'sacrificed to idols' (εἰδωλοθυτόν)." Could a Christian buy or eat such meat? This is the issue I n 1 Cor. 8, 10-11:1.

[102] Murphy-O'Connor, 161.

[103] Theissen, *The Social Setting,* 125-127.

[104] Meeks, *The First Urban,* 69.

[105] Theissen, *The Social Setting,* 131.

[106] Meeks, *The First Urban,* 69.

[107] Murphy-O'Connor, 164. He comments that "it is easy to perceive the dilemma that one of the weak would face if he received such an invitation to celebrate the marriage of his pagan brother. He could not decline on the grounds that his new faith did not permit it, because the strong were known to participate in such banquets. No matter how deeply rooted his conviction that Christians could not share in such meals there was no way he could make it either comprehensible or palatable to his family. To refuse could only appear as a gratuitous insult to a family he still loved. If he ceded to the legitimate desires of his family, he would be going against his conscience, and all because the strong participated in such occasions."

[108] Walter Schmithals, *Gnosticism in Corinth,* trans. J. Steely (Nashville: Abingdon Press, 1971), 230-232. See also U. Wilckens, *Weisheit und Torheit* BHTh, 26 (Tübingen: J.C.B. Mohr (Paul Siebeck), 1959.

[109] S. Pétrement, "Le Colloque de Messine et le problème du gnosticisme," *Revue de Métaphysique et de Morale* 72 (1967): 371. *A Separate God: The Christian Origins of Gnosticism* (San Francisco: Harper & Row, 1984), 1-27. See also E. M. Yamauchi, *Pre-Gnosticism* (London: Tyndale Press, 1973), 16.

[110] R. Mcl. Wilson, "Gnosis at Corinth," in *Paul and Paulinism* by M. D. Hooker and S. G. Wilson, eds. (London: SPCK, 1982), 108. He says that E. M. Yamauchi distinguishes two divergent views of Gnosticism, and writes: "Those who will accept only a 'narrow' definition of Gnosticism do not find any conclusive evidence of pre-Christian Gnosticism, whereas those scholars who operate with a 'broad' definition of

Gnosticism find it not only in the New Testament but in many other early documents as well."

[111] Theissen, *The Social Setting*, 132. "Yet that simply underlines the problem of how to interpret the obvious analogies. The opinion that in Corinth we are dealing with an incipient Gnosticism is of itself unsatisfactory. Gnosticism's beginnings can be dated much earlier if by that is meant the initial appearance of concepts which play a role in the later Gnostic systems."

[112] Schmithals, 224-229.

[113] heissen, *The Social Setting,*, 133.

[114] John W. Drane, *Paul: Libertine or Legalist?* (London: SPCK, 1975), 105.

[115] Malherbe, *Social Aspects*, 81.

[116] Ralph P. Martin, "The Setting of 2 Corinthians," *Tyndale Bulletin* 13 (1986): 8.

[117] Theissen, *The Social Setting*, 123-125.

[118] Ibid., 125.

[119] Malherbe, *Social Aspects*, 82.

[120] Ibid., 83.

[121] Theissen, *The Social Setting*, 138.

[122] J. Murphy-O'Connor, *Becoming Human Together: The Pastoral Anthropology of St. Paul* (Wilmington: Michael Glazier, Inc., 1982), 209.

[123] John C. Brunt, "Rejected, Ignored, or Misunderstood? The Fate of Paul's Approach to the Problem of Food Offered to Idols in Early Christianity," *New Testament Studies* 31 (1985): 114.

[124] Malherbe, *Social Aspects*, 84.

[125] Bruce W. Winter, "In Public and in Private," In *One God, One Lord*, eds. Andrew D. Clarke and Bruce W. Winter (Grand Rapids: Baker, 1992), 125-126.

[126] Stambaugh, and Balch, *The New Testament*, 139-140.

[127] Theissen, *The Social Setting*, 125-127. See also Winter, 143-148.

[128] Murphy-O'Connor, 125-126.

[129] Talbert, *An Introduction*, 56-60.

Chapter 4

The Problem of the Meat Sacrificed to Idols In
1 Corinthians 10:14-22

Having laid the necessary foundation, we may turn now to examine the impact of these pagan social meals in the Greco-Roman world and their influence upon Paul and the Corinthians. To what extent had Paul encountered and adapted this social custom, and what can be known of its effect upon the city of Roman Corinth? In addition, our focus will be the issue of idolatry, eating of idol meat in a pagan temple, and Paul's treatment of the fellowship meal in 1 Cor. 10: 14-22.

Introduction to the Problem in Roman Corinth

The problem of Christians eating meat sacrificed to idols appears first in 1 Corinthians 8. Scholars generally acknowledge that a sound interpretation of 1 Corinthians 8-10 must investigate the real social issue and the situation in Roman Corinth to which Paul is responding.[1] Peter Tomson has observed that First Corinthians 8-10 is essential for the right understanding of Paul's concept of the practical teaching on the Law and idolatry.[2] In addition, Bruce Winter points out that primitive Christianity interacted with the Hellenistic social world and its religious pluralism in two main spheres, in public and also in private.[3] The issues involved are complex and require an understanding of the social situation in Roman Corinth. In answer to the Corinthians, the apostle Paul, in a diatribe manner used in schools, cites "those in the know" (γνῶσις),[4] and then qualifies their proclamation in a running dialogue.

The traditional statement of the problem is in terms of the two parties, the "weak" and the "strong" within the church, usually related to the divisions in 1 Cor. 1:12 and their letter to Paul asking his advice. Recent commentaries (such as Fee, Conzelmann, and Watson) still portray this kind of interpretation. The Corinthians inquired in their letter to Paul whether it was right to eat the flesh of animals that had been sacrificed to the pagan idols.[5] The traditional interpretation is inadequate. In the first place, the Corinthian epistle was a letter asking Paul's advice on a series of questions. Paul's answer and defence appears in 1 Cor. 8:1-13; 10:1-23; 11:1 and 9:1-22, where in the response itself, Paul discusses three important issues: (1) In 1 Cor. 8:1-13 Paul is dealing basically with the eating of meat offered at the pagan temples. (2) In 1 Cor. 10:23-11:1 he deals with meat sold in the market place, and says that such meat may be eaten freely without any question of conscience. (3) In 1 Cor. 9:1-22, he offers a strong defence of his apostolic authority, with special emphasis on his apostolic freedom.[6]

Recently, most scholars have taken the view that Paul is concerned here (Chapter 8) with the problem of food sold in the pagan shops, but Fee has argued that this point of view is difficult to accept. For instance, 1 Cor. 8:10 is the only verse in the chapter that refers to participation in a sacred meal in a temple. Furthermore, the manner of approach in chapter 8 is much less tolerant than that of chapter 10:23-11:1. In chapter 8 the apostle discourages the eating of food sacrificed to idols; in chapter 10:23-11:1 Paul seems to encourage it, unless someone points out that it has been sacrificed to the gods. Fee's conclusion is that in both chapters 8:1-13 and 10:1-2 Paul is addressing only one issue, the legitimacy of eating sacrificial meat.[7]

However, Fee's view is open to serious question. It is clear that Paul in chapter 8 does not discourage the Corinthians from eating, unless doing so could cause distress to a weak brother. But, in 1 Cor. 10:18-22, Paul is speaking about a practice that is contrary to tradition given to them and at the same time harmful, the act of partaking at the table of demons, thus bringing the participant into partnership with demons. Since in chapter 10 Paul is talking about the act of partaking in cultic meals, it would seem logical that in the earlier chapter (chapter 8) he must be talking about something less important, the eating of meat that has been sacrificed to the idols in the pagan temple.[8] Thus, obviously this practice divided the Christians at Roman Corinth on the morality of eating such meat.

Consequently, to get around the dilemma of the contradiction between 1 Cor. 8:1-13 and 1 Cor. 10:18-22, it is likely that Fee has to take the view in the latter chapter where Paul brings an argument of a different order to bear on the original problem.[9] But, we still have to deal with the difficulty that Paul begins by explaining the practice as not damaging, if his intention is finally to condemn or prohibit it entirely.

Two questions arise: How do these three important issues relate to each other? What were the Corinthians doing and what did they argue in their letter? It seems that the best solution to all these data is to view 8:10 and 10:1-22 as the basic problem to which Paul is responding throughout. This implies that εἰδωλόθυτα does refer basically to the food sold in the market place, but not necessarily the eating of meat offered at the cultic meals in the pagan temples. Therefore in 1 Corinthians 8 and 10 Paul deals with the problem of Christian participation in meals associated with pagan sacrifice in Roman Corinth.

Hence, the problem for the gentile Church's member at Roman Corinth and elsewhere was: how to live in a pagan society (pluralistic society) and not participated in idolatry?[10] They would have to think twice if they were to avoid partial union in Jewish society. In Paul's opinion the issue is not what kind of meat one eats. It is rather, the social and ethical effects in certain contexts.[11] The present study will investigate the meaning of εἰδωλόθυτα, the social interpretation of the cultic meals offered in the temple, and Paul's reply to the Corinthians' correspondence.

Idolatry in the Jewish and Christian Context

The term εἰδωλον and the other related terms such as εἰδωλόθυτον (from εἰδωλον and θύω), εἰδωλάτρη, and εἰδωλολατρία are characteristic Pauline expressions which appear especially in 1 Corinthians. Εἰδωλολατρία appears twice in Paul's letters; one of those occurrences is in 1 Corinthians.[12] Concerning the meaning of εἰδωλόθυτον it has been assumed that the term means "idol meat" wherever and whenever it may have been eaten. Ben Witherington has argued that the wrong use of the meaning of this word has caused difficulties in the interpretation of 1 Corinthians 8-10 and the so-called Apostolic Decree in Acts 15.[13]

In 1 Cor. 10:19 it seems clear that Paul is referring to sacrificial meat that is partaken in the pagan temple precincts. In order to understand the issue of idolatry (idol meat sacrificed in a pagan temple), it is good to remember that until the fourth and fifth centuries pagan worship was still practised in the Hellenistic world.

There were temples everywhere; in theatres and circuses the worship element was present, and the emperor's cult was one of them. Both Jews and Christians had difficulty with these practices and avoided being involved in any pagan cult. Certainly this was one of the main issues which Jews and Christians agreed upon.[14] In such a religious setting Paul and the Corinthians discussed the issue of idolatry. In the early development of the concept of sacrifice, the communal meal was held not for the simple intention of satisfying the need for food, but for the desire of entering into union with the mysterious Power of the deities.[15] It is interesting to notice that after they finished the sacrifice in the presence of the god in the temple, the whole ceremony was ended by a cultic meal.

The issue of meat (food) sacrificed to idols in 1 Cor. 8-10, is essential to understand Paul's practical and theological relationship with the Jewish Law.[16] In the Jewish Tora the prohibition of idolatry was conclusive. We can read it in the beginning of the Ten Commandments (Exod. 20: 3-5). In the Old Testament we can find these prohibitions repeated, especially in the covenant sections in Exodus 21-22 and 34 and in the book of Deuteronomy.[17] In addition, Brian Rosner argues that the most powerful and personal reason for having "no other gods" before the Lord is the fact that idol-worship provokes God's jealousy.[18] The basic explanation given for these prohibitions is that the Lord is "a jealous God" who cannot allow Israel to worship other gods (Exod. 20:5; 34:14). The Torah command that it is necessary to avoid completely the worship of pagan gods: "utterly detest and abhor" the heathen deities (Deut. 7: 25).

The post-exilic Jewish law on idolatry and pagan relations was more severe. The prohibition to marry gentiles also included to all non-Israelites. Further prohibitions were introduced, as mentioned in the book of Jubilees:

> Separate yourself from the nations, and eat not with them; and do not perform deeds like theirs; and do not become associates of theirs; because their deeds are defiled, and all their ways are contaminated, and despicable, and abominable; they slaughter their sacrifices to the dead and to the demons they bow down; and they eat in tombs.[19]

In this passage *idolatry*, means "sacrifices to the dead," and caused gentiles to be impure in all their ways. It was also prohibited for the Jews to eat idol meat while observing the laws of purity. Tomson mentions also that the *halakha* on the book of Jubilee is considered by many Jewish scholars very restricted on the issue of idolatry.[20] The notion of impurity caused by idolatry was a major subject both in the early and, through various transformations, in the later *halahka* governing relations with pagans. Idolatry for the Jews was a serious matter, why Paul sends an urgent warning. Christians who participate in meals alongside gentiles engage in idolatrous act of worshipping demons. Hence, the risk is to provoke God's jealousy.

The idolatry issue presented a challenge not only for Jews but also to primitive Christianity. Consequently it is no surprise that the early Church was unanimous in its basic prohibition of meat sacrificed to idols. P. Gardener points out that the term εἰδωλόθυτον originated at the Apostolic Council, which is summarized in Acts 15.[21] It appears to me that this assumption is a large mistake. Although, the apostolic decree in Acts 15 mentions food sacrificed to idols, this is not to say that the view originated in Jerusalem.

The issue was brought to Jerusalem from the Diaspora, especially from Paul's churches. 1 Corinthians 8-10 provides further evidence that this issue was a local one. For Paul, the well being of the local community came first. It is no accident that in precisely those areas of action non-Jews was forbidden. The Gentile community at Corinth was not an exception; food sacrificed to the gods was part of the daily ritual.

Another important issue along with the problem of idolatry is the local imperial cult that was established in the founding in the Roman colony of Corinth.[22] Winter raises two important questions: Do we have any proof that a local or provincial imperial cult had an impact on the theological beliefs of the Corinthian church? Does Paul's answer to the issue produced by the world of religious pluralism include the imperial cult?[23] These two questions are relevant to this thesis, but the limits of this study permit only a brief discussion of them.

According to E. Ferguson, contrary to the accepted view of New Testament scholars, emperor worship was subsequently neither rejected by Tiberius, nor did it lie dormant until the reign of Domitian.[24] It also has been suggested that some of the Roman Corinthian wealthy citizen showed devotion to the imperial cult.[25] Roman citizens worshipped the 'deified Julius Caesar and Rome. In the province they also worshipped "Augustus and Rome,"[26] as was part of the custom required in the whole Roman Empire.

Given that this was the case, it appears that Paul initially discusses the eating of meat in the temple in connection to pagan belief in the gods. Paul says that "for even if there are so-called[27] gods, whether in heaven or on earth [(as indeed there are many "gods" and many "lords")] yet for us there is but one God, the Father. . . and one Lord, Jesus Christ. . ." (1 Cor. 8:5-6). Paul cautions the Corinthians against participating in the pagan celebrations, based on his view that God is against the association of his people in idolatry, including the cult to the emperor (1 Cor. 10:1ff).

As we have seen in chapter two, the evidence for the practice of a meal in the temple is found in the following well-known Oxyrhynchus papyrus: "Chaeremon invites you to dinner at the Table of the Lord Serapis the name of the deity in the Serapeum tomorrow the 15th at 9 o'clock." R. P. Martin observes that Lietzmann regards the Serapis meal as "a striking parallel" to the reference in 1 Cor. 10:27.[28] Such practice was common and part of the ritual of sharing the food in communion with a deity. There was the notion of eating together when a god or goddess was thought to preside.[29]

However cautious A. D. Nock is on sacramental meals, he is trying to provide some evidence in the mystery religions for the common practice of these religious meals held in the temple precincts.   We found some important implications for some of those religious meals. However, the sacramentalism commonly accepted earlier this century, and still often understood today, is not convincing and certainly cannot be accepted as typical of the mystery religions.[30] It seems likely that even in the mystery religions, sacred meals were not considered sacramental occasions; in the earlier stages, the communal understanding may have been prominent.

A fact that cannot be overlooked is that cultic meals were normally considered essentially as occasions for social gathering[31] and conviviality like the *eranos*. As has been mentioned, converted pagans would have numerous social obligations, many of which might involve celebration and meals within or near a pagan temple or where the food served was sacrificed to the idols.

It has been suggested that the idol temple referred to in 1 Cor. 8:1 is the sanctuary of Demeter, where some small rooms of the Greek era were found.[32] However, Winter observes that the archaeological evidence points toward a different conclusion. It is clear that there was a break between activities in the temple during both the Greek time when there were small ceremonial dinners among, segregated groups of followers, and the Roman time.[33]

In any case, since 1 Corinthians 8:10 does not give any hint of a possible incident or a feast in the sanctuary of Demeter, this possibility is questionable. In addition, R. S. Stroud points out that "conceivably, there was still some kind of communal dining in the open air, but it seems clear from the excavated remains that in the Roman period small groups of segregated worshippers no longer assembled indoors for ritual dining as they had in Greek times."[34] It is not clear what we should make of the seemingly various dining facilities at the Corinth temple of Demeter and Kore.

The most recent archaeological evidence cast doubts on the earlier assumption that Paul's arguments in 1 Corinthians 10 were focused on these buildings.[35] Although these banquets were less common in the Roman period, the custom to commemorate them never stopped completely because of their importance and the connection with the local religious celebrations.

This invitation to sacred meals was done in the temple or in the house of a wealthy member of the Corinthian church. It seems to be a common practice of the social life of the city of Roman Corinth. Since meals were an important form of social communication and the practices surrounding them were often socially determined, there is little doubt as to whether one interprets this conflict sociologically.[36] It is clear that the Corinthian church had a real social-ethical problem about food offered to idols. For Paul and some of the church members, the idea of communion with an idol meant communion with the demons. This act was understood as idolatry. In the Didache, "food regulations are introduced as follows (6:3): περί δέ τῆς βρώσεως ὅ δύνασας βάστασον."[37] On the matters related to idolatry, no compromise was accepted: ἀπὸ δὲ τοῦ εἰδωλοθύτου λίαν προσέχε λατρεία γάρ ἐστιν θεῶν νερκῶν.[38]

According to Charles H. Talbert the restriction of the idol food was a clear matter to the Jews:

> Such food was prohibited to Jews because it was tainted with idolatry, it was not slaughtered in the proper way, and tithe had been not paid on it. So, instead of calling this meat "sacrificed for sacred purposes" (ηιεροτηυτον), Jews termed it "sacrificed to idols" (ειδολοτηυτον). Could a Christian buy or eat such meat? This was issue (1) in 1 Cor. 8.[39]

The expression περὶ τῆς βρώσεω in the Didache reveals that the author believed that to eat food sacrificed to idols was to fall into the unforgivable sin of idolatry.[40] The eating of meat sacrificed to idols, in the context of idol-demon food, constitutes the actual κοινωνούς τῶν δαιμονίων. In his article, Fee discusses a very crucial issue; he says that since eating the food in the temple surely means communion with the demons, the question is whether εἰδωλόθυτα should carry another meaning in chap 8. All who have written articles about idolatry in the N.T. assume that it refers to idol meat sold in the market place.[41] But Paul opposed participation in meals, which had been offered to idols, and eating meat, which was sold in the market after cultic ceremonies in the service of pagan gods.

N. T. Wright comments that this new Christian *Shema*[42] is exactly what the apostle needed at this point of his argument to reassert a proper "Christian" monotheism, the primacy of love, and to counter any underestimation of Christ that may have existed in Corinth.[43] It is clear that, for Paul, monotheism does not rule out the reality of lesser spiritual beings (demons), because some of them are malevolent.

Social Interpretation of the Cultic Meals and the "Parties" At Roman Corinth

It is well known that worship among Jews and Pagans in ancient times very often involved eating a meal in the presence of the deity. It is also important for this study to find out what significance pagan-cultic meals had in order to understand why some of the members in the Corinthian Church wanted to relate socially in such cultic meals. These meals had a social character in the majority of the cases; that is why some of the members were willing to participate. We can understand why because in 1 Cor. 8:4 they argue that the pagan deities were not really gods.[44] Paul, in this instance, has taken up their thesis just as in v: 1, and discusses it in the same way. There is evidence that, in general, cultic meals were linked with several social festivities. At the usual season of the festivity or at irregular but important times, like marriage, good fortune, and especially at death, worshippers would invite families or friends to join them at the temples or shrines to participate in worshipping the idols.[45]

For instance, Plutarch and Lucian place the philosophical feasts in the context of birthdays and wedding ceremonies; the references found indicate that such celebrations were very common practices.[46] There they would offer food to the gods; some of the sacrifice became the burnt offering for the deity, a portion was for the priest, but the majority of food was prepared for eating as a social event or a festive meal before the god.[47] In the O.T. there are examples (Deut. 14:22-26 and other references) where such sacrificial meals before God were enjoyed. This common practice was also found among the Canaanites (Judg. 9:27), Babylonians (Dan. 5:1-4), and Egyptians, including their several rituals (Exod. 32:6).[48] Socio-cultural customs, traditions and attitudes of different ethnic groups presumably would have been significant in influencing the behaviour shown by some of the members of the Corinthian church.

The socio-economic factor in Paul's day affected the relationship between the members who partook in some of the pagan cultic meals and also participated in the Lord's Supper. Paul himself suggests that we look for the weak among the lower strata. It is hardly an accident that the first chapters of the Corinthian letter already give voice to the distinction between strong and weak, connecting this with the social structure of the Corinthian congregation.[49] Paul says that among the Corinthians are not many who are "wise or powerful or of high social standing" (1 Cor. 1:26ff.). It has been argued that people of differing perspectives and social classes were also involved in another of the conflicts that perturbed Christians at Corinth: the issue of "meat offered to idols," addressed in 1 Corinthians 8-10. One can compare the divisions in the Corinthian Eucharist with two situations familiar to Roman society.[50] As has been seen in chapter three, the practice of the Greco-Roman *eranos* setting explains clearly the Christian *eranos* meal and the Corinthians' conduct.

It was common to have some special treatment among members of clubs and guilds. For instance, W. A. Meeks points out that "in collegia,.officers were sometimes assigned larger quantities of food than ordinary members."[51] It appears that some members in the church at Roman Corinth saw the meetings as some sort of association or *collegium*, especially in view of the fact that the primitive church had no temples, no priests, and no sacrifices. Most clubs and guilds were more socially homogeneous than the Corinthian congregation seems to have been, and therefore conflicting expectations might arise in the latter that would have no occasion in the former. Paul objects on quite different grounds, but Theissen has given good reason for looking for the origin of the wrong behaviour in the social status of such a stratified society. Indeed, in the city of Roman Corinth, social climbing was a major preoccupation.

Meeks does not reject the idea, but undertakes to show that there is a "social dimension of the conflict to which the ideological factor would have to be related."[52] It seems clear that the whole perception of what it meant to eat meat would have been different for people of different socio-economic levels. According to Theissen, the poor (including members of the church at Roman Corinth) rarely ate meat; the only occasion when they ate and attended a cultic meal associated with the sacrifice made in the temple, was in public celebrations or in private homes.[53] Theissen's view has been challenged recently by J. J. Meggitt. Additionally, Meggitt observes that the evidence that the lower-class ate meat comes from what it is known about the *popinae* and *ganeae*.[54] Although the quality of the meat was questionable[55] the fact is that Theissen overlooked the evidence. Whether or not the quality of the meat was good, the poor consumed it.

For some of the converts to Christianity, either Jewish Christians or Gentile Christians, the whole issue of eating meat sacrificed to idols brought similar difficulties, especially to those who belonged to the lower social classes.[56] Those who had been pagans must have found the issue perfectly natural because they were accustomed to attending those pagan meals and eating meat sacrificed to idols in pagan temples.

The fact is that the Corinthian social pretensions are not unexpected. Far from being a socially downcast community, the Corinthian are typical; they were dominated by a socially arrogant segment of the society of the big cities in the Roman Empire.[57] The relationship between high social status and idolatry is not ignored by early Christian paraenesis. Invitations to partake in sacrificial meals served basically as a means of communication. Families, associations, and cities came together on such occasions and in so doing expressed ceremonially their common membership in the community.[58]

Further, Lucian pointed out that private symposia could be considered a family affair, such as weddings and funerals. It could be an invitation to a member's home. It could also be an invitation scheduled by a member of a particular club or association commonly designated as ἔρανοι or θίασοι.[59] Those who expressed common membership automatically became part of that social group and participated with them in the common meals.

In summary, the restrictions on meat offered to idols were barriers to communication, which increased the problem of the relationship of Christians to the society of the ancient world and especially to the society of which the Corinthian congregation were members.

The letter from Corinth put this issue to Paul since there was a division of opinion among the Corinthians themselves. Paul labels the two sides as "the strong" and "the weak." The terms weak and strong used by Paul are often used in literature on factionalism, because they make clear who has the political advantage and who does not.[60] According to Dionysius of Halicarnassus the whole intention of a concordant political body is to make all members strong.[61] As Plutarch says: "The Greek states which were weak (ἀσθενεῖ) would be preserved by mutual support when once they had been bound as it were by the common interest (τῷ κοινῷ συμφέροντι), and that just as the members of the body (τὰ μέρη τοῦ σώματο) have a common life and breath because they cleave together in a common growth. . . ."[62] It was the common practice among the politicians and patrons to look out for the interests of the less fortunate (the weak) in the Greco-Roman world.

The specific counsel Paul gives in answer to the division between strong and weak is to urge a new attention for each other as fellow members of the body of Christ, specifically, not to humiliate one another.[63] It seems clear that Paul is dealing with two opinions (the opinions of the weak and the strong) on the problem of food offered to idols in Roman Corinth.[64]

Lake confidently suggests that this matter of two groups is clear from 1 Corinthians. H. D. Wendland says, "So teilt sie sich in zwei Gruppen, die 'Starken' und die 'Schwachen.' Diese Bezeichnungen werden in Korinth entstandene Schlagworte sein."[65] The way Paul introduces the problem in 8:1, περὶ δὲ τῶν εἰδωλοθύτων, clearly indicates that the issue was one of those referred to the apostle through the congregation (cf. 7:1). As we mentioned before, it is generally agreed that a quarrel or division arose within the Corinthian church and that an appeal for guidance was made to Paul.

This point is denied by J. C. Hurd, who maintains that the Corinthian were not divided on this issue, and they were protesting as a unified block Paul's effort to proscribe the eating of idol meat.[66] It is conceded that Hurd's reconstruction of the events has certain plausibility, but in the final examination it fails to bring conviction. No evidence contradicts the traditional viewpoint that there were two groups within the Corinthian church. As we can see, one group (the strong) had no doubts regarding the legitimacy of eating food offered to idols; the other (the weak) had serious problems in dealing with the subject of idol-meat.

However, it has been argued that it was common practice among the Gnostics to partake in pagan cultic meals from a willing Christian stance.[67] The above assumption about the Gnostic theory is improbable. In relation to the Gnostics at Corinth the most that one can find out is that there were isolated elements of the genesis of the development of what later was known as "Gnosticism."[68]   However, the observation of the Corinthians' slogan "we all possess knowledge" (1 Cor. 8:1) is no justification for accepting the notion of Gnostic intruders or their followers within the Corinthian congregation.

The main issue in 1 Corinthians 8 is not gnosis.[69] Idol meat[70] was the issue which concerned all the parties, and this issue dominates the agenda. Nevertheless, we can see that the libertines in Roman Corinth are in a sense like those (Gnostics)[71] who were indifferent with respect to Paul's establishment of proper moral behaviour, such as complete abstinence from eating εἰδωλόθυτα.

It has been pointed out that the whole case with regard to εἰδωλόθυτα was brought up by the Cephas party. Although we cannot specify the religions of the Gentile converts, the fact is that most of the church members at Roman Corinth were Gentile from a pagan background (1Cor. 12:2).

Archaeological evidence has been found in Roman Corinth which attests to the presence of a Jewish community.[72] Whether this Jewish community was influential in the Christian church at Roman Corinth is questionable. Paul says nothing of the Apostolic Decree, because to his mind it had no validity for purely Gentile-Christian communities.[73] This argument is not convincing because when the problem of the buying and eating of food offered to idols entered the debate, he could not have ignored it. The different situation of Paul and the Apostolic Decree, which is raised by 1 Corinthians 8-10, arises from a context known for the apostle, since he was present in the debate.

In other words, the Apostolic Decree was not to be imposed on the Gentile churches, but the agreement was that the Gentiles should abstain from what has been sacrificed to idols, from blood, from what is strangled, and from fornication.[74] These agreements between the Christians from Jerusalem and from the Gentile churches (Antioch, Corinth, and others) were intended to facilitate a good social relationship between Jewish Christians and Christians who came from a pagan background.

Paul's position concerning the eating of εἰδωλόθυτα put him into an uncomfortable debate with the Cephas group and the Corinthian Gnostics.[75] This is why many scholars have suggested that the problem in Roman Corinth is in fact to be connected to outside attempts to introduce the Apostolic Decree into the Corinthian Church. Nevertheless Paul is understood by some as being influenced by Hellenistic, Gnostic elements in his thought.[76]

On the contrary, we see Paul reacting to this Corinthian γνῶσις by appealing to the Corinthians' conscience. For the apostle Paul, human thought processes are unreliable and lead us to conclusions that are likely to be groundless.

It is easy to assume that a learning experience in the past (perfect infinitive in ἐγνωκέναι) has led us to hold a valid position in the present.[77]   Paul reverses their argument by telling them that a man should order himself, not according to his own γνῶσις and conscience, but according to that of his neighbour. Paul is careful to make clear that the principle of Christian freedom[78] is not to be jeopardized.

Paul's argument appears to be inconsistent. In chapters 8 and 10:23-11:1 he chooses in principle the argument of the "strong" that were inclined to see the food to the idols as harmless and that it could, consequently, be eaten. But, on the other side, the restriction on freedom is imposed not by the meat,[79] but by the conscience of and the bond with the "weak" brother. It is generally accepted that πάντες γνῶσιν ἔχομεν (8:1) was the slogan used by the "strong."[80] The strong adopt a weak position; they do not need restriction against idolatry in order to protect their Christian faith, because they know that the idols are not real; they are proud both of their γνῶσις and of the power and freedom which this knowledge, the grace they have received as believers in Christ, gives them. Dupont tries to demonstrate that the "weak" in Corinth were Jewish-Christians.[81]

We do not agree with Dupont because 1 Cor. 8:7 shows that they were Gentile-Christians and not Jewish-Christians as Dupont suggest. This also means that they had participated in pagan cultic meals.[82] Although we cannot precisely identify the religions of the Gentile Christians, we can probably detect evidence of their previous social and religious association (In 1 Cor. 12:2 Paul mentions the Corinthians' religious experience and says ὅτε ἔθνη ἦτε). According to C. K. Barrett, it is probable that some of Paul's members, prior to becoming Christians, had experienced religious ecstasy within the Hellenistic cults.[83]

This is precisely why Paul reacted to this Corinthian γνῶσις, because they felt free to eat everything, even the meat which came from the *macellum*. Further, those with γνῶσις claimed the ἐξουσία[84] (1 Cor. 8:9) to continue their pagan custom, despite their conversion to Christianity. What was this right that the Corinthian were claiming? Some Christians were exercising what Paul terms "this right of yours" (ἡ ἐξουσία ὑμῶν αὕτη). Apparently, it was the right that enabled them to sit at meat in an idol temple (1 Cor. 8:9). The same right was also possessed by the "weaker" at Roman Corinth though they did not think it was right to exercise it.[85] While, Paul did not deny that they possessed a degree of γνῶσις, he cautioned them that their γνῶσις (freedom) could easily become (γενέσθαι),[86] a danger to other Christians.

The idea of this group at Roman Corinth might be summed up as "knowledge is power and power gives freedom and certain rights," but, Paul counters them with his own logan: "Love builds up the *ekklesia* and gives opportunity and power for service to other." As Willis observes, for the apostle Paul freedom is not the first and main cry, which then is crimped or limited by love. Rather, love is the main thing, and it indicates how one's power ought to be used.[87] Paul does not understand freedom as liberation from obligations or from the controls of interpersonal relationship, which was the common belief in some parts of Greco-Roman society. For Paul, freedom means being free from sin, fear of death, and the law, in order to serve his Lord and his people.[88] The Christian's ἐξουσία will sometimes be selfish and destructive to others, but it need not involve idolatry.[89] It is most likely, therefore, that the weak were Gentile-Christians whose mental conviction, that there was only one God, had not been fully grasped emotionally.

In 1 Cor. 10:1-22, on the other hand, Paul seems to be in favour of the weak because it was dangerous to eat food offered to idols. Therefore, the strong were admonished. Paul uses imperative language in v. 14 to admonish all who are against the tradition, especially in the practice of the Lord's Supper. He says: "Διόπερ, ἀγαπητοί μου, φεύγετε ἀπὸ τῆς εἰδωλολατρία." The apostle Paul is very explicit and determined to let the Corinthians know that they should φεύγειν ἀπὸ τῆς εἰδωλολατρίας, for the sake of the weak brother and the Christian community.

Paul's Ethical Response

Paul's response is complex; to understand it one must distinguish between his attitude toward food offered to idols and his treatment of the problem. Paul does not simply conclude that food offered to idols is right or wrong.[90] Besides this dilemma mentioned above, the main difficulty in understanding Paul's response and the passage itself is that this rather pragmatic rule, which is oriented toward responsibility between persons, stands alongside an imperative prohibition of "idolatry" in 1 Cor. 10:1-22, backed by a biblical example (vss. 1-13) and by an illustration from the Lord's Supper (vss. 16-22).[91] Paul's argument throughout the three chapters (1 Corinthians 8, 10 and 11) seems to reveal some kind of inconsistency about the eating of idol-meat and the participation in the Eucharist meal. The questions arise; did Paul's argument have influence? Where does Paul stand concerning the issue of "idolatry" in relationship to the divisions of the Corinthian church?

1 Corinthians is in itself a social reality; the evidence of communication between Paul and the church community is obvious.[92] Paul was informed by the congregation of the socio-ethical issue, about idol-meat, and he begins the discussion making reference to at least two Corinthian slogans that were

included in their letter to him: 1 Cor. 8:1, "all of us have knowledge," and 8:3, "an idol has no real existence." From the starting point of the argument, Paul's own concern transcends the particular issue of idol-meat and places the attention on the wider ethical question, the interpersonal relationships that are involved in this situation. The "strong" appeal to their "γνῶσις": There is only one God; there are no idols and, therefore, "no meat offered to idols" is dangerous (1 Cor. 8:4ff.). Paul argues differently. He distinguishes cultic meals in an official setting (8:10) from meals in private houses (10:25ff). To be sure, his opinion about official cultic meals in a temple is not quite uniform, but the intention is clear.[93] Paul's reply to the Corinthians implies that they had affirmed that they possessed knowledge which, in a sense, justified the uninhibited consumption of idol-offered meat.

Paul insists, however, that the value of such knowledge is limited in that those who possess it have an almost irresistible tendency to become puffed up with pride. The feeling that the knowledge of God is precise and comprehensive may bring to some members of the Corinthian congregation a sense of superiority that is breaking a basic social element of human relationship in the community.

On the contrary, the "weak" argue against eating idol food as a matter of conscience.[94] But, the question arises: Are the church members at Roman Corinth converts from the pagan cults or from the Jewish religion? [95] Paul sees the weak as the ones who, lacking γνῶσις, because of their previous customs in paganism, regard the eating of sacrificed meat as a real and dangerous matter (8:7).

Many attempts have been made to define these positions in terms of their theological beliefs or ideologies. Theissen does not dismiss all these efforts, but tries to show that there is also a social dimension of the problem to which the ideological factors would have to be connected. In his interpretation, the "strong" are the socially powerful, also referred to in 1 Cor. 1:16f. It is probable that some, after conversion to Christianity, may still have had reasons to accept invitations to dinner where meat would be served (10:27), perhaps in the shrine of a pagan god [8:10]. Some of the wealthy church members would still have kept some social or business responsibilities. For them it was more important to their roles in the larger society than to their association among people of the lower class.

The whole perception of what it meant to eat meat would have been different for the members of different economic levels. The poor people in fact rarely ate meat. For the poor, moreover, the Christian community provided a more than adequate substitute for the sort of friendly association, including common meals that one might otherwise have sought in clubs, guilds, or cultic associations.[96] On the whole, Theissen's argument is extremely good in showing the conflict between the two groups as evidence of the social-ethical problem among the Corinthians. He tries to demonstrate that the "strong" are in a higher status than the "weak" and assumes that they are consequently better integrated socially into the larger society in Roman Corinth. The idea of freedom of conscience (or rather "consciousness"), far from being Paul's solution, was the real problem in the ethical difficulties created by the eating of idol-meat in Roman Corinth. Apparently Paul does not have a concept of "conscience" already worked out, as he confronts the conflict in Roman Corinth.[97]

If we analyze the polemical situation, it seems that Paul picks up the terminology of *syneidesis* from the enlightened Corinthians who were eating the idol-meat. *Syneidesis* is a significant word for Paul. Probably, this term comes from the pagan world not from Paul's Jewish background.[98] It is significant that here the term "conscience" is to some extent considered as attached to an assessment on grounds other than the quality of acts themselves. In some of the cases at Roman Corinth, the knowledge of the source of the meat used has brought pain, but actually, it is not the eating of meat. C. A. Pierce points out that "even in its negative and limited function, conscience does not so much indicate that an act committed is wrong, as that an act 'known' (by other means and rightly or wrongly) to be wrong has been committed."[99] But on the other hand, the Christian's behaviour is to be controlled by positive considerations toward his neighbour, and not negative actions.

Is it harmless to eat of it? Or is it beneficial for the edification of the church community? In chapter two we mentioned that some of the Corinthians might have considered participation in pagan cultic meals as social celebrations, not worship occasions. Consequently, these pagan cultic meals do not pose any problem of conscience to them. In any case, some Christians at Roman Corinth were familiar with these meals connected with pagan temples and some of them did not see any problem in participating in those meals.[100] This custom was part of their social background.

Paul argues that the very confidence that one has knowledge demonstrates that one has not made a proper adjustment to knowledge, for one has failed to realize that human knowledge is only partial. Paul's basic criticism is of a position which he was prepared to uphold: $\alpha\gamma\acute{\alpha}\pi\eta$ must always take precedence over $\gamma\nu\hat{\omega}\sigma\iota\varsigma$ (1 Cor. 8:1-3; 13:2; 8:9, 12ff.), and my brother's conscience is always more important than my own.[101] We can see that Paul builds up the whole community by the principle of love rather than knowledge. In his reply to the dilemma posed by the freedom of conscience, Paul insists on the real ethical question at the interpersonal level. The structure and the substance of Paul's reply make the effect of one's behaviour on others the criterion of ethics.

Paul's argument in both in 8:7, 13, and in 10:23-24 and 32-33 refers to those who would exercise their newfound spiritual freedom with their fellow members in the community. In chap 9 he speaks from this context, especially since the argument follows the same pattern of thesis and antithesis as in chap 8.[102] In summary, Paul presents himself in chap. 9 as an example of the necessity to be willing to give up one's own rights for the sake of others.

Thus, Paul treats the question by changing the focus to the issue of Christian love rather than simply giving an answer to the question. In so doing he presents the principle, that love and respect for others transcends the rightness or wrongness of the eating of the idol-meat, and participating in the communal meals which were part of the common practice of the society in which the Corinthian were living.

Paul's Treatment of the Fellowship Meal: 1 Cor. 10:14-22

As has been pointed out in this pericope, idolatry was a constant problem in the centres of Greco-Roman civilization where Primitive Christianity came to be found.[103] The reason for Paul's prohibition can be summarized in one main point: Paul was against eating food offered to idols because he understood that the Lord's meal was a fellowship with the Lord and with the believers.

The purpose of 10:14, 15 in the structure of 10: 14-21 is to introduce a reasoned argument against Christian participation in pagan cultic meals. In 1 Cor. 8 Paul responds to a defense of eating conveyed to him from the Corinthians.[104] Nevertheless, in 10:1-13 he makes known his own discussion, based on an explanation of Israel's history. Then in 1 Cor. 10: 14-21 Paul gives a second argument, this time based upon the significance of sacred meals. These two arguments are grammatically related by διόπερ.

Paul uses this very strong inferential conjunction διόπερ "therefore" ("for this very reason") to bring the previous argument to its sound conclusion. Διόπερ is stronger than διό and γάρ. "Wherefore" or "therefore" is not enough. Paul urges upon his readers the conclusion that flows from verse 13. An idol cannot rescue the believer from temptation. *Au contraire* idol worship has always been contributory to the grossest of sins. The idol is faithless. God is faithful. Paul shows in vv. 1-13 an example of how Israel's idolatry caused their destruction in the desert, despite their "sacraments."[105]

Paul makes spiritual applications of several incidents from the Pentateuch. God's extraordinary action for his people in the Exodus time did not prevent their destruction. Paul maintains that these events had a deeper meaning for the church and their practice. They are types which happened to the Israelites as examples. Thus confirmed, the Christian members at Corinth may confront the danger to which Paul addressed himself. Fee points out that "here the rule is the apodictic φεύγετε."[106] Max Zerwick says that the word means "flee, keep away."[107] Similar to Jewish belief, Paul is sure that idolatry is impossible for a Christian believer. No amount of γνῶσις of the nonexistence of an idol-god justifies participation in idol worship in any form. Paul now concludes the argument with a tender appeal, ἀγαπητοί μου, and a straight forward prohibition, φεύγετε ἀπὸ τῆς εἰδωλολατρίας.[108] Paul's admonition is clear: "they must not try to see how near they can go, but how far they can fly. *Fugite idolatriam: omnem ubique et totam.*" This might have been hard saying for some of them, especially after expecting a wide measure of liberty, so he softens it with ἀγαπητοί μου.[109]

Paul challenges the Corinthians to differentiate and give consideration to his argument. Paul calls them "wise" though their behaviour indicates otherwise. Paul like any good rhetorician knows that he must rely on the power of persuasion. Consequently, the only logical thing he can do is to exhort; the Corinthians must consider the situation and respond. He has warned them about the immorality that may entrap idolaters. He will now consider the contradiction of idol-association and participation in the Lord's Supper.

Paul continues: "ὡι φρονίμοιι λέγω" He is turning from an Old Testament parallel; he is now about to show them with a discussion based on their common experience the force of which, as sensible men, they will readily recognise, as this discussion is based on the parallel between the Christian Eucharist and an idol feast.[110] Now Paul is trying to show them that a sophisticated understanding of the nature of idols is not enough. They have plenty of intelligence and can see whether an argument is logical or not. It seems that the Corinthians made use of their common sense or γῶσις, so that is why Paul says to them κρίνατε ὑμεις ὅ φημι. The use of ὑμεῖς is emphatic. Paul's change from λέγω το φημι should be marked in translation, although Robertson says it may be made merely for variety: "Judge for yourself what I declare."[111] Once again Paul appeals to the power of discernment and good judgment.

In presenting the Lord's Supper as the norm, Paul turns to the traditional terminology and the acknowledgment of the Lord's Supper as a communal act. Conzelmann wonders, when Paul mentions the cup first, if he is then linking up with a form of celebration of the Lord's Supper in which the cup was distributed first. Or has he himself reversed the order for particular reasons as in the Didache?[112] We can say that his form of the celebration of the Lord's Supper depends on the tradition which appears in the expression "ποτήριον τῆς εὐλογίας."

Therefore, Paul is not reversing the order of the celebration, but is following the church's tradition. But it seems quite possible that the expression has some similarities to the one found in Joseph and Aseneth. The term for the cup of wine was a technical Jewish expression that came at the end of a meal used as its formal close.[113] H. L. Strack says that the Jewish custom at Passover was to bless the cup of wine three times and he explains:

> Becher des Segens. So heisst im Rabbinischen insonderheit der Becher Wein, über dem nach Schluss eines Mahles das Tischdankgebet gesprochen wurde, s. Exkurs: Ein altjüdisches Gastmahl. Bei der Passahfeier war es vermutlich der 'dritte' Becher Wein, üben dem als dem 'Segens Becher' jener Danksegen nach Tisch gesprochen worden ist, s. Exkurs: Feier das Passahmahles—Über den 'Segensbecher' beim Mahl der Gerechten in der zukünftigen Welt.[114]

The Lord's Supper was a meal in which the participants drink from a cup over which a blessing was pronounced. The Jewish cup of blessing (כּוֹס שֶׁל בְּרָכָה) corresponded to the cup of the interpretive saying (Mk. 14:23 par. Mt. 26:27; 1 Cor. 11:25; Lk. 22:20). At every meal when wine was drunk the prayer of thanksgiving was said over this cup after the main meal.[115] So, several prayers were offered as part of the ritual of the Jewish Passover.

Paul's use of the sequence of cup–bread is unique in the New Testament[116] because the evidence from 11:23-25 makes clear that the normal sequence, bread–cup, is the one which prevailed in the churches founded by Paul. It has been argued that the order presented by Paul should not make us overlook the fact that for Paul "body is not simply the correlate of blood." In Paul's mind the "body of Christ" is the church; therefore, Paul makes the reversal of bread and cup.[117]

Paul's statement that the cup "οὐχὶ κοινωνία ἐστὶν τοῦ αἵματος τοῦ Χριστοῦ" enlarges and describes, as Bruce says, "the dominical words of institution (cf. 11:25) as his description of the bread which we break as a participation in the body of Christ. . ." Bruce adds also that such participation amplifies and interprets the words of institution spoken over the bread (cf. 11:24).[118] Neither the blood nor the body has a material sense in this interpretation by Paul. The "cup of blessing," as we mentioned before, was the technical term for the final benediction at the end of the meal. This was the cup that Jesus Christ himself blessed at the Eucharist meal (cf. 11:25, "after the meal") and described as "the new covenant in my blood," (although in Mk-Mt the link with Jeremiah 31 is not so clear).

Goppelt observes that this expression can be understood as the eschatological saying from Jesus; that it was initially associated with the blessing of a cup (Lk. 22:17a) is implied by the use of the term "fruit of the vine" (Mk. 14:25).[119] We must understand that the interpretation of κοινωνία τοῦ σώματοι τοῦ χριστοῦ ἐστιν and the associated words have a central significance for Paul. A close analysis of the term shows that Paul never used κοινωνία in a secular sense but always in a religious one.[120] For Paul κοινωνία always refers to the relation of faith to Christ.

In the Lord's Supper Paul's concern is that the drinking of this cup is for the believers a sharing (κοινωνία) in the blood of Christ. The Christian communion service, therefore, is unique in its importance since it sets forth in symbol the unique sacrifice of the unique Son of God in his unique incarnation.

In a similar way, Paul speaks of "τὸν ἄρτον ὅν κλῶμεν," the sharing of the bread. This expression he takes to mean sharing in the body of Christ. It is doubtful that Paul here is talking about the physical aspect of the human body of the Lord.[121] Paul describes the human body of Christ in other terms: in Col. 1:22, he uses the word flesh, whereas for him the term "the Body of Christ" refers to the church. Paul says that in the Christian fellowship this is a communion with the body of Christ. So, we can conclude that κοινωνία means participation in the body and blood of Christ and thus union with the exalted Christ. Paul is leading his readers to understand the real meaning of being in communion with Christ.

ὅτι εἷς ἄρτος, ἕν σῶμα οἱ πολλοί ἐσμεν. The use of ὅτι, "because," is to be connected with verse 16. Paul brings together the notions of ἄρτοισῶμα, "bread/body" because in his mind he has the thought of the body of Christ. Conzelmann says that the sacred participation in Christ's body makes us into the body of Christ.[122] The Eucharistic κοινωνία in the body of Christ is the sacrament of the believers in unity, proclaiming common membership in the one body. Further, George Panikulam points out that "those who ate from the altar became κοινονοι of the altar; this is an allusion to the cultic unity of Israel."[123] It seems that the apostle is making a comparison between vv.17 and 18.

However, Paul's argument is from the fact that one loaf was broken and shared and consequently those who participate in the one loaf are, not withstanding their plurality, one body.[124] Paul's intention is to show that all who participate in the one loaf have communion with Christ. This is what follows next in the other part of v. 17b: οἱ γὰρ πάντες ἐκ τοῦ ἑνὸς ἄρτου μετέχομεν. Paul's main idea, therefore, is not the unity of the body that this supper represents, but the loyalty of the redeemed community as one body that makes all be united as one.[125]

The meaning seems to be that all have communion with the body (κοινωνία), but the body is not divided. The emphasis lies on the unity and the sharing of the one loaf. Paul adds οἱ πάντες, "all as one" "all the whole congregation." We agree when Robertson describes Paul's feeling concerning the social viewpoint. Robertson comments that it is remarkable how the apostle

Paul insists upon the social aspect of both the sacraments. Paul says: "For in one Spirit were we all baptized into one body" (12:13).[126] The Corinthian, in participating in the Lord's Supper, are having a social fellowship with the Lord. They are edifying not just one segment of the church, but the whole congregation becomes united to form the body of Christ.

Having made his main points clear, Paul adds the analogy of the sacred meals in Israel. τὸν Ἰσραὴλ κατὰ σάρκα. This verse brings a historical proof by citing the practice of Israel, which is unquestioningly recognized as valid.[127] The illustration used by Paul from the OT is from several sources, but Paul is especially referring to the meals prescribed in Deut. 14:22-27, not to the priest's share of the sacrifice mentioned in 9:13. Lev. 10:12-15 mentions that it was the priest's privilege to use up some part of the offering. The non-priestly worshippers also consumed part.[128] Paul says they were partners in the altar when they shared the benefit of it. S. Aalen points out that

> Der Terminus viel mehr am Opfer *bzw* am Altar orientiet. Die Letztere Möglichkeit ist die 1 Kor. x:18 vorliegender (koinwnoiv tou' qusiasthvriou). Der Unterschied zwischen Opfer und Altar ist jedoch in diesem Zusammenhang nicht gross. Das Opfer wird besonders dann hervorgehoben, wenn es um die Frage des Unterhaltes der Priester geht (so 1 Kor. ix:13), der Altar dagegen, wenn die religiöse Sicht betont werden soll.[129]

Paul's emphasis when he says "sharers in the altar" is that the ones who participate share together in the food on the altar. In this meal they are bound together in their everyday worship of God. By this analogy Paul is trying to say to the Corinthians that when they partake of the Eucharistic meal they become "partners" of the God of the altar. Thus table fellowship was established with God; the participants were established as his people.

According to Conzelmann Paul starts by assuming the reader already knows, as indeed he now wishes to confirm, that the κοινωνία τοῦ θυσιαστηρίου, "partnership in the altar," of the "one" God rules out fellowship with evil spirits or demons.[130] In other words, Paul wished to say to the Corinthian congregation, especially the "Libertine," that he rules out partaking with demons and their table. In doing so Paul has apparently involved himself in a certain inconsistency. Barrett seems not to agree with the other scholars when he says neither of these writers seems to do full justice to the facts in 1 Corinthians. That Paul found himself in some difficulty over the question of sacrificial food is certainly true.[131] Since Paul argues that there is sacred meaning in the Lord's Supper and the sacrificial meals in ancient Israel, he must continue that Christians should neither partake of nor participate in anything related to idolatrous worship.

It seems likely that it was not difficult for Paul as a converted Jew, trained in the Rabbinical school of Jerusalem, to accept the substance of the Jewish-Christian Decree even though he never mentioned it. For Paul the whole issue is not that the food offered to the demons changed into a demonic substance or represented demons. He is arguing that sacrifices to demons are evidence of yielding allegiance to them and entering into an unholy κοινωνία with them. Christians at Corinth must renounce this partnership, because they are exclusive partners of God in Christ. The following verses are explicit on the matter.

When Paul states, ἀλλ᾽ ὅτι ἃ θύουσιν τά ἔθνη, δαιμονίοις καὶ οὐ θεῷ θύουσιν, he alludes to the LXX in Deut. 32:17, δαιμονίοις καὶ οὐ θεῷ, θεοῖς οἷς οὐκ ᾔδεισαν. Robertson points out that "they sacrificed to demons (Shêdin) and to a no-god, to gods whom they knew not."[132] Paul's argument does not suggest that idols are real. But rather, the Corinthian have to understand idolatry in terms of OT revelation.[133] However, Paul considers them (demons) as real beings (1 Cor. 8:5).[134] The term demon used by Paul had provided him and other Hellenistic Jews with a helpful way of expressing a truth which otherwise would not have been easy to put into words. Because of the nature of the demons and their relation to pagan idols, Paul's view differs from that of the "intelligent people" of Corinth, who consider that idol-offerings and participation in table fellowship make no difference.

But, that is why he goes on and clearly says in v. 20b: οὐ θέλω δὲ ὑμᾶς κοινωνοὺς τῶν δαιμονίων γίνεσθαι. In what sense does Paul regard those who participate in such sacrificial feasts as partners with demons? Paul thinks of feasts to the idols as explicitly under the patronage of a pagan god, involving in some degree the acknowledgment and even worship of that deity.[135] So, Paul's point is simple: these pagan meals are in fact food sacrificed to idols (demons) and, therefore, the worship of demons is involved.

This is why he says in v. 21: "οὐ δύνασθε ποτήριον κυρίου πίνειν καί ποτήριον δαιμονίων." Drinking a cup dedicated to the Lord and at the same time drinking a cup dedicated to demons must be unthinkable for Christians. Note that both κυρίου and δαιμονίων are anarthrous, but the context makes clear what Paul means. The Christian communion table is divine; the pagan idol temple is demonic. It is impossible to relate both to Christ and to demons. Conzelmann clearly points out that "verse 21 expresses with fundamental sharpness the impossibility of participating in the pagan cult, and does so with special reference to participation in meals, drinking and eating."[136] The Eucharistic formula used by Paul and handed down in the community clearly shows us that it is thus impossible to drink both the cup of the Lord and the cup of demons.

The reference to the cup of demons is Paul's main argument for this prohibition. The Christian should not share lordship with demons because in the Christian observance this is a partnership of the body of Christ. As in the case of the wine, this has been understood to mean some identity with the flesh of Christ, whether actually or symbolically; and so the participant would gain his divine characteristic by a kind of sacred "Christophagy." This partnership with demons Christians must renounce and be sole partners of God in Christ.

Paul is arguing here, not from pagan notions, but from the OT principle that every sacrifice which is not offered to the living God is dedicated to demons.[137]   On the basis of the Lord's Supper Paul warned the Corinthian libertines concerning participating in drinking of the cup of the Lord and the cup of demons; and he adds what we can call a second warning: "οὐ δύνασθε τραπέζης κυρίου μετέχειν καὶ τραπέζης δαιμονίων." Μετέχειν" is a verb of sharing. At the Lord's Table we share with others the symbols of the body and blood of Christ and, in a deeper sense, we share participation in the Body of Christ.

To share in the table with the Lord and with demons is also impossible for one who is aware of being united with Christ. How then can the Christians also share with pagans in a service that is dedicated to the worship of Satan?

The two unions are absolutely incompatible. No basis for fellowship between them exists (cf. 2 Cor. 6:14-18), because, Fee says, "those who eat at the Lord's Table are proclaiming his death until he comes (11:26); they are thereby also bound to one another through the death of the Lord that is thus celebrated."[138] What harm could there be in attending these meals? [139] Verse 22 represents the turning point of Paul's argument.

Paul adds a final warning--ἢ παραζηλοῦμεν τὸν κύριον μὴ ἰσχυρότεροι αὐτοῦ ἐσμεν--a rhetorical inquiry which expects an emphatic negative answer. "Are we stronger than he?" The particle ἢ introduces the alternative, "Or (if you think that you can't eat of Christ's table and the table of demons) are we going to provoke His jealousy?"[140]   Fee is not the only one among the commentators accepting that "the precise intent of this question is 'puzzling."[141] Several of the commentators take this inquiry as an ironic, if not sarcastic, reference to "the strong" in the Corinthian church, which possessed the "knowledge" (1 Cor. 8:1).

According to Rosner this interpretation is improbable since the apostle Paul does not use the word "strong" in 1 Corinthians as he does in Romans 14.[142] However, it seems clear that Paul labels the two groups of the controversy as "the strong" and also "the weak." In fact Paul's warning mentions more than one group in Corinth; he asks, are we ἐσμεν (not are you, (ἐστὲ) stronger than he? (1 Cor. 10: 22).

The warning is to those Christians in Roman Corinth who think they have γνῶσις and ἐξουσία and become indifferent to Paul's teaching in following the right way to celebrate the Lord's Supper. Paul uses the word ἰσχυρότεροι ("stronger") not in an ironic way, but to describe a group.[143]

This word also describes the characteristic of the Corinthian attitude toward Paul's counsel. We may conclude by saying that Paul has given them a practical plan for Christian living in a pagan society. In verses 14-22 Paul also expressly condemns the attendance at pagan meals. Some things are constructive and others destructive, but the tradition handed down from the Lord cannot be changed for pagan practices. Paul had in mind the building up of the Body of Christ.

Summary

All of our difficulties in interpreting 1 Cor. 10: 14-20 seem to disappear when one acknowledges that Paul is not arguing *a fortiori* from the Jewish and pagan viewpoint of κοινωνία to the Eucharist, but rather the contrary. The parallelism with Israel's practice does not intend to build κοινωνία as a doctrine, but to lead us to understand better the example of avoiding idolatry (1 Cor. 10:7). The people of Israel had a similar κοινωνία of the altar because there is Christian κοινωνία (fellowship), just as manna is a "spiritual food" in view of the Lord's Supper (v. 4).[144] The fellowship of the altar saved the faithful ones; those worshipping idols perished. The usage of this pattern from the Old Testament argues against Christian participation in eating meat offered to idols, a frequent subject in 1 Corinthians 10. The real κοινωνία with Christ should avoid any confusion of the weak brothers united to Christ, if the strong brothers are also willing to recognise that the "little ones"[145] are also members of the body of Christ.

Furthermore, Paul concludes his teaching on the basis of human interaction. Paul is concerned with the well-being of the church's society and its members. We are to consider other people's feelings, sensibilities, and beliefs so as not to cause them to stumble or to offend them unnecessarily. Paul insists that his own life direction (*modus operandi*) is oriented to the advantage of the many. He delineated his principle of adaptability in 1 Cor. 9:22, "all things to all people," which has as its ultimate goal God's salvation of his people through the preaching of the gospel.

Notes

[1] G. Fee, "Εἰδωλόθυτα Once Again: An Interpretation of 1 Corinthians 8-10," *Biblica* 61 (1980): 179-197. He points out that "Paul's answer to the Corinthians' stance on εἰδωλόθυτα, food sacrificed to idols, has long posed difficulties for modern interpreters. The problems basically have to do with 1) the relationship of the various parts of Paul's answer to one another, and 2) the nature of the problem in Corinth and its relationship to the Corinthians' letter to Paul."

[2] Peter J. Tomson, *Paul and the Jewish Law* Minneapolis: Fortress Press, 1990), 187. We agree with Tomson's interpretation when he says: "We have seen that the prohibition of idolatry is firmly anchored in the Old Testament and Jewish tradition. It represented one of the commandments most vital to the existence of the Jews as a religious-ethnic community. The prohibition of food sacrificed to idols was obviously included. This meant that Christ-believing gentiles were forced to take a stand vis-à-vis a cornerstone of the Law of the Jews when confronted with the issue of idol food offering. Moreover, inasmuch as for Jews the prohibition against contact with idolatry included communication with those eating sacrificial food, the attitude of non-Jewish believers would directly affect Jewish-gentile relations, both within the Church and outside it." Whether this interpretation is right or not, the issue is at the very least a prominent one. Tomson is also right when he observes that "the modern assumption about Paul and the Law also predominates in scholarship: *halakha* is hardly taken into account as a positive source for Paul. Although far-reaching judgments are pronounced on Paul's practical attitude towards Jewish Law, nowhere is a comparison made with the essential materials: the *halakha* on idolatry." It appears according to Tomson that in First Corinthians *halakha* was of significant value for Paul's practical teaching on the issue of idolatry.

[3] Bruce W. Winter, "In Public and in Private: Early Christians and Religious Pluralism," eds., B. W. Winter, and Andrew D. Clarke. *One God, One Lord: Christianity in a World of Religious Pluralism.* (Grand Rapids: Baker, 1992), 125-148. "In public evangelistic preaching it was encountered in Lystra and Athens and actually discussed with the listeners (Acts 14 and 17). Some Christians participated in the public cultic activities in Corinth (1 Cor. 8:10). Paul discussed appropriate Christians' interactions in both public and private activities. These were to govern the church's conduct as it lived in the midst of a world which endorsed religious pluralism (1 Cor. 8-10)." See also Winter's article on the subject "Theological and Ethical Responses to Religious Pluralism: 1 Cor. 8-10." *TynB* 41.2 (1990): 209-226.

[4] S. K. Stowers, "Paul on the Use and Abuse of Reason," *Greeks, Romans, and Christians,* eds. D. L. Balch, E. Ferguson, and W. A. Meeks (Minneapolis: Fortress, 1990), 253-286. Stowers observe that the diatribe style is pedagogical in origin, not a form of mass propaganda used by Cynic preachers. See also A. D. Litfin, *St. Paul's Theology of Proclamation: An Investigation of 1 Cor. 1-4 in Light of Greco-Roman Rhetoric* (Cambridge: University Press, 1994), 137-146. According to Litfin the

significance point is that this style of teaching shows that Paul is working as an educator with pupils and treating these Corinthians as immature students.

[5] R. Kugelman,"The First Letter to the Corinthians," *The Jerome Biblical Commentary* (Englewood Cliffs, NJ: 1968), 266.

[6] G. Fee, *The First Epistle to the Corinthians* (Grand Rapids: Eerdmans, 1987), 359.

[7] Ibid, 363 n.23. Fee is aware of this issue and its difficulty. "The chief objection to this reconstruction lies in the tension some see between this section, where he appeals to love, and 10:14-22, where he forbids such behavior outright. How can he begin in this way if in fact he intends finally to forbid it altogether? It should be noted, however, that because of 8:10 this is a problem for all interpreters."

[8] Jerome Murphy-O'Connor, *1 Corinthians* (Wilmington: Michael Glazier, 1979), 76-82.

[9] Nigel Watson, *The First Epistle to the Corinthians* (London: Epworth Press, 1992), 82-89. But what about the difficulties which Fee considers being inherent in the traditional view? He points out that, "as for the alleged marked difference in tone between 8.1-13 and 10.23-11.1, this seems to be rather a matter of emphasis. As Bruce N. Fisk, "Eating Meat to Idols: Corinthian Behavior and Pauline Response in 1 Corinthians 8-10," *Trinity Journal* 10 (1989): 49ff. puts it, in a detailed critique of Fee's position to which my own is indebted, while the emphases of the two passages are different, the basic message is almost identical, Thus: 8.1-13: Eat idol meat unless someone will be scandalized. 10.23-11.1: Eat idol meat unless someone will be scandalized." Fisk's view is also open to objection. The emphasis of the two passages is different of course, but the message is not identical. Whereas in 1 Cor. 8:1-13 Paul discourages the eating of the food in question, in 1 Cor. 10:18-22 the apostle in a sense encourages it, unless someone points out that is sacrificed to the pagan idols. Paul's main concern in 1 Cor. 8:1-13 is the problem of the meat sold in the *macellum*.

[10] Tomson, *Paul,* 190. It seems clear that the idolatry issue was a very difficult issue to discuss and to agree upon it.

[11] After I had nearly completed this study, I discovered Ben Witherington's assessment of the social situation (*Conflict & Community in Corinth: A Socio-Rhetorical Commentary on 1 and 2 Corinthians* (Grand Rapids: Eerdmans, 1995), 187ff), which is essentially the same as mine. He maintains that the main discussion is regarding the interpersonal behaviour in certain contexts, not in regard to food *per se*. The Corinthian were, Witherington says, behaving like most of the Greek or Roman citizens and other aristocrats by indulging in boasting and preening as part of their status-seeking behaviour. Paul sought to deflate such attitudes and defuse such activities by offering models of accord and self-sacrifice. Paul's example and *modus operandi* was an *imitatio Christi* (1 Cor. 11:1).

[12] H. Hübner, *EDNT* vol. 1 (Grand Rapids: Eerdmans, 1991), 386ff.

[13] Ben Witherington, "Not So Idle Thoughts About Eidolothuton" *Tyndale Bulletin* 44.2 (1993): 240. "I will argue below that εἰδωλόθυτον in all its 1st century occurrences means an animal in the presence of an idol and *eaten in the temple precincts*. It does not refer to a sacrifice which has come from the temple and is eaten elsewhere, for the

Christian sources rather use the term ἱερόθυτον. In fact in all the 1st century AD references the association of εἰδωλόθυτον specifically with temples and eating seems very likely and is made clear by the context of these references in one way or another." We will argue that Witherington has the better of this argument about the right meaning of this term.

[14] Tomson, *Paul,* 177-186.

[15] R. K. Yerkes, *Sacrifice in Greek and Roman Religions and Early Judaism* (London: Adam & C. Black, 1953), 26.

[16] Tomson, *Paul,* 151.

[17] See also Lev 19:4, 26:1; Deut 4:15-20; 13:6-18; 17:2-7; 27:15.

[18] Brian Rosner, "No Other Gods: The Jealousy of God and Religious Pluralism," eds., B. W. Winter, and Andrew D. Clarke. *One God, One Lord: Christianity in a World of Religious Pluralism.* (Grand Rapids: Baker, 1992), 149. Rosner observes also that "the jealousy of God lies at the heart of the Old Testament's conflictual stance towards other religions (and more to the point, other gods) and has obvious relevance to the subject of religious pluralism. It is therefore surprising that the notion of God's jealousy is conspicuous by its short treatment, if not its absence, from the literature on all sides of the current debate."

[19] Jubilees, 22:16f.

[20] Tomson, *Paul,* 153. For a detailed study of the subject see also the section on *Tannac Halakha,* 154-176. "Correspondingly early post-exilic sources mention Jews, either in Palestine or in the Diaspora, abstaining from wine, oil, bread and other food deriving from or prepared by gentiles. Likewise the idea of the impurity of gentile territory and dwellings must date back to somewhere early in the Second Temple period." The difference between idolatry committed by Jews and the gentiles is basic to Rabbinic *halakha.* There is a reference in the Mishna that defines the exact way of punishment. The majority were of the opinion that the right punishment for idolatry was stoning. See introduction to Avoda Zara in Albeck, *Mishna* 4, 321-3.

[21] P. Gardner, *The Gifts of God and the Authentication of a Christian* (PH. D. diss., Cambridge University, 1981), 15.

[22] D. Engels, *Roman Corinth: An Alternative Model for the Classical City* Chicago: University of Chicago Press, 1990), 100.

[23] Bruce W. Winter, "The Achaean Federal Imperial Cult II: The Corinthian Church," *Tyndale Bulletin* 46.1 (1995), 171ff. For a detailed discussion of the imperial cult see B. W. Winter's article "Acts and Roman Religion," eds. D. W. J. Gill and C. Gempf, *The Book of Acts in Its Graeco-Roman Setting* (Grand Rapid: Eerdmans, 1994), 93-103.

[24] E. Ferguson, *Backgrounds of Early Christianity* (Grand Rapids: Eerdmans, 1987), 163.

[25] Engels, *Roman Corinth,* 102.

[26] Dio Cassius, 51.20.6-7. Dio clearly mentions that "Caesar (Καῖσαρ), meanwhile, besides attending to the general business, gave permission for the dedication of sacred precincts in Ephesus (Ἐφέσῳ), and in Nicaea (Νικαίᾳ) to Rome and to Caesar, his father, whom he named the hero Julius (Ἰούλιον). These cites had at that time attained chief place in Asia (Ἀσίᾳ) and in Bithynia (Βιθυνίᾳ) respectively. He commanded that

the Romans resident in these cities should pay honour to these two divinities; but he permitted the aliens, whom he styled Hellenes ({Ελληνάς), to consecrate precincts to himself, the Asians to have theirs in Pergamum (Περγάμῳ) and the Bithynians theirs in Nicomedia (Νικομηδείᾳ). This practice, beginning under him, has been continued under other emperors, not only in the case of the Hellenic nations but also in that of all the others, in so far as they are subject to the Romans."

[27] Winter, "In Public and in Private," 143-145. "The term 'so-called' referred to gods (οἱ θεοὶ λεγόμενοι) and indicated that the attributing of deity 'in heaven and on earth' which was made by the non-Christians in Corinth was not true--the ascription was popular but erroneous. They had 'no existence in the form their worshippers believe them have." Winter observes that "in 1 Cor. 8-10 Paul discussed how Christians should live in the world of religious pluralism. His teaching stood in contrast to that of Rabbinic Judaism and its prime concern with maintaining personal ritual purity for the adherents. Paul's teaching was also in contrast with the response to religious pluralism by some of the Corinthian Christians (1 Cor. 8:7ff). Their actions, he argues, were not only self-centred but perilous for their spiritual well-being (8:9-13, 10:4). His discussion was not simply a proscription but in it he also set out clear prescriptions for the church on how its members were to conduct themselves in the Christ-like way in their society."

[28] R. P. Martin, "Meats Offered to Idols," *The New Bible Dictionary* (London: Inter-Varsity Press, 1972), 554.

[29] A. D. Nock, *Early Gentile Christianity and Its Hellenistic Background* (New York: Harper & Row, 1964), 57-69. mentions that "The orator Aristides, writing in the second century of our era, says in his speech 'Concerning Serapis' (viii. vol. i, p. 39 sq., Dindorf), 'Men have perfect communion in sacrifices with this god alone in a peculiar degree, inviting him to their hearts and causing him to preside over their feasts:' two invitations to dinner 'at the couch of the Lord Serapis' (one of these adds "in the Serapeum") have been found at Oxyrhynchus. A citizen of Bologna built a dining-room for Jupiter Dolichenus: This implies perhaps the god was supposed to be present at the common meal of a cult society, as Zeus of Panamara may also have been at the communal banquet held in the course of his mysteries."

[30] W. L. Willis, *Idol Meat in Corinth* (Chico: Scholars Press, 1985), 47.

[31] Bruce N. Fisk, "Eating Meat to Idols," 62ff. Part of the problem was that lines between religious and civic (social) ceremony were not so clear, if drawn at all. As has been mentioned in chapter two Willis' findings cannot be disregarded. Gill's findings support Willis' argument. He points out that the earlier Greek writings suggest that the god himself participated at the temple meal, but later on, in the early centuries C. E. the focus was more horizontal, on the table-fellowship enjoyed by the human participants. The god is more in the background, more spectators at than a partaker in the sacral banquet. D. Gill, "Trapezomata: A neglected Aspect of Greek Sacrifice," *Harvard Theological Review* 67 (1974): 137. These findings have important implications for this study for they suggest that significant, conscious worship of deities during these meals was at times minimal or non-existent. Indeed, the social aspect was the most significant part of the *eranos* Greek dinner.

[32] J. B. Salmon, *Wealthy Corinth: A History of the City to 338 B.C.* (Oxford: Clarendon Press, 1984), 403.

[33] Bruce W. Winter, *Seek the Welfare of the City: Christians as Benefactors and Citizens* (Grand Rapids: Eerdmans, 1984), 170.

[34] R. S. Stroud, "The Sanctuary of Demeter on Acrocorinth in the Roman Period," ed., T. E. Gregory, *The Corinthians in the Roman Period*, Journal of Roman Archaeology Mono. Supp. 8 (Ann Arbor: Cushing-Malloy, 1994), 69.

[35] Earlier reports by Bookidis among others support the assumption that this is the place Paul had in mind when he wrote 1 Corinthians 10. However, Bookidis' most recent work cast doubt on such an assumption, and so the issue must be approached with caution. N. Bookidis and J. E. Fischer, "The Sanctuary of Demeter and Kore," *Hesperia* 41 (1972): 283ff. It looks as if Willis has ignored some of Bookidis' warnings. The dining facilities at the Demeter sanctuary now seem mainly to be under the level of the Roman floor.

[36] G. Theissen, *The Social Setting of Pauline Christianity* trans. J. H. Schütz (Edinburgh: T. & T. Clark, 1982), 122-123.

[37] Didache, 6.3.

[38] 2 Clement, 1.6; 3:1. and also see Justin Martyr, *Trypho,* 34. According to Justin the issue of idolatry is the touchstone of orthodoxy. He commented that Gentile Christians (and it will apply to Jewish Christians as well) πᾶσαν ἀδικίαν καὶ τιμωρίαν μέχρι ἐσχάτου θανάτου ὑπομέουσι περὶ τοῦ μήτε εἰδωλόλατρῆσαι μήτε εἰδωλόθυτα φαγεῖν. Trypho answers (35) that he has found many who profess to be Christians ἐσθίειν τὰ εἰδωλόθυτα καὶ μηδὲν ἐκ τούτου βλάπτεσθαι λέγειν. Justin commented that these are those false Christians whose coming Jesus himself foretold.

[39] Charles H. Talbert, *Reading Corinthians: A Literary and Theological Commentary on 1 and 2 Corinthians* (New York: Crossroad, 1987), 57.

[40] C. K. Barrett, *Essays on Paul* (London: S. P. C. K., 1982), 43.

[41] Fee, Εἰδωλόθυτα 181.

[42] N. T. Wright, *The Climax of the Covenant: Christ and Law in Pauline Theology* (Minneapolis: Fortress Press, 1991), 129. "Paul, in other words, has glossed 'God' with 'the father', and 'Lord' with 'Jesus Christ', adding in each cases an explanatory phrase: 'God' is the Father, 'from who are all things and we to him', and the 'Lord' is Jesus the Messiah, 'through who are all things and we through him'. There can be no mistake: just as in Philippians 2 and Colossians 1, Paul has placed Jesus within an explicit statement, drawn from the Old Testament's quarry of emphatically monotheistic texts, of the doctrine that Israel's God is the one and only God, the creator of the world."

[43] Ibid. 120-131.

[44] Willis, *Idol Meat,* 48.

[45] Fee, "Εἰδωλόθυτα," 184.

[46] Plutarch, *Table Talk* 717B; Lucian, *Symposium* 5. "When an individual wished to get together with his friend or businesses or religious associates, he would generally do so by inviting them to his home for a banquet. Banquets were also held on important family occasions, such as birthdays, weddings, and funerals." See also D. E. Smith and E.

Taussig, *Many Tables: The Eucharist in the New Testament and Liturgy Today* (Philadelphia: Trinity Press International, 1990), 28.

[47] M. H. Pope, *Song of Songs* (AB: Garden City, 1977), 210-229. See also Talbert, 56-65.

[48] H. H. Rowley, *Worship in Ancient Israel: Its Forms and Meaning* (London: S.P.C.K., 1978), 125-126.

[49] Theissen, *The Social Setting*, 124.

[50] Ibid, 127. See comments on chapter three, 73-77.

[51] W. A. Meeks, *The First Urban Christians* (New Haven: Yale University Press, 1983), 68.

[52] Ibid, 68-70.

[53] Theissen, *The Social Setting*, 128. See also J. K. Chow, *Patronage and Power* (Sheffield: Sheffield Academic Press, 1992), 145.

[54] J. J. Meggitt, "Meat Consumption and Social conflict in Corinth," *Journal of Theological Studies* 45 (1994): 138-39. "The meat from all these outlets tended to be in forms that have historically been associated with the poor: sausages or blood puddings appear to have been common, as was tripe, and various off-cuts that might appear unappetizing to the modern palate."

[55] Ammianus Marcellinus 28.4.34. *"nauseam horridae carnis."*

[56] Theissen, *The Social Setting*, 128-143.

[57] E. A. Judge, *The Social Pattern of the Christian Group in the First Century* (London: The Tyndale Press, 1960), 59-60.

[58] Theissen, *The Social Setting*, 128. He mentions the example of social aspect such as the case of Aelius Aristides: "Moreover, in sacrifices men maintain an especially close fellowship with this god alone. They call him to the sanctuary and install him as both guest of honor and host, so that while some divinities provide portions of their common meals, he is the sole provider of all common meals, holding the rank of symposiarch for those who at any time are gathered about him."

[59] Lucian, *Symp.* 8. Private *symposia* were of two major types, those for which the cost was divided among the participants, and those to which the guests were freely invited. The Corinthian *eranos* could be classified as a free common meal.

[60] Aristid. *Or.* 24.14 on Solon: "He was most of all proud of the fact that he brought the people (δῆμος) together (καταμῖξαι) with the rich (οἱ δυνατοί), so that they might dwell in harmony (ὅπως ἄν μιᾷ γνώμῃ τὴν πόλιν οἰκῶσιν), neither side being stronger (ἰσχύοντες) than was expedient for all in common (κοινῇ συμφέρει)."

[61] Dionysius. *Ant Rom.* 4.26.1. ". . . and declaring that concord (ὁμοφροσύνη) is a source of strength to weak states (τοῖς ἀσθενέσιν), while mutual slaughter reduces and weakens even the strongest (ταῖς ἰσχυραῖς)."

[62] Plutarch. *Arat* 24.5

[63] Margaret M. Mitchell, *Paul and the Rhetoric of Reconciliation* (Tübingen: J. C. B. Mohr, 1991), 127.

[64] K. Lake, *The Earlier Epistles of St. Paul:: Their Motive and Origin* (London: Rivingtons, 1914), 199-200. He pointed out that "pparently there were two opinions on

the matter in Corinth: One party maintained that an idol was nothing, and that therefore things offered to idols had no importance: They thought that the whole matter was indifferent, and that Christian freedom justified them in doing as they wished. Another party held the opposite opinion and thought that, cost what it might, Christians ought to abstain absolutely from the contamination of things offered to idols."

[65] H. D. Wendland, *Die Briefe an die Korinther* (Göttingen: Vandenhoeck & Ruprecht, 1962), 62.

[66] J. C. Hurd, Jr., *The Origins of 1 Corinthians* (London: S.P.C.K., 1965), 115-149. Hurd exaggerates the importance of 1 Cor. 10:1-22, and puts aside the force of 1 Cor. 8:7, but his hypothesis, as he himself acknowledges, leads to "he somewhat strange conclusion" that "Paul devoted the major part of his reply to vigorous disagreement with them, and only at the close did he give them permission to behave as in fact they had been behaving."It is not strange, therefore, that this hypothesis has not been accepted. See J. Murphy-O'Connor, "freedom or the Ghetto,"*RB* 85 (1978): 543ff.

[67] W. Schmithals, *Gnosticism in Corinthians*, trans. J. E. Steely (Nashville: Abingdon Press, 1971), 223. Conzelmann argues that this so-called Gnostic element in the church at Corinth is "Gnosticism *in status nascendi.* The Corinthians could be described as proto-Gnostics."H. Conzelmann, *1 Corinthians* (Philadelphia: Fortress Press, 1975), 15.

[68] Murphy-O'Connor, 544. "The former possessed 'knowledge' the later (at least in some sense) lacked 'knowledge.' The first group could be termed 'Gnostic,' and many commentators in fact use this designation. Even though it is justified etymologically, I prefer not to use it because it is susceptible of interpretations that are to say the least, misleading."

[69] Heinz O. Guenther, "Gnosticism in Corinth? in *Origins and Method* ed. B. H. McLean (Sheffield: Sheffield Academic Press, 1993), 54f. "Gnosis-knowledge was not a bone of contention between Paul and the Corinthians." Both parties took for granted that 'all Christians possess knowledge." Baird point out that "since the enlighten claimed γνῶσι, they have sometimes been identified as Gnostics. The γνῶσι of the enlightened, however, demonstrates some few elements of the kind of esoteric knowledge that is characteristic of gnosticism. Instead, according to 1 Corinthians 8:6 the Corinthians γνῶσι is based on a very clear understanding of the fundamental Christian confession "of God as creator and Jesus Christ as Lord." Baird, 125.

[70] Sacred meat (idol meat) is also meat offered to pagan deities. Later it was sold in public meat shops across the city. Paul is not concerned with the eating of such meat in private homes. The real issue at question was whether it should be consumed in public, in other words, in front of everybody, at fellowship meetings open to all the church members.

[71] I use the word here in its general sense of those "who have knowledge," not to allude to the second-century heresy.

[72] William A. McDonald, "Archeology and St. Paul's Journeys in Greek Lands, III-Corinth," *Biblical Archaelogist* 5 (1942): 41.

[73] T. W. Manson, "The Corinthian Correspondence," *Studies in the Gospels and Epistles* ed. M. Black (Manchester: Manchester University Press, 1962), 190-209.

[74] Acts 15:28f. "The decision against imposing circumcision on Gentile Christians must have given great satisfaction to the church of Antioch, especially to Paul. He was not likely to change his practice or policy whichever way the verdict went, but his work would have been rendered immeasurably more difficult if Jerusalem had gone on record as insisting on circumcision. No longer would it be possible for "trouble-makers" to visit his churches and claim that the circumcision of Gentile believers was official policy in the church of Jerusalem. That question was now closed. See F. F. Bruce, *Paul: Apostle of the Heart Set Free* (Grand Rapids: Eerdmans, 1986), 184.

[75] Barrett, 54ff. In the notes Barrett clarifies that when he uses the term "Gnostics" he is making reference to the one who uses the word too often and not to the use of the term *per se.*

[76] J. Dupont, *Gnosis: La Connaissance Religieuse dans les Epîtres de S. Paul* (Louvain: Nauwelaerts, 1960), 282-327.

[77] Talbert, *Reading Corinthians,* 57.

[78] W. F. Orr and J. A. Walther, *1 Corinthians* (Garden City, NY: Doubleday & Co., 1976), 255-256. Orr states the point clearly that "a free Christian is not to be judged by the conscience of another person; he must not allow his own conscience to think that he is doing something evil by the mere act of eating the food. In order not to damage the other person's conscience, he will refrain from eating; but in his own mind he knows he has the right to eat this food as food nothing has happened to it, it has not been changed, it has no particular power. He must not, however, let anyone think that he believes in idols; nor must he do anything to establish table fellowship with demons nothing to him, but everlastingly fatal to the other person."

[79] Conzelmann, *1 Corinthians,* 137.

[80] J. Murphy-O'Connor, "Freedom of the Ghetto," *Revue Biblique* (1978): 543-574.

[81] Dupont, *Gnosis,* 282-290.

[82] Baird, 121.

[83] C. K. Barrett, *The First Epistle to the Corinthians* (HNTC; New York: Harper, 1968), 278.

[84] The Corinthian's rights were based on: (1) pagan gods have no spiritual reality (1 Cor. 8:4-6 10:19-20); (2) food does not matter to God (1 Cor. 8:8, 10:23-27, 31); (3) partaking in baptism and the Lord's Supper maintained one safe from lapses into idolatry (1 Cor. 10:2-14, 20-22).

[85] Winter, *Seek the Welfare of the City,* 170-171. "It could not be to eat meat in the idol temple of Demeter or Asclepius, since attendance at a meal there was not seen as a 'right'. Access to activities in the temples of Demeter and Asclepius were open to everyone." See also B. W. Winter, "he Achaean Federal Imperial Cult II: The Corinthian Church," *Tyndale Bulletin* 46.1 (1995), 169-178.

[86] Fisk, "Eating Meat," 60.

[87] Willis, *Idol Meat,* 98.

[88] Witherington, 196-197.

[89] This point has been discussed by H. von Soden, "Sacrament and Ethics in Paul," in *The Wrintings of St. Paul,* ed. W. Meeks (New York: W. W. Norton, 1972), 264., H.

Conzelmann, *1 Corinthians*, 177, and J. Brunt, "Love," 25. Paul's change from εἰδωλόθυτα (1 Cor. 8:1, 4, 7, 10) το εἰδωλολάτρης (1 Cor. 10:7) and εἰδωλατρία (1 Cor. 10:14) is important. The former is morally neutral; the latter are detestable.

[90] J. C. Brunt, "Rejected, Ignored or Misunderstood? The Fate of Paul's Approach to the Problem of Food Offered to Idols in Early Christianity," *New Testament Studies* 31 (1985): 113-124.

[91] Meeks, *The First Urban*, 98.

[92] Theissen, *The Social Setting*, 137.

[93] Ibid, 122.

[94] Fee, *The First Epistles*, 359ff.

[95] Murphy-O'Connor, *Revue Biblique* 552. He comments that "the weak, therefore, are those who 'up to now have been accustomed to idols,' and who as a result of this conditioning see such meat as having been really offered to an idol. Are they converts from paganism or from Judaism? It is a question of a habitual attitude toward idols which remains up to the present moment (cf. 4:13; 15:6). The continuance of this attitude is what makes some 'weak.' It is not, therefore, a good thing in itself. It is part of the baggage of one's past which should have been left behind at conversion."

[96] Theissen, *The Social Setting*, 121-140.

[97] R. A. Horsley, "Consciousness and Freedom Among the Corinthians: 1 Corinthians 8-10," *Catholic Biblical Quarterly*, 40 (1978): 574-589.

[98] Robert Jewett, *Paul's Anthropological Terms* (Leiden: J. B. Brill, 1971), 421ff.

[99] C. A. Pierce, *Conscience in the New Testament* (Chicago: Alec R. Allenson, Inc., 1955), 77. Vv. 24 and 33 sum up the decisive principle, "The answer, therefore, to the question 'why is my liberty judged of another's conscience?'- - a question put into the controversialists' mouth by St. Paul-- is that it is a duty incumbent on love to protect the brother from pain of conscience. Conscience in this question is of course the same here as elsewhere in this passage: it is the pain consequent upon committing the (supposedly) wrong act, into which the little one has been led by the example of his more knowledgeable brother."

[100] I. Howard Marshall, "Lord's Supper" in *Dictionary of Paul and His Letters* eds. R. P. Martin, G. Hawthorne and D. Reid (Illinois: InterVarsity Press, 1993), 2. "Christian converts could well have been familiar with any of these types of meal and also with some of the practices of the different mystery religions. . . . There was a complicated mix of religious practices in Corinth. Some members of the church were familiar with meals associated with pagan temples and some believe that it was right to continue to participate in these. It does not, of course, follow that they viewed what happened at these meals and the Lord's Supper in the same way. Further, it is important to note that the very strong explicit criticisms that Paul makes of the Corinthians church meal do not appear to be connected in any way with pagan beliefs or practices that had been carried over into it. It may be that the Corinthian Christians felt that participation in the meal of itself protected them from divine judgment, but Paul's instruction to them is not about misunderstanding the meal but about refraining from idolatry."

[101] Barrett, *The First Epistle*, 56.

[102] Schmithals, *Gnosticism,* 228.

[103] R. P. Martin, *Eucharist Teaching in St. Paul's First Letter to the Corinthians* (M.A. Thesis, University of Manchester, 1956), 32.

[104] Willis, *Idol Meat,* 182.

[105] Fee, *The First Epistle,* 464.

[106] Conzelmann, *1 Corinthians,* 170.

[107] Max Zerwick, *A Grammatical Analysis of the Greek New Testament* vol. 2, trans. M. Grosvenor (Rome: Biblical Institute Press, 1979), 517. The use with the accusative and with ajpo; have the same meaning. G. B. Winer in his grammar, mentions that the same verb in the infinitive φεύγειν governs the accusative, as in 1 Cor. 6:18, 2 Tim. 2:22 in a figurative sense (to flee, to shun a vice)"; but is once followed by ἀπό, in 1 Cor. 10:14. This latter construction is very common in the New Testament.

[108] Fee, *The First Epistle,* 464.

[109] Tertullian, *De Cor.* 10., and see also A. Robertson and A. Plummer, *A Critical and Exegetical Commentary on the First Epistle of St. Paul to the Corinthians* (Edinburgh: T. & T. Clark, 1911), 211.

[110] F. F. Bruce, *1 and 2 Corinthians.* New Century Bible (London: Marshall, Morgan & Scott, 1971), 94.

[111] Robertson, 211.

[112] Conzelmann, *1 Corinthians,* 171.

[113] Barrett, *The First Epistle,* 94.

[114] H. L. Strack and P. Billerbeck, *Kommentar zum Neuen Testament aus Talmud und Midrasch* vol. 3 (Munich: D. H. Beck, 1926), 419.

[115] Goppelt, *TDNT* 6, 154.

[116] Fee, *The First Epistles,* 466ff.

[117] Conzelmann, *1 Corinthians,* 172ff. He does not consider Lk 22:17f. As evidence (as others do; see Gordon Fee, n.19) to the form of celebration. The sequence there is, bread, cup wine, has come from a combination of the common (we should say the normal) course of the supper. He adds that,"Paul is aiming at an interpretation of the community by means of the Lord's Supper cf. the step from v. 16 to v. 17. This is the connection between the Eucharist meal and Paul's concept of the church which is a new element that he introduces to the Corinthian church to their understanding of the Lord's Supper as a sacrament."

[118] Bruce, *1 and 2 Corinthians,* 94.

[119] Goppelt, 153ff.

[120] Schattenmann, *NIDNTT* 1 (1971), 639-644.

[121] Barrett, *The First Epistle,* 233.

[122] Conzelmann, *1 Corinthians,* 172.

[123] George Panikulam, *Koinonia in the New Testament: A Dynamic Expression of Christian Life. An Biblica* 85 (Roma: Biblical Institute Press, 1979), 28. He also comments that, "the interpretation prevalent so far, which connected v.18 with v.19, can hardly stand with Paul's argumentation in the context. Instead, connecting v.18 to v.17 makes better sense insofar as Paul gets a confirmation for his understanding of the Lord's

Supper in the Jewish world." The Lord's Supper in its sacramental meaning has more affinity to the Jewish meal than the mystery religious meals. Though in the social practice, the Lord's Supper (as has been discussed already in chapter six) at Corinth was not significantly different from those in their culture, especially the *eranos* from the social custom of the Greco-Roman world.

[124] Barrett, *The First Epistle*, 234.

[125] Fee, *The First Epistles*, 469.

[126] Robertson and Plummer, 215.

[127] Conzelmann, *1 Corinthians*, 172.

[128] Barrett, *The First Epistle*, 235.

[129] S. Aalen, "Das Abendmahl als Opfermahl im Neuen Testament," *Novum Testamentum* 6 (1963): 137.

[130] Conzelmann, *1 Corinthians*, 173. He mentions Weiss's position on v. 19: "The conclusion drawn by the opponents is reflected in the ou\n, 'then' of the question."

[131] Barrett, *The First Epistle*, 43ff. He mentions the case of scholars like A. A. T. Ehrhardt, T. W. Manson, and E. Molland. According to Dr. Ehrhardt, Paul changed his attitude on the issue of eating food offered to idols. He goes further and says, "It is remarkable that only a short time afterwards, namely after the visit of St. Peter to Corinth, St. Paul greatly changed his tune." He also says that Paul accepted the Apostolic Decree, in particular the prohibition of the eating of εἰδωλόθυτα. However, most of the scholars do not agree with Barrett's view.

[132] Robertson and Plummer, 217.

[133] Fee, *The First Epistles*, 471ff.

[134] Conzelmann, *1 Corinthians*, 173.

[135] Bruce, *1 and 2 Corinthians*, 96.

[136] Conzelmann, *1 Corinthians*, 175.

[137] Goppelt, 157. In the light of the Old Testament outcomes Paul appeals to the Corinthians to escape from any kind of contact with the idols. "He sets absolute opposition between the Lord's Supper and idol meals. It is in this background that we are expected to understand Paul's development of the Eucharistic theology." See G. Panikulam, *Analeta Biblical* 85 (1979): 29.

[138] Fee, *The First Epistles*, 473.

[139] A. J. B. Higgins, *The Lord's Supper in the New Testament* (London: SCM Press, 1964), 70. He explains that "though communion with Christ in the Eucharist may be secondary chronologically to union with Christ by faith, it is questionable whether Paul recognized any inherent precedence of the latter over the former . . . For he held the Eucharist to be essential to the church as the command from the Lord himself."

[140] Robertson and Plummer, 218.

[141] Fee, *The First Epistles*, 474.

[142] Rosner, "No Other Gods," 149-159.

[143] Conzelmann, *1 Corinthians*, 174.

[144] John M. McDermott, "The Biblical Doctrine of KOINWNIA," *Biblische Zeitschrift* 19 (1975): 220.

[145] Pierce, 80ff. He comments that "while it is perhaps not always easy to accept the arguments of Thornton yet there can be little doubt that he is right in his contention that the weak are the same people as *the little ones*, those to whom St. Paul elsewhere refers as babes. These babes are those who have not yet reached full maturity in Christ; so that is not implausible to suggest further that while the *little ones*, the weak, are sometimes those for whom the apostles are responsible, and whom they scandalise at their peril, at other times it is the weakness of the apostles themselves which is stressed."

Chapter 5

Paul and the Last Supper in 1 Corinthians 11:17-26:
The Social Significance of the Meal

We begin this chapter with a warning. Drawing a comprehensive picture of the Corinthian situation is beyond the scope of this study. The following section is designated instead to highlight only those aspects of the Corinthian situation we must understand if we were to grasp Paul's argument throughout 1 Cor. 8-11, especially the social and moral issues in the Lord's Supper.

We must examine, albeit more briefly now, at least the remainder of our literary unit, 1 Cor. 11: 17-26. If our treatment of 1 Cor. 8:1-13, and 10:14-22 is sound, it may have some bearing upon the interpretation of the remainder of 1 Cor. 11. It will be useful, therefore, to trace the Apostle's view through the end. Our primary goal will be to highlight those aspects of Paul's argument which may gain a deeper meaning in the light of what we have discovered in 1 Cor. 8:1-13 and 10: 14-22 in relationship with the Lord's Supper. We turn now to examine the details of 1 Cor. 11:17-26.

Introduction and Aim of This Chapter

As we concluded in the previous chapter, Paul was trying to show the Corinthians the correct practice of the Lord's Supper as a united body with one purpose in mind, to build up the body of Christ and to eradicate the divisive elements in the congregation at the Eucharistic Meal. However, there are those who argue that Paul's tradition was a direct revelation to him; others observed that he was not just correcting a sociological problem at Roman Corinth, but he was concerned with the social causes and consequences of the bad behavior in the church meal and also with the theological meaning of what was happening at the Lord's Supper.

Thus, part of Paul's strategy is to show those wealthy Corinthians the logical consequences of their un-Christian behavior, rather than just condemning them. In this section our aim is to continue the discussion of the social abuses and excesses of some of the Christians at Roman Corinth, and the way they celebrated the Lord's Supper. Paul is trying to correct the wrong behavior of the Corinthians; he does not provide a full exposition of his views of the Lord's Supper. Nonetheless, we learn a great deal in 1 Cor. 8-11 (especially in 1 Cor. 11:17:26) about how the Lord's Supper was celebrated at Roman Corinth and about Paul's socio-ethical beliefs of the Supper.

The Lord's Supper at Roman Corinth

In 1 Cor. 11:20, Paul calls the meal that was professedly partaken by the Corinthian church members "The Lord's Supper" (κυριακὸν δεῖπνον), but the phrase that became frequently used is "Eucharist" (εὐχαριστία, which means "a giving of thanks"). This term can be found in the Didache. Ignatius and Justin clearly indicate that in the Didache the prayers were spoken at the celebration of the meal and then in the whole sacramental celebration.

In addition, Ignatius knows the name 'Agape' (Sm. 8:2, Rom. 7:3? ἀγαπᾶν, Sm. 7:1='hold the Agape') which also occurs in Jd. 12.[1] From Paul's comments on the practice of the Lord's Supper in the church of Corinth, we may have an idea that the supper was held continually at possibly weekly intervals and not merely as an annual recollection of the Lord's death during a Christian Passover. In the church at Corinth there were two sections of the cultic service: a collective meal, taken for the purpose of nourishment (cf. Didache x.1: "after you are filled". . .), followed by a solemn service of the Eucharist meal.[2] Paul regarded the behavior of the Corinthians in the Lord's Supper as a disorderly act that led to its being mentioned in his letter. The problem in the church obviously arose from social disagreement within the congregation.[3] The Corinthians' behavior seems to be quite normal with the social standards of the day; although some church members were acting according to the rule of the society, they were not acting according to the rule and the standards of the Christian community at large.[4]

It is also possible to deduce something about the social stratification from several of the conflicts found in the Pauline communities. Paul's rebukes in 1 Cor. 11:17-34 make clear the divisions which appeared when the Corinthian Christians gathered for the Lord's Supper.[5] With their attitude, the Corinthian disdain the sacrament, possibly on grounds of spiritualism, and see it as a mere symbol. They commemorate it as a common meal.[6] Thus, we can assume that the Lord's Supper was held as a meal where all the members participated and the meal was being celebrated in a selfish way. This is why Paul warned them to go home and eat and later gather together around the Lord's Table with reverence and orderly conduct (1 Cor. 11:22, 30-34). Furthermore, in Paul's view, the sacred tradition regarding the Last Supper is recited specifically to encourage social equality, to overcome factionalism created by stratification. In Paul's mind the main purpose of gathering together in the Lord's Supper is to create unity and harmony in the assembly.

The Church Meal and Its Social Context

The church at Roman Corinth was composed of people from different social strata, the wealthy and the poor, as well as slaves and former slaves. It was customary for participants in the Lord's meal to bring from home their own food and drink. The wealthy brought so much food and drink that they could indulge in gluttony and drunkenness. The poor who came later, however, had little or nothing to bring, with the result that some of them went hungry and could not enjoy a decent meal.[7] This conflict at the Lord's Supper is seen in Paul's comment: "It is not the Lord's Supper that you eat. For in eating the meal each one goes ahead with his own meal" (1 Cor. 11:20-21). The allegation could be taken to signify that a distorted gluttony and drunkenness of the groups is the main cause of the conflict, as if each individual had eaten independently of the others.[8] The Corinthians' meal *eranos* [9] had become a social problem for the Christian community: (1) The meal made beforehand apparently differed in quantity and quality. (2) Some members began eating before the others arrived and before the Lord's Supper took place. (3) Murphy-O'Connor[10] observes that the one who arrived late found no room in the *triclinium*, which was the dining room where regularly only twelve could recline for the meal.

The problem with the space and discrimination against those provided with second-class facilities prepared the atmosphere for the tensions that appear in Paul's account of the Eucharist meal at Roman Corinth (1 Cor. 11:17-34). Nevertheless, Paul's statement that "one is hungry while another is drunk" (v.21) tell us those tensions was presumably provoked by another possible factor, clearly, the type and quality of food offered.[11] These private meals have to be eaten at home according to Paul's comments in 1 Cor. 11:22-34. He also reminded them that the Lord's Supper was meant to commemorate the Lord's sacrificial death.[12]

Nevertheless, in trying to be more specific, what behavior is it that, in Paul's view, disturbed the Lord's Supper? The crux of the dilemma seems to be stated in v. 22 in a list of rhetorical questions. This form, of course, is used when the speaker wants the readers to draw conclusions for themselves; here he seems to want them to acknowledge certain unacceptable inferences from their own behavior.

Their behavior implies that they reject the congregation of God, because they humiliate those who do have little.[13] Furthermore, if we add to the scene Paul's warning at the end of chapter 11 ("So then, my brothers, when you gather together to eat the Lord's Supper, wait for one another" [v. 33]), then it becomes obvious that the neglected are especially the poor and the slaves. Neither group could easily leave their work to attend the evening meal; especially was this true of the slaves because they were not the masters of their time.

However, from the text we may assume still more about the degeneration of this Corinthian celebration. The question arises: What have the Corinthians made of the Lord's Supper? According to the common view point, the Corinthian have abolished the concept of receiving the body of Christ.[14] For them the blessed bread was no longer the body and they ate the Eucharistic meal as an ordinary food.

P. Neuenzeit argues that "Würde die Brothandlung noch am Beginn der Feier gestanden haben, so hatten die später Kommenden nur an der Bechereucharistie teilnehmen können. Einen solchen Ausschluss der Armen von der Broteucharistie würde Paulus scharf tadeln."[15] Neuenzeit's argument is right because this bread, Eucharist, did not come at the beginning of the ceremony, neither did it come after some ordinary meal. It came after the private supper (*eranos* meal) of which Paul did not approve.

An attempt to explain the whole social issue has been made by Theissen. He explains that when Paul says, in v. 21, "during the meal each takes his own food," it means that in the process of the actual fellowship meal, the wealthy were supposed to give bread and wine away and keep some for themselves. Social distinctions were reflected in the quantity of food consumed.[16] It is also argued that there was a separation in the kind of food brought and eaten. The rich brought meat, fish, or other delicacies; [17] however, Theissen thinks that they did not see the need to share these goods because Paul's instructions on the Lord's Supper mentioned only bread and wine as part of the Eucharist meal.[18]

Such lack of concern for the needs of the poor seemed to distress Paul.[19] He says that when the members of the church of Roman Corinth come together, they should not start eating, one after another as they arrived, but the members should wait until they all arrived to hold the fellowship meal. In conclusion, Paul condemned drastic abuse because they despise the church of God by making a truly communal meal impossible. This was the crisis that made him appeal to the original tradition of the Lord's meal.

Paul's Account of the Last Supper in 1 Cor 11:17-26

The Christians at Roman Corinth came together in order to celebrate the Lord's Supper and to have fellowship and a nourishing meal. It is well-known that some ate a lot and even got drunk, while others, however, went hungry. The Eucharistic tradition in 1 Cor. 11:23-25 presents the following sequence of events: (1) The Eucharistic bread was blessed and broken. (2) The meal took place. (3) It finished with the blessing of the cup and the drinking from it.

In addition, in order to understand the social-cultural context of the Gentile Christian meal at Roman Corinth, it is necessary to know what happened in a typical Greco-Roman dinner party (*eranos*). A comparison of the common practice of both the Greco-Roman and the Corinthian meal would allow us to see some similarities.[20]

The Greco-Roman Dinner Party	The Corinthian Eucharistic
(Dinner + Symposium/Eranos)	"Potluck Dinner" (Eranos)
- **Dinner at "First Tables"**	- The richer Corinthians eat "early" (1 Cor. 11:21)
Break	
Start of the	
"Second Tables"	
- a sacrifice, invocation of the house gods and of the geniuses of the host and of the emperor	- Blessing and Breaking of the Bread, invocation of Christ
-Second Tables	- The sacramental eucharistic
(often with guests who had newly arrived)	meal (some stay hungry)
- a toast for the good spirit of the house, the tables are removed	
- the first wine jug is mixed, libation, singing	- Blessing of the Cup
- drinking, conversation	- drinking
music, singing, entertainment in a loose sequence	- Maybe the worship activities of 1 Cor. 12-14 (espec.14:26-32): singing, teaching, prophesying, glossolalia (with translations); no orderly sequence

Obviously, the religious factors were present at a dinner party and it was not new for the Gentile Christians at Roman Corinth. It is most likely that they even had the opportunity to compare their Eucharistic meal with elements of the social dinners in the Greco-Roman dinner parties. Both the First and the Second Tables were started with the blessing and the breaking of the bread. The cup after the meal could be seen in parallel to the mixing of the first jug of wine. A formal shift was marked between the meal and the *eranos* drinking party by the wine ceremony. Smith suggests that the church members at Roman Corinth substituted for this cup of blessing of the Lord's Supper to mark this formal transition.[21] Both signal that all eating is finished now. Both were accompanied by religious ceremony, either by a blessing or libation.[22] Hence, it may be possible that these are the first resemblances that the Gentile Church members at Roman Corinth could draw. Looking back at the Corinthian scenario, they continued a Greco-Roman meal custom by dividing the evening into First and Second Tables, which led to problems in the Corinthian Church.

In addition, it seems quite logical to stress the fact that often the Corinthian Christians simply continued being a part of the Greco-Roman society to which they belonged before their conversion. Gradually, they realized that the church was a new socio-cultural setting where new practices and habits needed to be developed in some areas, especially the issues of status and divisions.

The Divisions at Roman Corinth

Paul uses the expression, in verse 17, Τοῦτο δὲ παραγγέλλων οὐκ ἐπαινῶ, to reprove the congregation regarding the parties or cliques, presumably the same groups as those that the apostle had dealt with earlier in his letter (in chs. 1-3). The participle παραγγέλλων is a temporal adverb. It introduces Paul's next part in which he points to bad practices in the observance of the Lord's Supper. There were groups that had broken the spirit of unity in Christ. Their practice which they had been holding regularly (present progressive retroactive tense in συνέρχεσθε) was doing more harm than good.

Apparently Paul had already anticipated this concern in his previous reference to the table in 10:17, where he reminded them that because they all eat of the one loaf, they together constitute the one body of Christ. Their "divisions" at the table denied the unity that their common partaking of the bread was intended to proclaim.[23] Indeed, the reading is somewhat doubtful, as also is the meaning of τοῦτο. If τοῦτο refers to the charge which he gives respecting the love-feasts, then the interval between this preface and the words which it anticipates is awkwardly prolonged.[24] Many scholars agree that this reading could be an accidental error.[25] Whether an error or not, the most important thing in this verse is that Paul was reminding them that they had to correct some practices, especially the lack of order and the division that attacked the very nature of the Eucharistic meal.

Paul's ideas in 1 Cor. 11:17ff. Do not simply presuppose certain social relationships within the Corinthian community. Above all, they express social intentions, the desire to improve interpersonal relationships. It is not accidental that Paul's statements issue a very concrete suggestion for the Corinthian congregation's behavior.[26] Social disparity was clearly one of the main problems leading to the lack of order in the Lord's Supper at Corinth.

As in the case of the division in the Corinthian Church, it was typical for ancient *symposia* or *eranos* meals to produce σχίσματα. Paul is not surprised by this (μέροι τι πιστεύω), since the divisions and factions were inevitable (δεῖ γὰρ καί αἱρέσεις) if those who were esteemed (οἱ δόκιμοι) were also to be considered (φανεροί). It is clear that these divisions were the result of jealousies and rivalries over such honors as place, and portion or quality of food and wine. Consequently, those who supplied houses and food were dishonoring (καταισχύνω) the poorer class.[27] Timon the brother of Plutarch spoke against these abuses "the rich lording it over the poor," but the majority who showed up at the banquet was upper class.[28] Juvenal also protested of the lot of the *pauper*; he means a lower class person who is at the hand of the richest:

> Is a man to sign his name before me, and recline on a couch above mine, who has been wafted to Rome by the wind which brings us our damsons and our figs? . . . Of all the woes of luckless poverty none is harder to endure than this, that it exposes men to ridicule. "Out you go, for very shame," says the marshall; "out of the Knights stalls, all you whose means do not satisfy the law." Here let the sons of panders, born in any brothel, take their seats.[29]

It is more likely that Paul meant that the result of their practising the Communion service as they had been doing was bad rather than good. In the remainder of the chapter he points out the flaws in their observance and what they should do to eliminate the social conflicts.

This social tension led Paul to say to the Corinthians in v. 18: πρῶτον μὲν γὰρ συνερχομένων ὑμῶν ἐν ἐκκλησίᾳ ἀκούω σχίσματα. A. T. Robertson takes μέν in its original use, as emphasizing πρῶτον. Hence he translates "from the very outset" meaning that this sad situation of division had characterized the Corinthian church since its beginning.[30] This may indeed be the meaning, but it is difficult to believe that the Corinthians, during the first years of Paul's revival there, were so plagued with division.

The σχίσματα that make themselves manifest at the Eucharistic meal are, in part at least, the result of the social or class differences among the wealthy and the poor. It is possible to believe, according to Barrett that some Jewish Christians may have insisted on kosher food, with the result of separating themselves from their Gentile brothers and sisters.[31] The above statement is difficult to accept because the influence of Jewish Christians at Roman Corinth was not felt. Although this situation introduced some difficult crises into the church, the whole congregation of believers still came together in one assembly.[32] The Corinthians still had common meals and participated in the Lord's Supper.

Allo clearly explains that Paul uses the phrase πρῶτον μέν to emphasise what he calls Paul's "premier reproche." He further says that

> Le premier reproche (πρῶτον μέν) concerne des divisions, contraires à la charité, qui se faisaient dans leurs assembliés, et dont Paul à eu vent (même si rien ne lui à été écrit à; ce sujet). On pense naturellement d'abord à un effet de ces disputes dont il à été parlé au premier chapitre, lequel aurait pu être dénoncé aussi par les gens de Chloé l'effet de ces divisions serait apparu jusque dans le banquet eucharistique (20-22), et, à plus forte raison, dans les rivalités entre "inspirés" (voir ch. xiv). Paul dit, avec quelque ironie peut-être, que "il le croit pour une part"; síl le croit, c'est qui' 1 connaît l'état d'agitation des esprits, qu'il a décrit dès le commencement de son épître.[33]

Consequently, the assembly of the church at Corinth (ἐκκλησία) is characterized by σχίσματα. The apparent unity of 1 Cor. 10:17 are not yet worked out and this disunity has shown itself at the Lord's Supper. Paul's main concern is very clear and he describes the real danger in the Eucharistic meal on the fundamental points: First, the earlier divisions were further described as quarrels and jealousy on the part of the members of the church (1 Cor. 1:11; 3:4), which are missing from this chapter, where we find social problems (vv. 21-22; 33-34). Second, Paul notes in 1 Cor. 1:12 the names of four people involved in the dispute which took place; moreover, there is an anti-Paul feeling in that dispute. Third, in the passage that we are studying Paul says, "When you come together as a church, there are divisions among you." This language implies that the divisions are especially related to their gatherings, not simply to false allegiances to their leaders or to wisdom.[34]

The situation in the church at Corinth was a negation of a true Eucharist in a sense. The divisions among the church members jeopardized the unity of the body of Christ, symbolized in the Eucharistic loaf (10:17); the excessive self-indulgence of some of the church members in the Lord's Supper denied the principle from which it took its name and demonstrated that they were entirely oblivious to the deeper significance of the common life in the body of Christ.[35] Paul's instruction begins with his "premier reproche," not that the Corinthian are profaning a holy rite, but that they are dividing the holy community.

In the first four chapters of the epistle, Paul demonstrated how seriously he regards schisms. With apparent resignation he accepts the inevitability of the divisions as a means of testing, but in no way does he approve the divisions that result from their practice in the celebration of the Lord's Supper. In addition, it seems that the Corinthians were faithfully observing the ordinance of the Lord's Supper as Paul had taught them (1 Cor. 11:2), but they were ignoring the need for spiritual preparation before they approached the Lord's Table.

In v. 19 Paul states, γὰρ καὶ αἱρέσεις ἐν ὑμῖν εἶναι. Paul, however, speaks not only of individual Christians, but also of divisions (σχίσματα) and factions (αἱρέσεις). He apparently thinks not in terms of a string of individuals, but of groups. He has already used the same term σχίσμα in 1 Cor. 1:10 to refer to such groups.[36] The meal serves as a boundary marker in the church gatherings at Corinth. In other words, Paul states that the meal is a locus both for the identification of divisions within the church and for their perpetuation.[37] So something about the Corinthians' meal created social boundaries and brought αἱρέσεις among the members which Paul did not like. All these elements are considered in Paul's rebuke. The fact is that he raises the issue for discussion and deals critically with it (1 Cor. 11:17, 22).

Paul introduces an element of judgment and self-examination: ἵνα (καὶ) οἱ δόκιμοι φανεροὶ γένωνται ἐν ὑμῖν. Paul introduces an eschatological element, combining, the notion of testing by difficult circumstances, so popular with pagan moralists as well, with the eschatological notion that the Day of the Lord alone reveals one's true worth.[38] Therefore, every member of the Corinthian Church must meet the test (οἱ δόκιμοι). The idea of testing is summarized in verses 28-32. Each one as single individual, not as a church or group member must test himself and herself before eating and drinking.

Paul was trying to warn them about their own behavior that they might not fall in God's judgment. Divisions could be unavoidable, not edifying to the church in which they take place. The proper observance of the Communion, if carried on in complete conformity to the social Christians rules that regulate it, will correct this situation of division within the church. That the Corinthian were not observing it properly is apparent from what follows.

The Social Private Meal

The struggle at the Lord's Supper is disclosed when in fact Paul says in verse 20: "Συνερχομένων οὖν ὑμῶν ἐπὶ τὸ αὐτὸ οὐκ ἔστιν κυριακὸν δεῖπνον φαγεῖν." What is happening? They assemble together not to eat the Lord's Supper, but to eat their own meal. The supper, as it was conducted in the church at Roman Corinth, did not bring honor and did not belong to the Lord, but to the church members. The Greek adjective used (κυριακόν) which qualifies the term "supper" means "pertaining to the Lord" (κύριος)[39] or "belonging to the Lord." Paul is censuring and questioning the kind of celebration of the community meal which they called or described as the "Lord's Supper." The Corinthians violated the nature of the Eucharistic meal by their behavior. So, for Paul it was no more possible for the Lord's Supper to be eaten in an environment of social unfairness than it was for the same church members to participate in the table of the Lord and the table of demons (10: 21).[40] The Lord's Supper could be unsanctified by divisions as well as by idolatry. Before Paul describes in detail (verses 23-26) what belongs properly in the Lord's meal, he points out in further detail (verses 21-22) their evil practices.

Paul attacked the social discrimination (11: 21, 22) that existed at Corinth because the wealthy began to eat without any consideration of the others; especially, they did not wait for the arrival of the poor brethren, who usually came late from their jobs. Besides, they ate and got drunk while others did not have the chance to eat anything. According to C. H. Talbert "the purpose of the supper forgotten by the Corinthians, customary social convention prevailed and divisions resulted."[41] Lucian and Athenaeus observe that gluttony was another form of self-indulgence typical of many *symposia*.[42] That is why Paul says that instead of the Lord's Supper (κυριακὸν δεῖπνον), "each proceeded with his private supper" (τὸ ἴδιον δεῖπνον), and "one goes hungry and another gets drunk" (καὶ ὃς μὲν πεινᾷ ο} δὲ μεθύει). This statement and the one in v. 20 could be understood to mean that gluttony and drunkenness was the root of the strife, and it seemed that each person had eaten without regard to the others.[43]

Another point we should keep in mind is the problem of the famine in Roman Corinth.[44] This situation obviously increased the tension in the church. P. Garnsey observes that the market was controlled, and that the "have-nots" had gained advantage from a reduction in the price of the grain. The non-slave workers and artisans who have Corinthian citizenship were most in danger.[45] These were common citizens who, in time of famine were the most exposed.

The slave and freedman citizens connected to a household were, economically speaking, more secure than these citizens whom Paul called οἳ μὴ ἔχοντες.[46] So, clearly, the richest members of the congregation were the hosts of the meeting and most likely provided the food for everybody. This was in accordance with the practice of various ancient clubs and with the custom followed in the society of those days.

The hosts in many cases provided both large amounts and better quality of food and drinks to the ones who were socially equal to them than to participants of lower status. So, the struggle was between "different standards of behavior," between "status-specific expectations and the norms of a community of love."[47]

Paul's answer, Theissen suggests, is an agreement which asks that the rich brothers have their own private meal at home, so that in the Eucharist meal the norm for equal portions of food to all the members can prevail. Plutarch always emphasized the view that there should be equality among the guests, ἡ ἰσότης τοῖι ἀνδράσι.[48]   Contrary to Plutarch's view, Athenaeus thought that there should be a difference among the guests as there is a difference in age, outlook and social status, calling it "a factor which might add both interest and variety to the proceedings."[49]

However, it is in 1 Cor. 11: 22 that we find two groups against each other: those who have no food, the μὴ ἔχοντες, and those who can bring their own meal, ἴδιον δεῖπνον.[50] Euripides describes them: the first group were identified as "those who have not" and it is this people which "save the city," σῴζει πόλεις, by keeping the order which the state ordains. The second group, the rich, was those whom he describes as useless and "always lusting after more."[51] In Paul's mind, in these gatherings the sacred element was far more important than the social, but the Corinthians had destroyed both. Κοινωνία is destroyed when a large group of members suffers want and another group is drunk. It is clear that we have here not a sacramental rite, but an ordinary meal taken in the church.

Paul's ecclesiological desire is presented in 1 Cor. 10: 16:   The transformation of a multiplicity of individuals and different backgrounds into a unity.   In other words, the *communitas* experienced in baptism, in which separation of role and rank are replaced by the unity within the congregation as a whole in a new society where love reigns, is Paul's intention in the Supper. For Paul, unity among members is synonymous with unity in the body of Christ. That is why group unity caused strong group boundaries.[52] Thus, even if the expression ἕκαστος γὰρ τὸ ἴδιον δεῖπνον προλαμβάνει ἐν τῷ φαγεῖν leads to the conclusion that Paul is addressing certain individuals' behavior it is a form of behavior which in the situation is restricted to a certain group.

Those members of the church at Roman Corinth who ate their own private meal may have had a high social rank, not only because they differed from other Christians, but because they could bring food for themselves. Their social position is also clear in Paul's question: μὴ γὰρ οἰκίας οὐκ ἔχετε εἰς τὸ ἐσθίειν καὶ πίνειν. Paul poses the question, "Do you not have houses (οἰκίας) to eat and drink in?" He addressed this question to those that probably were the owners of the houses and, therefore, the heads of the households. It seems quite logical to conclude that the divisions were among households or members of households with the dominant part composed of the wealthy household heads.[53] Thus, we can see that social relations at Roman Corinth would be affected, that the church supper had become a centre of these household rivalries.

But Paul's point, expressing outright condemnation, is that the wealthy should eat and drink their own meal at their homes because if they cannot wait for others (11:33), if they must satisfy their own appetite, they can at least maintain the church's ordinary meal free from such malpractices as can only bring disgrace to the celebration. Their behavior, makes the church meal lose its character of a love-feast. Paul's condemnation is clear and sound: ἢ τῆς ἐκκλησίας τοῦ θεοῦ καταφρονεῖτε, καὶ καταισχύνετε τοὺς μὴ ἔχοντας. The attitude of Paul is filled with such indignation that he makes a series of rhetorical questions with the desire to reduce the "sated" to a position of humiliation similar to that which they have been trying to reduce the poor members of the church.[54]

The poor member, who can bring hardly anything for himself, will, of course, feel ashamed when he sees the food brought by his Christian fellows. The wealthy member's attitude is not controlled by love, but rather by selfishness. It is by failure in Christian love that the Corinthian profane the sacramental aspect of the supper, not by liturgical error.

This congregation, which should be a congregation of brothers and sisters, shows clearly that, in their meeting for worship, they portray a shameless view of social cleavage.[55] What is happening in the church is so notorious a repudiation of some Christian standards of conduct and practice that even the apostle was puzzled about it. He says, Τί εἴπω ὑμῖν their unbrotherly conduct in this regard could not have any praise, but only obvious disapprobation from the apostle (ἐν τούτῳ οὐκ ἐπαινῶ). Paul attacks the system indirectly, yet at its very core. To be a genuine Christian in participating in the Lord's Table means to be concerned with the needs of others; this goes along with Paul's own principles and is also part of the believer's life. We can see that the apostle's main concern is the significance of the Lord's table vis à vis their unity in Christ.[56]

In summary, to dine alone at church means to decline to join with the church in this great expression of common fellowship and Christian social life; and it, therefore, manifests contempt toward the sacrament. The fellowship meal should unite the members as a joint family who gather together with a common purpose in mind, to build the church in brotherly love, regardless of the social status of the ones who partake of the Lord's Meal. Paul now proceeds to explain to them how the Lord's Supper was introduced by Jesus, a model which they should follow.

Paul's Tradition of the Last Supper

Paul makes it clear in verse 23 that the tradition of the Lord's Supper involved a historical memory, which immediately distinguishes the Lord's Supper from all pagan memorial meals.[57] Paul introduces the formula of the Last Supper in this way: Ἐγὼ γὰρ παρέλαβον ἀπὸ τοῦ κυρίου, ὃ καὶ παρέδωκα ὑμῖν. The phrases he uses, παραλαμβάνειν and παραδιδόναι, are considered similar in meaning to two well-known rabbinical terms, קבל and מסר. This is a tradition that Paul has inherited from his predecessors. J. Jeremias argues that this is a notion of an old, established tradition that Paul was reminding the Corinthians of, seen in 1 Cor. 15:3. Here the apostle uses the same technical terms παραδιδόναι and παραλαμβάνειν (παρέδωκα γὰρ ὑμῖν ἐν πρώτοις, ὃ καὶ παρέλαβον).[58]

At this point the most important issue to take into consideration is whether the apostle himself is claiming to know about the Lord's Eucharistic word through a personal revelation, or through a tradition handed down to him from some members or leaders of the church at Jerusalem. In our earlier discussion, we found that the difference between Paul and the Synoptic Gospels (especially Mark) focused on the question: In what way is Paul's account linked to that of Mark? Clearly, both accounts have their similarities and differences. Paul's account of the Last Supper in 1 Cor. 11:23-26 is considered the earliest written account by some, although not by Jeremias, who opts for Mark's account. It was, he says, written in the early fifties; however, some scholars[59] argue that Mark's Gospel, which was written later, has many Aramaic expressions and could be considered an older text than Paul's version. Lietzmann mentions the fact of several independent accounts, but coming from the same original source.[60]

Paul begins the words of institution as "tradition" which the apostle has received from the Lord and later communicated to the members of the church at Corinth. "What does *paradosis* mean here?"[61] It is known that Paul introduces a formula given to him beforehand, but which is common to the Corinthians and which later he gave to them. H. Maccoby points out that Loisy and Lietzmann argued that Paul was speaking, especially in this verse (v. 23), of a private or personal revelation which has been too easily dismissed.[62] However, Talbert observes that "Paul used the technical terms "to receive" and "to deliver" for learning and teaching the oral traditions (cf. 1 Cor. 15:3). He does not claim that the tradition to follow was given him personally by the earthly or the risen Christ."[63] Several theories have been proposed but no agreement has been reached among scholars.

For instance, one theory sees Paul's declaration, which was rejected by some scholars and more recently reopened by Maccoby (see note 71), to mean that Paul claims to receive his version of the Lord's Supper by direct personal revelation, just as it occurs in Gal. 1: 12: "I did not receive it from any man, nor did anyone teach it to me. It was Jesus Christ himself who revealed it to me." This is a reference to Paul's encounter with the resurrected Lord on the Damascus road.

The addition of the phrase ἀπὸ τοῦ κυρίου raises at least two questions: Where did Paul hear about this tradition? And when did he hear about the Lord's tradition? We do not have to take this to mean that Paul received a special divine revelation given in a private way to him.[64] It seems probable that when Paul says, "For I received from the Lord," he is not claiming a direct personal revelation ἀπὸ τοῦ κυρίου, though this idea is often assumed. It is more likely that a tradition has been given to him, as from the Lord.[65]

A second theory is proposed by Lietzmann: "Paul is the creator of the second type of the Lord's Supper." He explains that Paul received the revelation from the Lord, that is, the prototype of the Eucharist, as a memorial of the death of the Lord. However, it is unnecessary to look for parallels in the Hellenistic memorial meals of the dead when we can find Jewish parallel sources which are available. The Supper must be repeated in remembrance of Jesus. By emphasising Christ's atoning death, the apostle becomes the true originator of a type of the Lord's Supper which is different from the one he calls the Jerusalem type.[66]

Kümmel disagrees with Lietzmann. He believes that Paul considers himself to be handing down the tradition, unmodified by the church, which ultimately goes back to the historical Jesus. Higgins points out that this point of view is accepted by the majority of scholars such as M. Goguel, J. Weiss, A. Schweitzer, M. Dibelius, F. L. Cirlot, E. Gaugler, Théo Preiss, R. Bultmann, and J. Héring.[67] More recently Marshall agrees with Kümmel's view and adds that Paul was talking about an existing tradition that he considered a kind of formal account. Paul reflects Rabbinic terminology as in the handing on of Rabbinic tradition.[68] This notion of Jewish oral tradition, received (παρέλαβον) and handed on (παρέδωκα), has been challenged by Barrett. He says that we have to be careful in emphasising the Jewish usage because both terms were used in the same sense in ancient Greek long before these expressions had been in any way influenced by Jewish custom;[69] however, it is not correct, without more evidence, to perceive a full rabbinic content in them.

Lohmeyer's viewpoint can be categorized as a third theory. He disagrees with Lietzmann's position in saying that the command, "Do this in remembrance of me," forms the crux of the new emphasis on the essence of the Lord's Supper which Paul received as part of the tradition. But he considers the language of the account as un-Pauline. The phrase "remembrance" (ἀνάμνησις), Lohmeyer says, is not used by Paul in any other place.[70]

Finally, the last view or theory which is worthy of mention is O. Cullmann's. He cites some passages (for example, 1 Cor. 7:10, 25; 9:14; 1 Thess. 4:15) in connection with the idea that "the Lord" takes the place of "tradition." 1 Cor. 11:23, "I received (by tradition) from the Lord." For Cullmann the Lord, in this passage, is not only the historical Jesus as the chronological origin of the tradition, but the glorified Lord who is behind the communication of the tradition, who works in it.[71] Thus, the term ἀπὸ τοῦ κυρίου, in a sense, can be understood to mean a direct revelation from the exalted Lord, without necessarily connoting of a vision or denying the possibility of its being transmitted through human beings. Paul considers himself a link in a chain of tradition (as he says in 1 Cor. 15:3ff.), yet he breaks this traditional chain by saying that he received the tradition (ἀπὸ τοῦ κυρίου). Another evidence that Paul found the liturgical words already in existence is the fact that they speak of a "communion" with the body and the blood of the Lord. Therefore, it seems clear that Paul did not receive the Lord's Supper tradition by direct revelation as Maccoby and others claim.

We come back to the question, where did Paul hear about this tradition? We know Paul received it from the Lord. The manner of revelation is debatable. Scholars like Bornkamm and others express the view that Paul received the tradition when he was in Antioch, before he began his mission.[72] On the contrary, when Paul says that he gets it "from the Lord," he is not claiming special divine revelation.

Rather, he is alluding to a tradition that was prevailing in the church. Clearly Paul had heard about it before coming to the Corinthians. We must consider three possible places: Antioch, Damascus, and Jerusalem. Antioch and Damascus were founded by Christians from Jerusalem; therefore, Jerusalem was the place where Paul heard about the tradition.[73] But, even though the churches in Antioch and Damascus were founded by Christians from Jerusalem, could it be that Paul's formula may go back to Damascus instead[74] (where he spent according to Acts 9:19-31 several days with the believers)? How long was he there? The Scripture does not say specifically; the fact is that after his encounter with the exalted Lord, he stayed in Damascus before he went to Jerusalem. The probabilities are that the apostle's knowledge of the tradition goes back to Greek-speaking Christians in the Diaspora (so that Damascus seems most likely), rather than in Jerusalem as is proposed by Marshall.

They had translated it out of the historical account of the Last Supper used by Hebrew or Aramaic-speaking Christians living in Damascus. Thus, Paul's instruction of how the Eucharist meal was celebrated probably goes back to the practice of the rite of the Lord's Supper in the early church through the believers in Damascus. Jeremias' argument that Paul did not receive the formula of the words of institution is correct, but that Paul used a formula in use at Antioch, where he settled down years later after his conversion (according to Acts 11:26,)[75] is not quite right.

The view of earlier scholarship is that Paul is speaking of a direct revelation about the tradition of the Lord's Supper, has been accepted once again by Maccoby. He also says that the argument for the use of the two words παρέλαβον ἀπό has been discussed to show that ἀπό is not the correct word to use but παρά. First of all, Maccoby agrees that the preposition παρά is more usual in a context of transmitting information, but ἀπό is also very frequently used and found in such contexts (e.g. Matt. 11:29; Col. 1:7). He further adds that Jeremias argues that the preposition ἀπό does not indicate the source of Paul's account, rather the use of the verb παραλαμβάνω. This verb is similar in meaning to the Hebrew verb קבל, which normally refers to transmission as part of a process of tradition. So, he says that when "Paul indicates sufficiently that his account of the institution of the Eucharist is derived from the tradition of the church, not from a personal vision," it is debatable. In order to refute the argument, he quotes the use of the verb קבל in the Rabbinic literature and quotes the opening of the Mishnah tractate *Abot*: "Moses received (קבל) the Torah from Sinai." For Maccoby this argument is enough to prove that the verb קבל refers to the transmission of tradition, but also mentions the first step in that process, the receiving of the tradition from God himself. Thus, he concludes by saying that when Paul says, "I received (παρέλαβον) it from the Lord," Paul possibly considers himself as starting a process of tradition, not from other human beings, but rather from the exalted Lord himself.[76]

A second view stressed by Maccoby is that Jesus is the initiator of the tradition instituted by himself; Paul was not present at the Last Supper, so he was not a witness of Jesus' actions and words at the Last Supper. The witnesses did not receive it, they saw and heard it happening. Therefore, "it makes perfect logical sense for Paul, who was not present at the Last Supper, to say that he received an account of it 'from' the heavenly Jesus."[77] In spite of Maccoby's argument, it makes much more sense to say that even though Paul was not present at the Last Supper and not a witness of the actions and words of Jesus, he may well have attributed the tradition he received to the Lord himself and at the same time interpreted it. As a result he may have even changed some aspects of the tradition which did not affect its practice. Paul was quoting technical terms from his own Jewish heritage. Furthermore we are not to understand from Paul's version of the Last Supper that he is quoting the *ipsissima verba* of Jesus, but we are to find there the precipitate of those words percolated through the mind of a Rabbi trained at the feet of Gamaliel.[78]

This explanation of Paul's account of the tradition of the Last Supper makes it possible for us to comprehend why it is, as has usually been pointed out, that the basic meaning of the Markan and Pauline accounts is similar, although the forms are different. The Pauline account (quoting Davies) of Jesus' Last Supper tradition is "a Rabbinization of the tradition."[79] In summary, Paul can put the revelation received on the Damascus road, and the church tradition,[80] on the same level because in both cases the revelation and the tradition came from the same Lord who is the originator of both.

The Saying over the Bread

The formula by Paul in v. 24 $\mu o \acute{u} \, \acute{e} \sigma \tau \iota \nu \, \tau \acute{o} \, \sigma \hat{\omega} \mu a$--with the possessive pronoun at the beginning--is strong evidence that Paul received the church tradition in the Greek language.[81] Paul's introduction of the phrase "which is for you" possibly is a secondary Hellenization that cannot be retranslated back to the original Aramaic. It is a "Haggadistic addition" in explanation of the saying of the Lord about his body.[82] One of the two words is joined to the saying on the bread and the other to that on the cup; both are alterations of an original tradition.

However, it has been pointed out that neither the Gospel of Mark, Matthew, nor the shorter Lukan text have the adjective clause "which is for you"; the longer Lukan text (22:19) has it in expanded form, "which is given for you" and follows it, as Paul's account does, with the command: touto $\pi o \iota \epsilon \hat{\iota} \tau \epsilon \, \epsilon \grave{\iota} s \, \tau \grave{\eta} \nu \, \acute{e} \mu \grave{\eta} \nu \, \acute{a} \nu \acute{a} \mu \nu \eta \sigma \iota \nu$. In the biblical sense memorial (remembrance) is more than a mental exercise; it suggests a realization of what is to be remembered.[83]

There is, therefore, a deep intellectual truth in Paul's communication of the words of the institution of the Lord's Supper. He brings together the words, "Do this in remembrance of me," with Jesus' description of the bread as his "body," and the words, "Do this, as often as you drink it, in remembrance of me," to Jesus' reference to the cup as "the new covenant in my blood." These same words of Paul's account are added in some versions to Luke's account of the Last Supper. Paul's use of the words $\epsilon \grave{\iota} s \, \acute{a} \nu \acute{a} \mu \nu \eta \sigma \iota \nu$ is the equivalent of the Hebrew term זכר or לזכר of the Haggadah, but "there seems to be no unanimity as to who is to do the 'remembering' and what the 'remembering' signifies."[84]

The command to repeat the rite is found (aside from the addition in Luke) only in Paul, especially when he mentions both the bread and the wine. It probably did not belong to the earliest form of the account of the Last Supper. Jeremias considers the command to repeat the rite as a separate tradition which Paul received in Antioch.[85] As the Passover meal was, in the words of the paschal narrative, "a remembrance of the going out of Egypt" (cf. Ex. 12:12; 13:3,9; Dt. 16:3), so the notion of the breaking of bread was to be an ἀνάμνησις" of the Lord after "his departure" which he was going to fulfill at Jerusalem (Lk. 9:31). This command is unique to the Paul/Luke version of the bread-saying. Because this notion is absent in Mark/Matthew, there has been some question as to its authenticity.[86]

It looks as though the earliest tradition described such a command by the Lord with the saying of the bread and the cup, in which case, no matter what its relative age, the Pauline account is reasonably prior to the Lukan one. We have seen that Paul is concern with the problem of εἰς ἀνάμνησιν within the context of the Passover meal. This point of view of Dalman and Davies, contra Jeremias, that the verb זכר (which the Lord instituted) was, according to the apostle, a זכר by which the disciples were to remember Jesus and his redemptive act rather than a prayer that they may remember him.[87]

The significance of the rite is explained by the words εἰς τὴν εμὴν ἀνάμνησιν, "in memorial of me"; the term ἀνάμνησις, "remembrance" (memorial) expresses much more than a mere celebration; it means a sacramental presence in the Lord's rite. It seems that this expression is found in the Greek memorial feast for the dead.[88] Paul concludes that the way they celebrated the rite, it does not have to do with a rebuilding of the continual table fellowship of Jesus and his disciples, but with a reproduction of the Lords Supper. Unlike Lietzmann, Jeremias holds that there is no evidence for the words εἰς ἀνάμνησιν in Greek remembrance feasts, but that they are found in the Old Testament and Judaism.

One example given is from the testament of Epicurus, who made preparation for a yearly celebration "in memory (εἰς τὴν μνήμην) of us (i.e., μέ) and Metrodorus."[89] The earliest tradition of the church did not include this kind of tradition but we owe much too Hellenistic custom even though it is true that the pagan memorial meals seem to have been less frequent than the Christian.

Differences among Christians and pagans are not surprising because, for instance, Epicurus was not believed, as Jesus was, to have risen from the dead.[90] Therefore, the Christian meal also brought to mind an act of deliverance; it was closely linked with a more significant Person, and the memorial was surely his memorial. Jesus gave himself on behalf of his people; so, when they share in eating a piece of bread in a meal, they eat and drink in his memory.

The Saying over the Cup

The saying over the cup, as it appears in Paul's account (ὡσαύτως καὶ τὸ ποτήριον μετὰ τὸ δειπνῆσαι), becomes plain, with minor modification, in the longer Lukan account (Lk. 22:20: καὶ τὸ ποτήριον ὡσαύτως μετὰ τὸ δειπνῆσαι). The saying of the cup is placed where not only Paul/Luke differs from the one of Mark/Matthew, but also where, in the second part, Paul and the Gospel of Luke differ from each other. As we see with the saying over the bread, both formulas in the tradition start with the word "this" and, in both cases, Jesus identifies the cup with his blood in a covenantal terminology. However, there is no agreement among the scholars as to which tradition represents the more ancient form.[91]

There is a difference in meaning and terminology between the sayings: "This is my blood of the covenant" (Mk. 14:24), and "This cup is the new covenant in my blood." (1 Cor. 11:25). Each of the expressions presupposes that the shedding of the blood of the Lord Jesus Christ marks the beginning of a new covenant between God and humans. In Paul's account the ascription is made directly to the covenant (διαθήκη), in this case the "new covenant" which is mentioned in Jer. 31:31. Mark's version refers to the old covenant explicitly and the new covenant implicitly.[92] In both formulas, the idea is almost the same. It is that the wine of the cup means Jesus' blood poured out in death, which ratified the new covenant.

In the Markan version διαθήκη, "covenant" is an explanation of αἷμα, "blood"; but in Paul's it is the contrary: αἷμα is an explanation of διαθήκη.[93] The reference to blood contains the notion of sacrifice. The blood of Jesus Christ plays a very important role in Paul's own soteriology, but a traditional role. The term appears only in Rom. 3:24ff, and in one further passage where the same tradition is mentioned, Rom. 5:9. The cup is the sign and pledge of a share in the new covenant, and so in the kingdom. The formula in the Gospel of Mark is the end of a liturgical tendency to make the saying equal with that about the bread, and to take it up to Exod. 24:8 (LXX: ἰδοὺ τὸ αἷμα τῆς διαθήκης).[94] In other words, Jesus said, "This is my blood," but he spoke of the covenant in his own blood. The word "blood" in Mark is the equivalent of the body. Though they are not exact parallels the correlative of blood is supposed to be flesh; and besides, Jesus had already mentioned his blood in speaking of his body.

The question is: how could the wine in Mark's gospel have been called "his blood" by the Lord, and then be mentioned as "the fruit of the vine"? The answer is that the latter comes from historical tradition; the Gospel of Mark is indebted to the former by liturgical custom.[95] Concerning the argument by Leenhardt, that the Pauline form of the word of institution over the cup is more reliable than that in the Gospel of Mark, Behm says that the fact that it is the only occurrence of καινὴ διαθήκη (new covenant) in the teaching of the Lord cannot be taken as an argument against its validity, and that this is the very saying of Jesus which explains the main idea of the covenant in Paul.[96] But perhaps the opposite is true; Paul's concept of the covenant is very important as is reflected in his own thought throughout several of his epistles (see Rom. 9:4; 11:27; 2 Cor. 3:6ff; Gal. 3:15ff; 4:24ff and Eph. 2:12). This has played its part in the formation of his own version of the cup saying.

Second, the thought that the genuine correlative of blood is not body, but flesh, and that Jesus himself did not say "this is my blood," would not be relevant, as presumably "body" stands for "flesh" in this saying. Therefore, the phrase "this is my blood" would have as strong a claim of being authentic as the phrase "this is my body," and the addition to it of the words "of the covenant" is under the influence of Exod. 24:8. The Pauline and the Markan formulas of the words of Jesus about his blood are independent. The third point is related to Leenhardt's reference to the two different descriptions of the wine (Mk. 14:24, 25) as against the validity of this is my blood." It is possible that the Lukan version is more precise in preserving the Lord's tradition by putting the saying about the fruit of the vine at the outset of the meal, when Luke mentions a cup before the saying of the bread and the cup "after the supper," though the latter is doubtless a harmonizing addition.

When the participants all drink of the cup of blessing in the meal, it becomes part of the covenant through the covenant blood of Jesus. To drink the cup is to enter into the covenant by means of Christ's blood; consequently, the believer becomes a covenant partner with God. The Lord enters at the same time into the covenant, and a covenant with the community is established. The order for repeating the rite is given in an extended form: τοῦτο ποιεῖτε, ὁσάκις ἐὰν πίνητε, εἰς τὴν ἐμὴν ἀνάμνησιν here it is clearly formulated as a "command for repetition." The effort is made to show that the word which the apostle Paul understood Jesus to have used to order the repetition of the Lord's Supper does not have just a sacrificial association, but a more exact Jewish origin. In the command "Do this, as often as you drink it, in remembrance of me," the critical word is ἀνάμνησις; in biblical usage this is a liturgical term with a Godward reference.

The word ἀνάμνησις on each occasion of its use in the LXX has a particularly Godward reference. The four instances of the use of the word "memorial" in the Greek Old Testament, together with Heb. 10:3, are said to point to the conclusion that the phrase "ἀνάμνησις," in biblical usage, is unmistakably a ritual and liturgical term.[97]

The repeated command after the institution of the saying of the cup, "Do this, as often as you drink it, in remembrance of me," is unique to Paul, being absent from even the longer Lukan text. The longer Lukan version possibly combines an independent short tradition with the tradition reproduced by Paul here.[98] Furthermore, the double command is absent from the Gospel of Mark. It surely means that this "command for repetition" was unknown to Mark; it is hard to understand why Mark would have omitted it; perhaps it had fallen out from the tradition.

Higgins goes further and asks: "Does the injunction to repeat what was done at the Last Supper belong to a tradition utilized by Paul, or is it his own creation?"[99] It was Paul who interpreted the Lord's Supper at Roman Corinth as a continuation of the fellowship meal of Jesus and his disciples as a commemoration of his death. Lietzmann points out that in effect the Lord's Supper assumes the character of a meal of memory influenced by the sacred meals in the Greco-Roman period.[100]

Thus, the passage indicates that the Supper of the Lord involves a body of believers who participate in the meal as his followers and who receive the cup as an indication of conscious participation in the benefits of the new covenant with the Lord. Paul recalls the exact words of the institution to make the emphasis that as often as they eat this meal and drink from the cup, it is in the Lord's remembrance.

The Proclamation and the Parousia

The celebration (in the Primitive Church) was a thanksgiving meal which looked forward to the return of Christ. This partaking of the bread and wine is for Paul a proclaiming of the death and resurrection of the Lord "until he comes." Paul further assumes, in agreement with the early Christian Church's idea, that eating and drinking in the Eucharist Meal in fellowship with Christ is an anticipation of the table fellowship with the Lord at the Messianic banquet. It is along this line that Paul calls the celebration a drinking of the cup of the Lord and eating at the table of the Lord (1 Cor. 10:21).[101]

As Schweitzer says, "It is the death that is preached at the table, not the dying of Jesus that is re-enacted. And this emphasis has obvious links with the Passover liturgy."[102] Thus, this eschatological motif and proclamation is what Paul has in mind, when the bread is broken and the cup is shared.

Furthermore, the Corinthian church members did not have a "duty" of proclaiming; rather they proclaimed by the very fact that they got together in the name of the Lord.[103] The expression of happiness and gratitude in 1 Cor. 11:26 is described by the use of the verb "proclaim." The proclamation is done when the believers gather together, and partake of the elements according to the Lord's command. Before the birth of Jesus, prophets proclaimed his coming, and angels proclaimed his glorious advent. Jesus Christ proclaimed the kingdom, God's βασιλεία. In his ministry he taught his disciples that he would rule by and from the cross. At Jesus' last meal, the disciples were promised that only after the Parousia would they eat together with the exalted Lord.[104]

Even though Paul did not record exactly the words of Jesus in 1 Cor. 11:26 ("For whenever you eat this bread and drink this cup, you proclaim the Lord's death until he comes"), they reveal that Paul's tradition of the Last Supper maintained its eschatological character. The use of the word "for" indicates that Paul is now giving the reason why he is repeating the tradition at this point in the argument. It is not because the Corinthians have forgotten the words of the institution, nor because they abandoned the practice of the Lord's Supper; it is because their own practice of the Lord's Supper misrepresents its original character.[105] Whether Jesus spoke the words "This do in remembrance of me" (and whether we take the longer text of Luke 22 or Paul as the authority for them), the view was very clear in Jesus' mind; his desire (as well as Paul's) was that the disciples go on doing it.[106] Thus, the focus of Paul's concern was that the Corinthian practise what they have received from him as part of the church tradition. The Lord's Supper was supposed to be a proclamation of Christ's death until he comes again, rather than self-gratification of their own bodies.

Paul uses the verb καταγγέλλετε and it could be indicative or imperative. Since Paul uses the word γάρ, it is more likely to be indicative. Is Paul trying to say that the Eucharistic action is a proclamation of the death of Jesus, or does he mean that the proclamation is an explicit idea in it?[107] Because there is no such thing as a liturgical rite without proclamation, we have to consider the latter[108] When the Christians held a common meal, they remembered aloud the event that took place an event upon which their existence was based. The command to repeat the story of Jesus' death is to continue until he comes again. The Greek phrase ἄχρις οὗ, used with the aorist subjunctive and without the particle ἄν, regularly introduces the eschatological idea.[109]

To celebrate the Lord's Supper is also to proclaim together as a community of believers, but Paul says only ἄχρι οὗ ἔλθη. The Lord's Supper will find its complete fulfillment when the Lord himself will gather together with his people and will provide the heavenly banquet in the company of God the Father. The expression "until he comes" can mean nothing but the looking forward to the future, to "the real" presence of the Lord himself.[110] Paul cites these traditional words of the institution to urge the Corinthian church members to mend their behavior and to restore the unity of the church in all aspects of the social community life, not just when they partake of their *eranos* meals.

This rite centers on the celebration of Jesus' death "for us." Indeed, the Lord is regarded as living, and the believers look forward to His return. Thus, Paul's conception coincides with that of the tradition (from the early Christian Church); the Lord's Meal is not an anticipation of the banquet of the blessed, but an establishment for the age of the church from the resurrection of Christ to his coming.[111]

As has been said, the final clause in 1 Cor. 11:26 specifies that this proclamation via the Lord's Supper goes on "until he comes" (ἄχρι οὗ ἔλθῃ). However, some commentators see in this merely the point at which observance of the Lord's Supper terminates.[112] That is to say that the believers will no longer partake of the Lord's meal when the parousia has occurred. On the other hand, this can be understood as a purpose clause ("in order that he might come"); thus, the supper reminds God of his promise and urges God to send Jesus.[113]

It is difficult to think that Paul would refer to the parousia of the Lord as a simple deadline. Most of the time, when Paul mentions the expectation of the Lord's coming, he does so in connection with the triumph of God (1 Cor. 15:24-28) or the life of believers together with the parousia of the Lord (1 Thess. 4:14-18). An event of such magnitude does not readily become a way of marking the end of a present custom.

Nevertheless, Paul is clear that the time of the parousia is a matter of God's choosing (1 Thess. 5:1-3), "not an event that can be hurried by means of human action."[114] B. Gaventa raises the question: How are we to understand the phrase "until he comes" if it is not a deadline or a way of urging God to hasten Jesus' return?

Accordingly, to explain that Paul quotes them correctly does not mean that he also understands their views here correctly. C. K. Barrett points out that the Corinthian were acting "as if the age to come were already consummated. . . . For them there is no "not yet" to qualify the "already" of realized eschatology."[115] However, E. Ellis rightly asks: Would Paul attack an eschatological view which he himself seems to adopt?[116] Three important questions could be raised here: First, did Paul misunderstand the Corinthians? Second, did the Corinthian deny the resurrection of Christ and the sacraments? And third, did the Corinthian believe they had already been resurrected?

From different sources (1 Cor. 1:11; 5:1; 7:1; 16:17) Paul had become aware of serious problems within the church and of major differences of viewpoints between himself and certain factions at Corinth. A very sensitive and vital problem was that of the resurrection. Furthermore, the topic that was discussed by the church in Roman Corinth unquestionably had to do with Paul's manifesto of the resurrection. Obviously some of his readers were inclined to doubt Paul's placing the resurrection at the centre of his message. It is possible to gather from verse 12 that what was in contention was not Christ's resurrection, but the resurrection of believers.[117] Some members of the Corinthian church were saying that there was no resurrection of the dead (1 Cor. 15:12).

However, as has been observed "implicitly or explicitly, consciously or unconsciously, their proponents are saying that Paul misrepresents or misunderstands the Corinthians."[118] The deniers of the resurrection mentioned in verse 12 were some church members who accepted the Gnostics' view.[119] They were not unbelievers, since they were church members (1 Cor. 15:12). Who these deniers of the resurrection were it is very difficult to establish with precision.   It is difficult to see, however, how Paul misrepresents or misunderstands the Corinthians; it is possible to see the problem the other way around.

Moreover, Paul taught at Roman Corinth for some eighteen months, and the members of the church at Roman Corinth would, therefore, be well aware of Paul's own eschatological emphasis. On the other hand, it seems that "the Corinthians had misunderstood the Christian eschatological message. . . believing that eschatology had been 'realized'."[120] Even after eighteen months in one another's company, it seems possible that both the church members and Paul could not understand one another, so that the true message about the resurrection was not clear to the Corinthians. Probably, the Corinthians, in emphasizing a realized eschatology, felt that they were truly developing Paul's view on the resurrection.[121] One might also inquire how well Paul understood their position when he wrote to the church members at Roman Corinth.[122] On the other hand, Wedderburn argues that Paul misunderstands the Corinthians on the issue of the resurrection of the body.[123]

One matter is clear; Paul did not waste time in getting to the centre of the problem. It seems probable that some of the church members at Roman Corinth were syncretistic in their beliefs. It is further argued by F. F. Bruce that they "thought that the respectable Greek belief in the immortality of the soul. . . was perfectly adequate, and that the resurrection of the body was an embarrassing Jewish handicap."[124] However, this is not "realized eschatology" as it was understood among the deniers of the resurrection in the church at Roman Corinth.[125]   It seems clear that some of the deniers of the resurrection were arguing against Paul's view about the resurrection issue at Roman Corinth.

Evidently, their views of new life and the hereafter are, therefore, a confusion of Christian thought with a Hellenistic view of immortality. The Corinthians were acting as though the triumph over death was a reality now in this present age. Paul does not have anything to do with such eschatological emphasis. He accused these Corinthians of being illogical. How could they affirm the Gospel and deny the reality of the future resurrection (1 Cor. 15:12)? Paul did not agree to divide our resurrection (or eschatology) from that of Christ.[126]

Neither did he make an attempt to deny the eschatological reality of the Christian's situation. Furthermore, he brings into play the idea of a future resurrection, just as earlier in the same epistle he called attention to the future judgment and to a future inheritance of the kingdom (1 Cor. 6:2, 3, 9. 14). Barrett points out that "only the future provides the argument that Paul needs."[127] The complete argument of 1 Cor. 5 and 6 depends not just on the idea of corporate solidarity with Christ, but also on the view of eschatological destiny.[128] Christians must strive to live now and await the resurrection with judgment for deeds done in the body.

However, the tendency among some of the members of the Corinthian Church was to regard the prize as already won (1 Cor. 9:24). But the death of believers before the return of Christ constituted a grievous problem for the Corinthians; this is evident from the fact that Paul explains cases of death in the church of Roman Corinth as a punishment by God for the unworthy behavior and celebration of the Lord's Supper (1 Cor. 11:29-32). This is not to say that such deaths before the return were interpreted in the early church (especially in the case of the Corinthians) as meaning that those who died early were refused the Messianic blessedness[129] in spite of their belief in Christ.

The most interesting point, which is generally omitted, is that these groups who denied the resurrection had no doubt at all about the resurrection of Jesus.[130] This is why Paul refutes them by the argument that, if there is no resurrection of the dead, Christ himself cannot have risen.

1 Cor. 15:13: "But if there is no resurrection of the dead, then Christ has not been raised (οὐδὲ Χριστὸς ἐγήγερται)." 1 Cor. 15:16: "For if the dead are not raised, then Christ has not been raised.

Therefore, these deniers of the resurrection were not *sceptics*,[131] but they have been called representatives of the "ultra-conservative eschatological view"[132] that said there was no resurrection. Schweitzer's suggestion has been rejected.[133] What solves the problem of the dying among the believers at Roman Corinth received in general we do not know. However, when death was seen to be the rule, if the Christian hope was not to fail, then Paul's eschatological view and solution was the one to take, that the dead in Christ arise at his return.

With regard to those who feel that they have won the prize already, Paul reminds them that the final victory has not yet been achieved. Indeed, the Lord's Supper has a distinct reminder quality, for it looks forward to the parousia (ἄχρι οὗ ἔλθῃ, 1 Cor. 11:26). The Lord's Supper was instituted even before the death and resurrection of Christ, which was the first of the last events. Paul also suggests not to think of attempting to anticipate the final judgment.[134] As a matter of fact, it is the Lord's death, and the believer's share in it, which is central in the Lord's Supper (1 Cor. 11:26; 1 Cor. 1:18-31 and 2 Cor. 1:9; 4:8-12). Furthermore, the intention of Paul's apology is not to argue for an eschatology which achieves a metaphysical unity (such as was debated by the later Gnostics).[135] His main purpose is to provide those "in Christ" with a sense of hope and security in their salvation, a sense of trust in the coming Lord.

Finally, a further question is raised: Who were the Corinthians who denied the resurrection? It is highly probable that they were people who had accepted Paul's original view and proclamation that Jesus had been raised and they believed it. But they had understood this in the sense of exaltation to heaven, not a bodily resurrection. If Jesus were raised, so also were his followers, through participation in the sacraments.[136] Against this non-somatic idea of the resurrection Paul set forth his own view that the resurrection was both future and bodily, but not fleshly (1 Cor. 15:1-19).

What Paul is trying to say to the believers at Corinth is that when they gather together to partake of the Lord's Supper, they announce the death of the Lord in its eschatological meaning. The celebration itself demonstrates the proclamation of his parousia. The expression "hasta que él vuelva" ("until he comes") does not merely indicate a chronological event which limits a certain time, but also has a sense of finality. For this reason, "ἄχρι οὗ ἔλθῃ" means also "para que él vuelva."[137] This understanding of the eschatological motif in verse 26 is important because it allows us to see more clearly the relationship between what happened the night of the betrayal and the day of the final parousia.

The Lord's Supper has value only by reference to future realities which will be accomplished when he comes. We might conclude that Paul's view of worship, then, is consistent with the position he takes throughout the letter.[138] The celebration of the Lord's Supper is not a time for rejoicing in one's salvation. Instead, the celebration of the Lord's Supper proclaims the death and resurrection of Jesus and awaits his parousia. However, Jeremias interpreted the expression εἰς τὴν ἐμὴν ἀνάμνησιν ας δαμιτ Γοττ μειϝερ γεδεϝκε." His viewpoint is that the Lord Jesus instituted the celebration of the Lord's Supper not in order that Jesus' disciples might remember him, but to remind God that Jesus may bring about the kingdom at the parousia. Jeremias says when Paul mentions the expression "you proclaim the Lord's death until he comes," he found an element of purpose in the last clause. So, it means that Paul is saying that "you proclaim the Lord's death until the goal is reached when he comes" ("in order that he may come").

Furthermore, Jeremias relates this hope with the prayer of the early church, "Maranatha."[139] It should be noticed that Jeremias is trying to make a point which is rather different from the older Catholic interpretations. We found nothing in his argument which tells us about a doctrine of the real presence of the Lord or a Eucharistic sacrifice. Its emphasis is eschatological. Also, this interpretation can be considered as basically Jewish and Palestinian in background; it is then "very probable that the command goes back to Jesus himself."[140] Although Jeremias' thesis has not been widely accepted, perhaps the clause "until he comes" contains some element of purpose; but the proclamation which is explained is a proclamation of the good news to humans and there is no mention that it is a proclamation directly to God. The support for Jeremias' argument is thus weak and doubtful, and it is probable that the remembering of the death of Jesus is to be done by Jesus' own disciples.

Therefore, "the action is to remind them of Jesus."[141] This is the interpretation that arises from the context. The next issue will be the problem of how Jesus' disciples were to continue remembering their Master during his absence. The solution to the problem is that by celebrating the Eucharistic meal the disciples remember him by proclaiming his death whenever they partake of the fellowship-table until he comes again. The eschatological hope is always fulfilled when the church fulfills Jesus' command to repeat the rite as a memorial of his death.

Nevertheless, communion with Christ, which some of the believers at Corinth enjoyed at his table, excluded communion with a pagan god at his table, and such communion with a pagan god excluded the real communion with the crucified Lord. Whenever the believers gathered together as a community and partook of the bread and wine, they proclaimed and looked forward to the Messianic banquet in unity with their Lord.

Summary

The tradition which Paul received from the Lord is recalled to show that the present abuses of the Lord's Supper result from failing to continue the Master's practice. The basic agreement between the Synoptic records is evidence that the Apostle Paul's claims of dominical continuity are well founded, but it does not prejudice the interpretation of the tradition and the practice of the rite. It is not hard to see how Paul's summary statement in verse 26 contributed to the cultic, sacramental understanding of the bread and wine: "as often as" easily becomes a rite. Furthermore, it appears that the gospel tradition preached by Paul, in all probability, was the same gospel tradition preached by the Palestinian *Urgemeinde*.[142]

It is likely that the very structure of the Christian gathering at Roman Corinth has been influenced by the *eranos* (symposia) pattern. The δεῖπνον is clearly set at the beginning, and starts with what can easily be understood to be a 'sacrifice' of a portion of the food to be eaten and concludes (μετὰ τὸ δεῖπνον,

1 Cor. 11:25), with a ceremony which contains wine (1 Cor. 11:20-26). Regardless of the Jewish custom, they were obviously adaptable (especially the practice of the communal meal at Roman Corinth) to the structure of the Greco-Roman *eranos* "potluck dinner" party.

The emphasis on Paul's eschatological message to the Christian Church at Roman Corinth is clear and the eschatological nature is not removed from the Lord's Supper by Paul.[143] On the contrary, Paul's emphasis is that he who is present (the Lord) and who gives himself in the Lord's Supper is the crucified, glorified One and as such the One who is to come. When the believers participate in the Lord's Supper, they look backward to the crucifixion and forward to the return. But at the parousia of the Lord, the Lord's Supper will come to an end, for the celebration of the absent Lord ceases when the absent Lord comes back.

Then, instead of their eating and drinking in memory of the Master, he will eat and drink with them in his Kingdom (1 Cor. 11:26). The action for Jesus' remembrance is expanded to announcing (proclaiming) the death of the Lord until he comes again, thus specifying the meaning of the cup and placing the remembrance in the ongoing worship and social life of the church. Paul's emphasis shows how each common meal is to become a recollection and proclamation of the tradition of the Gospel.

Finally, it is altogether likely that the early Christian Church worshipped Jesus as the exalted Lord and Messiah and that in this Christian confession of Jesus as Lord we find the essential elements of all later Christology, including Paul's Christology. "Jesus is Lord" was the message of the early Christian Church and Paul's message as well.

Notes

[1] Ignatius, *Letter to the Smyrnaeans* 8:2; 7:3. See also R. Bultmann, *Theology of the New Testament* vol. 1, trans. K. Grobel (London: SCM Press, 1952), 144.

[2] Didache X. 1. See also R. Martin, *NBD* 751.

[3] I. Howard Marshall, *Last Supper and Lord's Supper* (London: The Paternoster Press, 1980), 109.

[4] G. Theissen, *The Social Setting of Pauline Christianity* trans. J. H. Schütz (Edinburgh: T. & T. Clark, 1982), 147. He observes that "analysis of the social conditions surrounding human behavior presupposes that this behavior will be described with the greatest precision, but in our case a great deal remains unclear. Four questions require an answer. 1) Were there different groups at the celebration of the Lord's Supper, or is it a

matter of a conflict between the congregation and some of its individual members? 2) were there various points at which the meal began, and what is the sequence of the various actions mentioned in 1 Cor. 11:17ff? 3) Were there quantitative differences in the portions served at the meal, or 4) qualitatively different meals for different groups? To answer these questions we must also draw on other contemporary texts to understand better what kinds of behavior were possible at this time."

[5] W. A. Meeks, *The First Urban Christians* (New Haven: Yale University Press, 1983), 67. He adds that these divisions about which Paul "hears" (v.18) may be connected in some way with the incipient factions reported by Chloe's people (1:10f.), but nothing that is said here hints that either the jealousy between followers of Apollos and partisans of Paul or the "realized eschatology" of the πνευματικοί is involved.

[6] H. Conzelmann, *1 Corinthians* (Philadelphia: Fortress Press, 1975), 194.

[7] Marshall, *Last Supper,* 109.

[8] Theissen, *The Social Setting,* 147.

[9] Homer, *Odyssey* 1.226-227. See also Aelius Aristides, *Sarapis* 54.20-28., and Lucian *Lexiphanes* 6,9,13. The *eranos* practice existed since the time of Homer and also in the second century C.E. The guests bring either money or meals baskets. "Aristophanes describes this custom nicely (*Acharnenses* 1085-1149): Come at once to dinner," invites a messenger, and bring your pitcher and your supper chest. The hosts provide wreaths, perfumes, and sweets, while the guests bring their own food which will be cooked in the host's house. They pack fish, several kinds of meat, and baked goods in their food baskets before they leave home. Also Xenophon (*Mem* 3.14.1) describes how the participants of a dinner party bring *opson*, e.g., fish and meat, from home. "Whenever some of those who came together for dinner brought more meat and fish (*opson*) than others, Socrates would tell the waiter either to put the small contributions into the common stock or to portion them out equally among the diners. So the ones who brought a lot felt obliged not only to take their share of the pool, but to pool their own supplies in return; and so they put their own food also into the common stock. Thus they got no more than those who brought little with them. . ." Here we have a close parallel to the Corinthian problems. See also Peter Lampe's *Affirmation*, 4. It seems that the apostle Paul and Socrates are protecting the communal meal (*eranos*) practice from such abuse. This practice should not lead some to overeat while others stay hungry.

[10] J. Murphy-O'Connor, *St. Paul's Corinth* (Wilmington: Michael Glazier, 1983), 158-159. The ones who arrived late had to sit in the atrium or in the peristyle, which was another inconvenience for them. "The mere fact that all could not be accommodated in the *triclinium* meant that there had to be an overflow into the *atrium*. It became imperative for the host to divide his guests into two categories; the first-class believers were invited into the *triclinium* while the rest stayed outside. Even a slight knowledge of human nature indicates the criterion used. The host must have been a member of the community and so he invited into the *triclinium* his closest friends among the believers, who would have been of the same social class. The rest could take their places in the *atrium*, where conditions were greatly inferior. . . . The space available made such

discrimination unavoidable, but this would not diminish the resentment of those provided with second-class facilities."

[11] Pliny The Younger, *Letters* 2:6. The practice to serve different types of food to different categories of guests was the popular Roman custom. Pliny tells the following experience: "I happened to be dining with a man, though no particular friend of his, whose elegant economy, as he called it, seemed to me sort of stingy extravagance. The best dishes were set in front of himself and a select few, and cheap scraps of food before the rest of the company. He had even put the wine into tiny little flasks, divided into three categories, not with the idea of giving his guests the opportunity of choosing, but to make it impossible for them to refuse what they were given. One lot was intended for himself and for us, another for his lesser friends (all his friends are graded), and the third for his and our freedmen. . . ."

[12] I. Howard Marshall, "Lord's Supper" in *Dictionary of Paul and His Letters* eds., R. P. Martin, G. Hawthorne and D. Reid (Downers Grove: InterVarsity Press, 1993), 1.

[13] Meeks, *The First Urban*, 68. The καί here is epexegetic; that is, the second clause explains the first.

[14] G. Bornkamm, *Early Christian Experience* trans. P. L. Hammer (London: SCM Press, 1969), 126.

[15] P. Neuenzeit, *Das Herrenmahl* (München: Kösel-Verlag, 1960), 71.

[16] Theissen, *The Social Setting,* 153.

[17] Marshall, *Last Supper,* 109. Several of Theissen's ideas were already expressed by earlier authors, but he provides very comprehensive material and gives important background to the whole social issue.

[18] Theissen, *The Social Setting,* 153-162.

[19] Charles H. Talbert, *Reading Corinthians: A Literary and Theological Commentary on 1 and 2 Corinthians* (New York: Crossroad, 1987), 74.

[20] Lampe, *The Corinthian Eucharistic*, 2-3. He observes that "Religious ceremonies accompany even the regular, non-cultic dinner party. The dinner at "First Tables" starts with an invocation of the gods. After the dinner there is a break; new guests can arrive. The house gods and the geniuses of the host and the emperor are invoked and a sacrifice is given. People recline again and eat and drink at the "Second Tables"; often not only sweet desserts and fruit but also spicy dishes, seafood, and bread are served. The "Second Tables" end with a toast for the good spirit of the house. The tables are removed, the floor is swept; in a jug, wine and water are mixed and a libation to a god is poured out while people sing a religious song. Slaves pour the wine from the jug into the participants' cups. Whenever the jug is empty, a new one is mixed, another libation is sacrificed, and people continue drinking, conversing, and entertaining themselves. This can go on until dawn."

[21] D. E. Smith, "Meals and Morality in Paul and His World," *Society of Biblical Literature 1981 Seminar Papers*, ed. K. H. Richards (Chico: Scholars, 1981), 323.

[22] Ibid, 325.

[23] Fee, 531. See also Talbert, *Reading Corinthians*, 74. Talbert points out that "such divisions associated with the common meal would be viewed as tragic by Paul, who saw the meal as the catalyst for Christian fellowship (1 Cor. 10:16-17)."

[24] Robertson, 238. τοῦτο cannot be precisely defined. Weiss ascribes the section to the older letter, on the ground that ἀκούω, "I hear," shows that Paul is referring to a first report about the σχίματα, "divisions," whereas in 1:10ff. (ἐδηώθη μοι), "I have been told") he is in possession of further information.

[25] C. K. Barrett, *The First Epistle to the Corinthians.* HNTC. (New York: Harper & Row, 1968), 260. Barrett comments that the text translated παραγγέλλων οὐκ ἐπαινῶ is read by a G and the majority of MSS; A C* and the Latin and Syriac have παραγγέλλω οὐκ ἐπαιῶν; B has παραγγέλλων οὐκ ἐπαινῶν D* and a minuscule have παραγγέλλω οὐκ ἐπαινῶ. See also E. B. Allo, *Saint Paul: Première Epître aux Corinthiens* (Paris: J. Gabalda et Cie., 1934), 269-270.

[26] Theissen, *The Social Setting*, 163.

[27] Stephen M. Pogoloff, *Logos and Sophia: The Rhetorical Situation of 1 Corinthians* (Atlanta: Scholars Press, 1992), 254. He comments that "this last reference to bringing shame or dishonor upon those who "have not" is somewhat puzzling if we imagine them to be poor, since honor and shame were normally much more a concern for the upper class. But οἱ μὴ ἔχοντες need not refer to the poor, since in literature about meals a common *topos* had developed in which the "poor" who suffered at the hands of the rich were not actually poor, but upper class persons who were not as rich as their hosts."

[28] Plut. *Quaest. conv.* 1.2

[29] Juvenal. 3.81, 152-156.

[30] A. T. Robertson, *A Grammar of the Greek New Testament in Light of Historical Research.* 4th edition. (Nashville: Broadman Press, 1934), 1152.

[31] Barrett, *The First Epistle*, 261.

[32] William Ellis, "Some Problems in the Corinthian Letters." *ABR* 14 (1966): 34.

[33] Allo, *Saint Paul*, 271.

[34] Fee, 537.

[35] Martin, *Eucharist*, 83. He argues that "Paul has already dealt with the dissensions within the church in his teaching on the one bread (10:16, 17). He counters the other defects by recommending that the claims of hunger and thirst should be met at home (vvs. 22, 34) and that the common meal should be true to its name--a *sharing* of the common table, as the whole church gathers at the same time (v. 33.). The recommendation of verses 33-34, while not discrediting the Agape altogether, was the first step in the process which eventually separated the Eucharistic or Cultic service from a fellowship meal."

[36] Theissen, *The Social Setting*, 147.

[37] Stephen C. Barton, "Paul's Sense of Place: An Anthropological Approach to Community Formation in Corinth," *New Testament Studies* 32 (1986): 225-246. He says that Paul's comments are punctuated by rhetorical questions and exclamations (11:22), by solemn warnings (11:27-29), and by ominous promises (11:34b). Paul

obviously believes that the meals upon which he is commenting are surrounded with danger to the participants: "For anyone who eats and drinks without discerning the body eats and drinks judgement (κρίμα) upon himself. That is why many of you are weak and ill, and some have died" (11:29, 30; cf. 32a). He also makes clear that ritual action is the only way both to avoid the danger arising out of contact with the sacred (meal) and to appropriate its power for the community and the world (11:23-32).

[38] Meeks, *The First Urban*, 67.

[39] Barrett, 262. He comments that "The Lord's Supper" is familiar, but that the possessive case fails to make clear the relation of the supper to the Lord. "In memory of the Lord," "under the authority of the Lord, "and "in the presence of the Lord," might all be used to help out the rendering chosen here; in fact, the sense in which the Supper is "the Lord's" can only be brought out through the ensuing paragraph as a whole.

[40] Bruce, 110.

[41] C. Talbert, *Reading Corinthians,* 75. It is well-known that the meals of other religious communities of the periods had similar problems. For instance, "from a bacchic society of the second century B.C., one finds regulations like, disruptive behavior at the meetings is not to be tolerated. If anyone starts a quarrel, he is to be excluded until a fine paid. From the regulations of the guild of Zeus Hypistos of the first century B.C., one hears: 'it shall not be permissible. . . to make factions."

[42] Lucian, *Par.* 5; Athenaeus, *Deipn.* 5. 178; 12. 527. Basically, a *symposion* was a drinking party and normally tended to finish in intoxication.

[43] Theissen, *The Social Setting,* 147ff.

[44] B. W. Winter, "Secular and Christian Responses to Corinthian Famines," *Tyndale Bulletin* 40 (1989): 100. He comments that "the important point to note is that food crises in Corinth were alleviated during the period of the early days of the church in the traditional way of the East by the curator of the grain supply."

[45] P. Garnsey, *Non-Slave Labour in the Graeco Roman World.* (CPS Supp. 6; Cambridge University Press, 1980), 44-45. In times of grain shortage it is clear that the slave had security because of his place in the household. It is appropriate to think in terms of the secure and insecure. The latter was the group exposed to steep rises in the price of the grain, and these were the freedman artisans and workers.

[46] Winter, "Secular and Christian,"101. He also comments that "the mechanism by which Corinth assisted the "have nots" in times of grain shortage must have benefited that class mentioned by Paul in his enigmatic comments of 1 Corinthians 11:21, 33-4."

[47] Meeks, *The First Urban,* 158-163.

[48] Plutarch, *qu. conv.* 613F.

[49] Athenaeus, *Deipn.* 5. 177. In some occasions, both the slaves and masters found themselves at the same symposium.

[50] Theissen, *The Social Setting,*148. This does not, however, absolutely exclude a more "individualistic" interpretation which might find support in the words ἕχαστος and ἴδιον.

[51] Euripides, *The Suppliant Women* 238-244.

[52] Meeks, *The First Urban,* 159. Consequently, Paul uses traditional language from the Supper ritual, which speaks of the bread as "Communion of the body of Christ" and the "cup of blessing" as "Communion of the blood of Christ" to warn that any participation in pagan cultic meals would be idolatry.

[53] Barton, 237. He explains that the rich distinguished themselves from the poor by timing of their meal--they ate first and without waiting for others to arrive (11:21, 33); by its quantity and quality (11:21); and by their refusal to share, since "each one goes ahead with his own meal" (11:21). By these means also, the rich sought to extend their influence in the church. Their eating practices were a demonstration of status, both to themselves and to the others, and an attempt to dominate by imposing shame (11:22).

[54] Fee, 543.

[55] Bornkamm, *Early Christian,* 126ff.

[56] Fee, 544.

[57] The Corinthians may have seen the Lord's Supper as such a funerary meal. But the tradition as Paul records it demonstrates that what Jesus did at the Last Supper was not to institute a funerary rite.

[58] Joachim Jeremias, *The Eucharistic Words of Jesus* trans. Norman Perrin (London: SCM Press, 1966), 129.

[59] Higgins, *The Lord's Supper,* 24. See especially the fine discussion of the Semitisms in Mark's narrative by J. Jeremias, 118ff.

[60] Lietzmann, *Mass,* 206-207.

[61] Bornkamm, *Early Christian,* 130.

[62] H. Maccoby, "Paul and Eucharist," *New Testament Studies* 37 (1991): 247-267. He comments that "the argument, then, turns on the meaning of the two words παρέλαβον ἀπό. It has been held by some scholars that if direct revelation had been intended, the preposition παρά would have been more suitable than the preposition ἀπό which allegedly signifies a remote or ultimate source of information. This contention has given rise to a whole literature, for and against. The upshot seems to be that while παρά is more usual in a context of the direct imparting of information, ἀπό is also quite frequently found in such a context (e.g. Matt. 11:29; Col. 1:7). The argument from the remote ἀπό is thus inconclusive, and one cannot help feeling that it has been pressed so hard for theological, rather than strictly grammatical, reasons."

[63] Talbert, *Reading Corinthians,* 76.

[64] Bornkamm, *Early Christian,* 130.

[65] Bultmann, 150. Another indication that Paul found the liturgical words already in existence is the fact that they speak of a "communion" with the (body and the) blood of the Lord. Then, it cannot have been by direct revelation.

[66] Lietzmann, *Mass,* 208. He emphasizes that "the liturgical words τοῦτο ποιεῖτε εἰς τὴν ἐμὴν ἀνάμνησιν characteristic of the Pauline text and omitted in Mark, formulate the crucial revelation which exalted this new type of the Lord's Supper above the Jerusalem type." As has been discussed in a previous section in this same chapter,

Lietzmann denies that there was any connection between the Jerusalem type and the Last Supper. Furthermore, he considers Paul the creator of the Pauline type of Eucharist. As argued before, we have to show that Paul's explanation of the Lord's Meal was his own private revelation from God and came to him uniquely and independently of other Christians. Recently, Smith also observes that "the proposal that the early Jesus tradition is related to Cynic themes and motifs provides the best explanation for the context in which the table fellowship texts developed. This need not suggest that Jesus was himself a Cynic or identified with Cynic traditions. But it does suggest that certain early Christian communities utilized Cynic traditions to characterize and idealize Jesus as a hero." D. E. Smith, "The Historical Jesus at Table," *SBLSP* (1989), 485ff.

[67] Higgins, *The Lord's Supper*, 26.

[68] Marshall, *Last Supper*, 32. The fact that Paul was quoting a tradition in this passage, 1 Cor. 11:23-25, "is further evident from an examination of the wording; analysis has shown that the vocabulary and style are not that of Paul himself, and, since there is not the slightest reason to suppose that the words were added by somebody else after Paul had finished the letter, and indeed everything points in the opposite direction, we can be quite certain that Paul is quoting a statement which he had received from other Christians. This means that Paul's account was in existence within some twenty years of the death of Jesus."

[69] Barrett, *1 Corinthians*, 265. It is obvious that accounts of what Jesus had said and done were handed down from one to another in the early church; it is from such accounts that the Gospels developed. "To say this is itself to pass no judgment, whether favourable or unfavourable, on the historical value of the gospels (or of such passages as the present one), for traditions are sometimes accurately, sometimes inaccurately and tendentiously, preserved, and there is little evidence that the elaborated techniques of Jewish tradition were applied to the very different material, handed down in very different circles, by Christians."

[70] E. Lohmeyer, "Vom Urchristlichen Abendmahl," *ThR* 9 (1937): 168-227.

[71] Oscar Cullmann, "Kyrios as Designation for the Oral Tradition Concerning Jesus," *Scottish Journal of Tgeology* 3 (1950): 180-197.

[72] Bornkamm, *Early Christian*, 130. He mentions the names of scholars who agree with the hypothesis that Paul received the tradition of the Lord's Supper in Antioch (G. Kittel, A. Schlatter, J. Jeremias, R. Bultmann, E. Käsemann, and W. G. Kümmel). The formulae in 1 Cor. 11 and 15 which he learned there may therefore have been known at the beginning of the forties in the Antioch congregation.

[73] Marshall, *Last Supper*, 32.

[74] J. Héring, *The First Epistle of Saint Paul to the Corinthians* trans. A. W. Heathcote and P. J. Allcock (London: Epworth, 1963), 100ff.

[75] Jeremias, *The Eucharistic*, 131.

[76] Maccoby, "Paul and The Eucharist," 247-248.

[77] Ibid., 248.

[78] W. D. Davies, *Paul and Rabbinic Judaism* (London: SPCK, 1962), 249.

[79] Higgins, *The Lord's Supper,* 27, especially the saying of the cup.

[80] O. Cullmann, *The Early Church* ed. A. J. B. Higgins (London: SCM Press, 1956), 95.

[81] Martin, *Eucharist* 87.

[82] Higgins, *The Lord's Supper,*28. He ascribes it to the apostle, who is explaining the meaning he himself would attach to the cultic practice of the breaking of the bread in the church. Paul is not conscious, however, of adding anything more to the traditional saying of Jesus, but is making clear what he holds to be its essential meaning.

[83] Bruce, 110.

[84] J. J. Petuchowski, "Do This in Remembrance of Me (1 Cor. 11:24)," *Journal of Biblical Literature* 76 (1957): 293-298. He quotes Davies, who feels that "Christ has been substituted for 'the day thou camest forth out of Egypt' to the haggadah, and would understand the words in the sense in which they have been rendered in the RSV: 'Do this in remembrance of me.'"

[85] Jeremias, *The Eucharistic,* 160.

[86] Fee, 552. See also the discussions by Jeremias, 168, and Barrett, 267.

[87] Petuchowski, 295. But J. Jeremias, basing himself on other uses of זכר in Jewish liturgy as well as on the eucharistic prayers of the Didache, makes the phrase mean "that God may remember me." "That means the Eucharist is an ἀνάμνησις of the *Kyrios*, not because it reminds the church of the event of the Passion, but because it proclaims the beginning of the time of salvation, and prays for the inception of the consummation."

[88] Lietzmann, *Mass,* 148.

[89] Jeremias, *The Eucharistic,* 161ff. In particular, it is said of the feast of the Passover that it should be celebrated *lezikkaron* (Ex. 12:14; cf. 13:9; Deut. 16:3; Job. 49:15), and at the festival Kiddush, the one spoken by Jesus at the Passover meal, God is praised as He "who has given to His people Israel festal seasons for joy and *lezikkaron*"--as indeed the entire feast of the Passover is a feast of remembrance, and the Passover meal a meal of remembrance.

[90] Barrett, 267. There is another parallel in Lucian's account (*de Syria Dea* 6) of the feasts in "memory of the passion (μνήμη τοῦ πάθεο""; cf. Justin, *Trypho* 41) of Adonis. Pagan memorial feasts, however, may not have contributed the whole content of the clause, or provide a sufficient interpretation of it.

[91] Fee, 554ff.

[92] Ibib., 555. In contrast to the Gospels of Mark and Luke, Paul's account of the cup saying has no allusion to Isa. 53 ("which is poured out for many"), which has already appeared in the bread saying. In the Gospels the tie to Isaiah suggests the additional theological motif of the forgiveness of sins, made explicit in Matthew's account. But in Paul that motif is not tied to the blood as such, but to Christ's death, as pointed is in verse 26.

[93] Conzelmann, *1 Corinthians,* 199.

[94] Behm, *TDNT* 3 (1965), 730.

[95] F. J. Leenhardt, *Le Sacrement de la Sainte Cène* (Neuchâtel-Paris, 1948), 51ff.

[96] Behm, *TDNT* 2 (1965), 137.

[97] D. Jones, "ἀνάμνησις in the LXX and the Interpretation of 1 Cor. 11:25," *Journal of Theological Studies* 6 (1955): 183-191. He points out that D. Stone has the same view and uses some examples to explain the use of the word ἀνάμνησις. He mentions five occurrences of the term in the LXX; the first two (Lev. 23:243; Num. 10:10) are said clearly to denote a sacrificial memorial before God. The fifth (Wisd. 16:6) denotes "a memento to man." The third and fourth (Ps. 38:1 [Lxx 37:1] and 70:1 [LXX 69:1]) are obscure, but "the probability is very strong that a memorial before God is denoted." The conclusion is that "on the whole it may be said that the word 'memorial' naturally suggests, without actually necessitating, the sense of a sacrificial memorial before God; and that in the case of the institution of the Eucharist the probability of a sacrificial meaning is greatly strengthened by the use of the word 'covenant' just before and by the sacrificial surroundings when our Lord spoke."

[98] Bruce, 113. For a fuller discussion, see E. E. Ellis, *The Gospel According to Luke* 1966; and Jeremias, 110ff.

[99] Higgins, *The Lord's Supper*, 35.

[100] Lietzmann, *Mass*, 182.

[101] Schweitzer, 267.

[102] Ralph P. Martin, *Worship in the Early Church* (Grand Rapids: Eerdmans, 1975), 127. In that Passover liturgy, "the tale of deliverance is to be retold; and as it is recounted, each individual Israelite relives the experience and makes his nation's history and destiny his very own. At the table, the story of the greater redemption is reported as often as we eat the bread and drink the cup. . . . It confronts us as we sit at the table with all that the death of the Son of God meant then and means now."

[103] Léon-Dufour, *Sharing The Eucharistic*, 224ff.

[104] Barth, 47.

[105] Fee, 556ff.

[106] A. M. Hunter, *Paul and His Predecessors* (London: SMC Press, 1961), 63.

[107] Talbert, *Reading Corinthians*, 78. Talbert points out that "the stated purpose of the meal made it a public announcement of a certain cause. So a Christian meal held for the purpose of focusing on the sacrifice of Christ as the seal of the new covenant became a public proclamation of his death."

[108] Conzelmann, *1 Corinthians*, 201.

[109] Barrett, *The First Epistle*, 270.

[110] Léon-Dufour, *Sharing the Eucharistic*, 225.

[111] Conzelmann, *1 Corinthians*, 202.

[112] H. A. Meyer, *Critical and Exegetical Handbook to the Epistles to the Corinthians* trans. rev. W. P. Dickson, 5th ed. (New York: Funk and Wagnals, 1890), 266.

[113] Jeremias, *The Eucharistic*, 249-55.

[114] Beverly R. Gaventa, "You Proclaim the Lord's Death: 1 Corinthians 11:26 and Paul's Understanding of Worship," *Review Expositor* 80 (1983): 383.

[115] C. K. Barrett, *The First Epistle to the Corinthians* (New York: Harper & Row, 1968), 109.

[116] E. Earle Ellis, "Christ Crucified," in *Reconciliation and Hope* ed. Robert Banks (Exeter: The Paternoster Press, 1974), 73-74. Ellis argues that error in 1 Cor. 15 "offers doubtful support for an eschatological interpretation of 1 Cor. 4:8, and also that it is unlikely that Paul would criticize the Corinthians merely for appropriating an eschatological view that he himself has taught them." It seems to me that not necessarily did Paul teach them such a view, especially concerning the issue of the resurrection of believers. Conzelmann rightly observes that "Paul is not seeking to prove that Christ is risen. He can take this belief for granted. What he intends to elaborate is rather the expression 'from the dead.'" Hans Conzelmann, *1 Corinthians* (Philadelphia: Fortress Press, 1975), 261.

[117] Ralph P. Martin, *The Spirit and the Congregation: Studies in 1 Corinthians 12-15* (Grand Rapids: Eerdmans, 1984), 93.

[118] A. J. M. Wedderburn, "The Problem of the Denial of the Resurrection in 1 Corinthians VXV," *Novum Testamentum* 23 (1981): 230.

[119] Martin, 94. He comments that these deniers of the resurrection believe that "with the coming of the spirit and their baptism to initiate them to a celestial life here and now they had entered on a new existence. Their 'baptismal resurrection' (referred to in 1 Cor. 4:8) had given them the fullness of God's life; there was no more to come. They denied the 'eschatological proviso' that Paul's teaching set to mark the boundary between the 'already' of being saved and the 'not yet' of final redemption at parousia and resurrection of the dead in a new bodily existence (a theme handled in 15:35ff.)." Martin believes that the Corinthians embraced Gnostic ideas; however, this is not the most accepted view among scholars.

[120] R. M. Grant, *An Historical Introduction to the New Testament* (London: SCM Press, 1963), 204.

[121] Anthony C. Thiselton, "Realized Eschatology at Corinth," *New Testament Studies* 24 (1978): 512, further comments that "the question for Paul, however, was not, as Ellis seems to imply, whether realized eschatology contains truth; it certainly does. The question was, rather, whether it represented the whole truth. Even if it can be argued (and it probably can) that the Corinthians were simply underlining and developing Paul's own thought, this is not to say that any one aspect can be pressed and *ruthlessly* applied to the exclusion of other aspects without causing serious distortion. Paul is not attacking a straightforward falsehood, but a distortion of the wholeness of truth."

[122] Even if the apostle misunderstood what the Corinthians believed, this misunderstanding would be important as part of the background against which he put forth his own views on the resurrection.

[123] A. Wedderburn, "The Problem," 230. He comments that "this is true, for instance, of the suggestion that although they denied the resurrection of the body or flesh they looked

for a survival of the immortal soul beyond the grave. If that is the case then not only does Paul seemingly misrepresent them but this argument really misses the point: he fails to argue that disembodied survival is not an adequate hope. To that extent it is easier to say that he has misunderstood them, but would a Hellenistic Jew like Paul not be all too familiar with this idea?"

[124] F. F. Bruce, *1 and 2 Corinthians* (Grand Rapids: Eerdmans, 1971), 144.

[125] Martin, 130. He further observes that "they claimed as Greek-thinking individuals, that once their spirits were 'saved,' their bodies were irrelevant, and no evil could touch them (Paul answers this in 1 Cor. 15:1-13; 6:12-20; 10:6-13). They also imagined that their entry into a kingdom already present (1 Cor. 4:8) gave them a passport to a heavenly type of existence where such items as unusual marriage customs (1 Cor. 7:36) a kind of platonic union of minds, but imply a celibate relationship between the sexes, not unlike what they thought the angelic existence to be) and a privatized worship involving 'tongues of angels' (1 Cor. 13:1) prevailed. Most characeristically, they seemed to have thought that they would never die but were already enjoying--in Gnostic terms--life in a hidden body. Such a body lay beyond 'death' and simply continued to exist as a 'spiritual body,' a term (in v.44b) that as W. Schmithals and E. Schweizer remark, means for them a body composed of $\pi\nu\epsilon\nu\mu\alpha$, 'spirit'--man's original possession. To this 'body' they already laid claim as 'persons of the Spirit' (14:37, $\pi\nu\epsilon\nu\mu\alpha\tau\iota\kappa\omicron\iota$)." Thus, this is the background from where Paul addresses his reply to the issues being raised in the church at Corinth.

[126] Gerald L. Borchert, "The Resurrection: 1 Corinthians 15," *Review Expositor* 80 (1983): 406. "Too much is at stake, including the incarnation. Christ is still dead (15:13, 16) and there is no meaning to the Christian's proclamation--it is 'without any foundation' (*kenos*) and 'powerless' ($\mu\alpha\tau\alpha\iota\omicron$)--if there is no such reality as a resurrection from the dead (15:14, 17)." Moreover, if Christ has not been raised, the situation involves more than poor logic.

[127] Barrett, *The First Epistle*, 148.

[128] Thiselton, "Realized Eschatology," 517.

[129] Albert Schweitzer, *The Mysticism of Paul the Apostle* trans. W. Montgomery (New York: The Seabury Press, 1968), 92ff.

[130] Ibid., 93.

[131] Martin, *The Spirit and the Congregation*, 93.

[132] Schweitzer, 93. According to them, "only those have anything to hope for who are alive at the return of Jesus. They thus deny not only the resurrection to the Messianic Kingdom, but that to eternal blessedness. Their position is the same as that of the Psalms of Solomon and the eschatology of the Prophets."

[133] W. D. Davies, *Paul and Rabbinic Judaism* (London: S.P.C.K., 1970), 292. It is unlikely in the first place that there should be Christians of such exceptional conservative Jewish views in the Corinthian Church, "which was chiefly, though indeed not entirely,

Gentile in character. Secondly, there are other more plausible interpretations of the anti-resurrectionists at Corinth."
[134] Thiselton, "Realized Eschatology," 522.
[135] Borchert, 409.
[136] Schweitzer, 95.
[137] Guillermo J. Garlatti, "La Eucaristía Como Memória y Proclamación de la Muerte del Señor," *Revista Biblica* 47 (1985): 1-25. He further adds: "Lo cual equivale a afirmar que las cosas--con la acción eucarística--han llegado a un punto tal que el Señor debe venir porque, en cierta forma, ya se han consumado las realidades escatológicas del fin de los tiempos. Esto es lo que hace que la eucaristía sea igualmente una verdadera actualización 'en prospectiva' de la parusía de Cristo." Jeremias says also that in the New Testament the use of ἄχρι with subjuntive aorist without a[n introduces the perspective of the pursuit of the eschatological aim. Therefore, the expression ἔλθῃ is a "prospective subjunctive." See J. Jeremias, 316-317.
[138] Gaventa, "You Proclaim," 385.
[139] Jeremias, *The Eucharistic,* 115-118.
[140] K. H. Bartels and C. Brown, *NIDNTT* 3 (1975), 230-247. They say that even though Jeremias' view has not been accepted, he can point to Did. 10:5f, for supporting testimony to prayer in the early church for the eschatological remembrance of God, and to the OT for the idea of God remembering; his view does not rule out other interpretations. Τοῦτο ποιεῖτε ("This do") may be regarded as a summary of the procedure to be followed by participants in the Lord's Supper. They are to act as Jesus did, when instituting the Supper on the eve of his passion, according to the Synoptic account. All the words and actions are intended to be εἰς τὴν ἐμὴν ἀνάμνησιν.
[141] Marshall, *Last Supper,* 90.
[142] Hunter, *Paul,* 80. The questioned can be raised, Have we any reliable information on how those who were in Christ before Paul saw the master? "The early chapters of Acts purport to give an account of the first Jerusalem Christians, and of the manner which probably existed at first in Aramaic. For the primitive church Jesus is a man of Nazareth approved of God by might works (Acts 2:22), who after crucifixion and resurrection has been exalted to God's right hand as Lord and Christ (Acts 2:33ff) and has poured forth the promised Holy Spirit (Acts 2:33)."
[143] Bornkamm, *Early Christian,* 152.

Chapter 6

CONCLUSION

The importance of cultic meals and dining occasions has already been mentioned briefly in chapter two. It is obvious that how one understands the common meals in connection with the sacrifice in Paul's time (Hellenistic society) plays a major part in the interpretation of 1 Corinthians 8, 10 and 11. At the beginning of this century, scholars such as Lietzmann explained 1 Corinthians 11, 10 (especially the Lord's Supper in 1 Cor. 11:23-26 and 1 Cor. 10:14-21) by reference to similarities in pagan cultic meals.

Some scholars such as Bornkamm, Käsemann, Schmithals, and Jewett interpret the Christian cultic meals not as coming from the Hellenistic religions, but rather as being influenced by Gnostic ideas. This Gnostic notion is not embraced by the majority of scholars. We believe that there are some Gnostic elements that probably can be called "pre-Gnostic." It is also well-known that what later developed as "Gnosticism" at Roman Corinth was just Gnosticism *in statu nascendi*. Furthermore, it is clear that the gnosis issue was not the contention between Paul and the Christians at Roman Corinth.

Even among the Hellenistic Jewish meals (apart from the Jewish Passover) the similarities are too superficial to draw a solid conclusion on the matter. However, some social customs, such as the way the Corinthian Christians celebrated the Lord's Supper, reflect the common pattern of the *eranos* meal in the Greco-Roman society.

After studying sacred meals in the Greco-Roman world, we consider it proper that social meals should be studied as well. When we study ancient meals from the social perspective, it means that we no longer consider each meal as a separate item, but to some extent our purpose is to understand them as indications of a common social tradition. The Greco-Roman social tradition was very influential in the practice of meals in the early Christian church. Obviously, in some cases such as the Corinthians, churches adopted similar customs in the way they celebrated their meal. The Greek *eranos* meal, for instance, is a classic example of the social practice of the Christian *eranos* at Roman Corinth. Some practical patterns are shown in both meals. Of course, the motives and the main objectives of these meals were different.

The social factors of the customs in the Greco-Roman world give us sufficient explanation for the phenomenon of communal meals in early Christian communities (especially the Corinthian Church) and help to explain many of the social practices. They, furthermore, provide the foundation for the development of the beliefs and customs connected with their meals. So, it seems quite clear that the very structure of the assemblies of the Christian church at Roman Corinth has been influenced by the *eranos* pattern. The Greco-Roman social meal provided both the model and the main ideology for the development of the Christian *eranos* meal at Roman Corinth.

Chapter four shows that early Christianity, especially the Greco-Roman Corinthian Church, was neither a proletarian movement among the lower social classes nor a movement among the aristocrats of the Roman Empire. However, it is most likely that some of Paul's later converts belonged to the social high class spread through all segments of the society of the Greco-Roman world. Paul's words in 1 Cor. 1:26-28 cannot be used to argue that early Christianity was a lower-class phenomenon. However, terms like δυνατός make clear the political aspect and εὐγενής emphasizes the social aspect. In the Corinthian Church, we can see the educated, the influential, and people of distinguished family social background. Philo makes reference to rich citizens at Roman Corinth; it is most likely that some of them became Christians and were members of the Corinthian Church. It is our belief that Philo's statement gives a clear picture of the social status of some of the church members mentioned in 1 Cor. 1:26-29 as socially significant.

Furthermore, four criteria indicate the Christians' social status: (1) holding civil or religious office in the city; (2) owning a "house"; (3) serving the church or Paul; and (4) traveling (for the church). Although the last two criteria are not specifically sufficient in themselves to indicate social status, this prosopographical description shows that a section of the most active and influential church members belonged to the social high class. In spite of being a dominant minority, they represent the high social class in the church who appear to be very active. For this reason we need not cast doubt on Paul's statement that "not many" in the Corinthian Church belonged to a high social level. We may conclude that it is probable that the most active and important members of the church belonged to the "οὐ πολλοὶ σοφοὶ δυνατοί ανδ εὐγενειν." Consequently, a closer analysis of the problem of the Lord's Supper (1 Cor. 11) and the relationship between the "strong" and the "weak" clarifies the whole picture.

The study of the house churches is extremely significant, especially for a correct understanding of some of the issues related to the Lord's Supper. To fail to understand the house church of the New Testament is to close a window through which we may see more clearly how the primitive church functioned (Acts 1:13; 2:46; 5:42; 12:12). The house church has a prominent place in the formation of the early Christian church, and the life of the church takes place in houses. We strongly believe that it is in this context that the apostle Paul was exhorting and addressing the house churches, especially the Christian church at Roman Corinth where many problems arose because of the social and theological conflicts among the members. As a result, it is also in this social setting that the "strong" and the "weak" argue over the question of the legitimacy of eating meat sacrificed to idols (1 Corinthians 10 and 8).

The exegetical efforts in chapters five and six have shown that the whole issue in 1 Cor. 10:14-20 is caused by the gluttony and drunkenness on the part of the strong Christians who take advantage of their high social status over the poor, weak members. It thus appears that the main problem in the tension between the "strong" and the "weak" is not εἰδωλόθυτα *per se,* but the problem of the conscience of the "weak." It is well known that the meat came from the *macellum* where it was offered to the pagan gods and afterwards sold in the shops. Obviously, then, this is why such practices posed many problems to the weak Christians (eating the meat and participating in the pagan festivals as well).

The real κοινωνία with Christ should avoid any disturbance of the weak brother united to Christ if the stronger brothers are willing to recognize that the "little ones" are also members of the body of Christ. Paul also concludes his teaching on the basis of human interaction. He is concerned with the well-being of the church's society and its members. We are to consider other people's feelings, sensibilities, and beliefs so as not to cause them to stumble or to offend them unnecessarily.

The present exegetical approach has shown that in 1 Cor. 11:17-26 (in chapter six of this thesis) the Lord's Supper is presented as the tradition which Paul received from the Lord. The basic agreement with the Synoptic records is evidence that Paul's claims of dominical continuity are well founded, but it does not prejudice the interpretation of the tradition and the practice of the rite. Furthermore, Paul considered the behavior of the Corinthians in the Lord's Supper as a disorderly act that led to its being mentioned in his letter. The problem in the church arose from social and theological disagreement within the congregation.

Obviously, as it has been discussed, the real problem was the fact that some Christians at Roman Corinth had difficulty with the issue of how they should live in a Christian society and at the same time deal with former pagan customs and invitations. Several points may be made in support of the above contention: (1) Paul compares the Lord's Supper with pagan sacral meals with regard to their mutual implications for the partakers (1 Cor. 10:14-22). The force of the analogy is based on the actual similarities between the Lord's Supper and other socio-religious meals. It may be possible that some Corinthian Christians understood the Lord's meal in terms of the same conceptual framework from their own perspective. (2) The main reason for which the Christians assembled was to have dinner together (1 Cor. 11:33: ὥστε. . . συνερχόμενοι εἰς τὸ φαγεῖν. Although Paul thinks that members ought to satisfy their appetites at home (1 Cor. 11:22, 30), this does not mean the sacred meals were not real meals.

The important meaning of the sacred meal is emphasized in 1 Cor. 11:20-21, where Paul stresses the point that when the Christians get together, it is not the Lord's Supper that they eat, it is their own δεῖπνον. The apostle is offended by the behavior (disorderly manners) and decorum which marked the Lord's Supper of the Christian community. These were common problems of *symposia, convivia* or *eranos* dinner parties. The disorder at Roman Corinth seems fairly common to the real nature of such occasions. (3) Paul's main concern in 1 Cor. 10-14 is the necessity of a better behavior and decorum in the Christian gatherings. Paul, like Plutarch, is concerned that these gatherings exhibit such qualities as moderation, real Christian fellowship, order and decorum. (4) Paul's comments that some are drunk seem to be a note of realism, normal of Greco-Roman *symposia* or *eranos* dinners. (5) We have also observed that the δεῖπνον is clearly set at the beginning, and. . . . concludes (μετὰ τὸ δεῖπνον, 1 Cor. 11:25) with a ceremony involving wine. This was also a common pattern in the Greco-Roman *symposia* or *eranos* dinner parties.

It could be debated whether in 1 Cor. 11:23 Paul interprets the tradition he handed down to the Corinthians as a direct revelation from the Lord. When Paul says that he gets it "from the Lord," he is not claiming special divine revelation given to him. We believe that Paul is alluding to a tradition that was prevailing in the early church. He had heard about it before coming to the Corinthians. Where did Paul hear about this tradition? The argument is that there are three possible places: Antioch, Damascus, or Jerusalem. It has been argued that the churches at Antioch and Damascus were founded by Christians from Jerusalem; therefore, Jerusalem was the place where Paul heard about the tradition; this is debatable.

Furthermore, it is highly probable that Damascus (although it was founded by Christians from the Jerusalem Church) was the place where the converted Saul (Paul) was received into the Christian community. Since he was baptized there, it is also possible that he first came to know about the Eucharistic meal of the Christian church there. Thus, in tracing Paul's formula about the Last Supper back to the Primitive Church, one can develop a sense of assurance in the historical value of Paul's Lord's Supper account.

In contrast, the cult banquet was precisely that. The food had been offered to the god. The believer's Supper, on the other hand, celebrates a sacrifice, or more precisely, a death. It is eaten in memory of Jesus' death and in gratitude for its benefits. Paul never uses the word sacrifice (θυσία) to refer to the Supper. It is not eaten in a shrine or a temple before an image, but in a meeting, an ἐκκλησία. It is not eaten by worshippers participating in a cult, but by believers getting together in one another's homes. Therefore, whenever the believers met together as a community and participated in eating and drinking the bread and wine, the Christians proclaimed the death and resurrection of Jesus and looked forward to the Messianic feast.

Paul's emphasis on eschatology is clear, and the eschatological nature is not removed from the Lord's Supper. In an unmistakably theological argument, Paul, after learning that some church members at Roman Corinth were denying the resurrection as he had taught it to them, deals with the resurrection topic in a very lengthy manner. He reviews the message of the Gospel tradition and shows the Corinthians how necessary the resurrection is to that preaching tradition. He also is reminding them of what they should never have forgotten. "For what I received I passed on to you as of first importance: that Christ died for our sins according to the Scriptures, that he was buried, that he was raised on the third day according to the Scriptures, and that he appeared to Peter, and then to the Twelve" (1 Cor. 15:3-5). So, what was in question was not Christ's resurrection, but the resurrection of the believers. Paul's message to the Corinthians is that "Christ has indeed been raised from the dead, the first fruits of those who have fallen asleep" (1 Cor. 15:20f).

Nevertheless, it was in the Church at Roman Corinth that the dilemma of the state of the dead evidently most forcibly appeared as one of the main issues, and the manner in which the apostle dealt with it there shows his theological view on the resurrection. Paul's emphasis is on the one present, the exalted Lord, who is the one to come. When the believers partake of the Lord's Supper, they look backward to the crucifixion and forward to the return. But at the Parousia of the Lord, the Lord's Supper will come to an end, for the celebration of the absent Lord ceases when the absent Lord comes back.

It should be recognized that Paul takes the early church's idea of the Lord's Supper as an expectation of the table-fellowship with the Lord at the Messianic banquet, and from this conception Paul explains the word of Jesus at the meal about eating and drinking his body and blood. Moreover, Paul speaks of the table (τράπεζα) of the Lord and the table (τράπεζα) of demons. Though the idea of table was an accepted designation for the sacrificial altar, there is a logical sense in which the Supper of the Lord is a sacrificial meal, a memorial of the Lord's sacrificial death.

It may be concluded in this study that, the analysis of the social conflict in 1 Corinthians should not be restricted to a single method of study. The new insights gained from the sociological approach ought to be welcomed with enthusiasm. Nevertheless, the idea that all the issues are socially represented is another way of oversimplification, identical to the earlier theological way of oversimplification of the problem.

As it has been suggested, the conflict at the Lord's Supper in the Corinthian Church is primarily the problem of some of the members' difficulty in adapting themselves to their new social and religious community. They behaved as any normal citizen of the society of the Greco-Roman World. The socio-economic and cultural issues are involved in the conflict, but the dilemma of the meat offered to the idols in the pagan temple is religious, and the issue in regard to the resurrection of the dead is essentially theological.

Bibliography

Aesop. *Life of Aesop.* 51.
Ammianus Marcellinus. 23. 4. 34.
Apuleius. *Metamorphoses.* 11.
Athenaeus. 4.149c.
Betz, Dieter Hans. *Plutarch's Ethical Writings and Early Christian Literature.* Leiden: E. J. Brill, 1978.
Clement, *Protr.* ii. 16.18.
Cicero. *Ad Familiares.* 9.26.1.
Didache 10: 6.
Eusebius, *Historia ecclesiastica.* 5, 21, 1.
Homer. *Odyssey.* 1.226-227.
Ignatius. *Letter to the Smyrnaeans.* 8: 2; 7: 3.
Isidorus. *Orig.* XX 2.12.
Josephus. *Antiquities.* XV, 10. 4. 371; XVII, 13. 3. 346; B. J. i. 3. 5. 78.
Juvenal. *Satires.*15.40.
Lucian. *Symposium.* 5.
Martial. *Epigrammata.* 11.52, 10. 48.
Martyr, Justin. *Trypho.* 34.
Pausanias. 7. 27. 3.
Petronius. *Satyricon.* 67-69.
Philo. *De Vita Contemplativa.* Vol. IX. Translated by F. H. Colson. Loeb Classical Library. London: W. Heinemann, 1941.
_____. *Flacc.* 17. 136.
Plato. *Symposium.* 174 A.
Pliny. *Letter to Trajan.* 10.96.10.
Plutarch. *Is. et Os.* 364E.
_____. *Quaest. conv.* 616 E-F.
_____. *Table Talk.* 717B.
_____. *Symposium.* 174c.
Seneca. *Ep.* 82.
Tertullian. *Praescr. Haer.* 40.
Xenophon. *Symposium.* 238.

Commentaries in 1 Corinthians

Allo, E. B. *Saint Paul, Première Epître aux Corinthiens.* Paris: J. Gabalda et Cie., 1934.
Barrett, Charles, Kingsley. *The First Epistle to the Corinthians.* New York: Harper & Row, 1968.
Bruce, F. F. *New Century Bible: 1 and 2 Corinthians.* London: Marshall, Morgan & Scott, 1971.

Conzelmann, Hans. *1 Corinthians.* Translated by J. W. Leitch. Philadelphia: Fortress Press, 1975.

Fee, Gordon. *The First Epistle to the Corinthians.* Grand Rapids: Eerdmans, 1987

Héring, J. *The First Epistle of Saint Paul to the Corinthians.* Translated by A. W. Heathcote and P. J. Allcock. London: Epworth, 1962.

Lietzmann, Hans. *An die Korinther.* Enlarged and revised edition by W. G. Kümmel. Tübingen: J. C. B. Mohr (Paul Siebeck), 1949.

Mayer, H. A. W. *Critical and Exegetical Handbook to the Epistles to the Corinthians.* Translated by W. P. Dickson. New York: Funk and Wagnalls, 1 1890.

Murphy-O'Connor, *1 Corinthians.* Wilmington: Michael Glazier, 1979.

Orr, W. F. and J. A. Walther, *1 Corinthians.* Garden City, NY: Doubleday & Co., 1976.

Plummer, Alfred. *A Critical and Exegetical Commentary on the First Epistle of St.Paul to the Corinthians.* Edinburgh: T. & T. Clark, 1958.

Robertson, A. and A. Plummer, *A Critical and Exegetical Commentary on the First Epistle of St. Paul to the Corinthians.* Edinburgh: T. & T. Clark, 1911.

Watson, Nigel. *The First Epistle to the Corinthians.* London: Epworth Press, 1992.

Wendland, H. D. *Die Briefe an die Korinther.* Göttingen: Vandenhoeck & Ruprecht, 1962.

Modern Authors and Others Works

Aalen, S. "Das Abendmahl als Opfermahl im Neuen Testament." *Novum Testamentum* 6 (1963): 128-152.

Alexander, Loveday. "Luke's Preface in the Context of Greek Preface-Writing."*Novum Testamentum* 18 (1986): 48-74.

Alföldy, G. *Römische Sozialgeschichte.* Wiesbaden: Franz Steiner, 1975.

Aune, D. E. "Septem Sapientium Convivium," ed. Hans D. Betz. *SCHNT* 4 Leiden: E. J. Brill, 1978.

Avigad, N. and Y. Yadin. *A Genesis Apocryphon: A Scroll from the Wilderness of Judaea.* Jerusalem: Magnes, 1956.

Bahr, Gordon J. "The Seder of Passover and the Eucharistic Words." *Novum Testamentum* 12 (1970): 180-202.

Baird, William. "One Against the Other": Intra-Church Conflict in 1 Corinthians." in *The Conversation Continues: Studies in Paul and John* eds., R. T. Fortna and B. R. Gaventa. Nashville: Abingdon Press, 1990.

Balsdon, D. V. P. J. *Life and Leisure in Ancient Rome.* New York: Mcgraw-Hill, 1969.

Barclay, W. *The Lord's Supper.* London: SCM Press, 1967.

Barrett, Charles K. *Essays on Paul.* London: S.P.C.K., 1982.

_____. "Things Sacrificed to Idols." *New Testament Studies* 11 (1965): 138-153.

Bartels, K. H. and C. Brown, *NIDNTT* 3 (1971): 230-247.

Barton, Stephen C. "Paul's Sense of Place: An Anthropological Approach to Community Formation in Corinth." *New Testament Studies* 32 (1986): 225-246.

Barth, Markus. *Rediscovering the Lord's Supper*. Atlanta: John Knox Press, 1988.

Becker, A. W. *Charicles: Illustrating of the Private Life of the Ancient Greeks*. 8th ed. London: Longman Press, 1889.

Behm, J. *TDNT*. 10 vols. Grand Rapids: Eerdmans, 1965.

Benoit, Pierre. *Jesus and the Gospel*. 2 vols. Translated by B. Weatherhead. London: Darton, Longman & Todd, 1973.

Black, D. A. "A Note on the 'Weak' in 1 Corinthians 9:22."*Biblica* 64 (1983): 240-42.

Black, M. *The Scrolls and Christian Origins*. London: Thomas Nelson and Sons, 1961.

_____. "The Christological Use of the Old Testament in the New Testament." *New Testament Studies* 18 (1971-2): 9-15.

_____. *Apocalypsis Henochi Graece*. Leiden: E.J. Brill, 1970.

Blümmer, H. *The Home Life of the Ancient Greeks*. New York: Harper & Row, 1966.

Borchert, L. Gerald. "The Resurrection: 1 Corinthians 15." *Review and Expositor* 80(1983): 400-416.

Bornkamm, Günther. *Early Christian Experience*. Translated by P. L. Hammer. London: SCM Press, 1969.

_____. "On the Understanding of Worship." *Early Christian Experience*. New York: Harper & Row, 1969.

_____. *Paul*. New York: Harper & Row, 1971.

Bousset, W. *Kyrios Christos*. Göttingen: Vandenhoeck & Ruprecht, 1921.

Box, G. H. "The Jewish Antecedents of the Eucharist." *Journal of Theological Studies* 3 (1901-2): 357-369.

Broneer, Oscar. "Corinth: Center of St. Paul's Missionary Work." *Biblical Archaeologist* 14 (1951): 78-96.

_____. "Paul and the Pagan Cults at Isthmia." *Harvard Theological Review* 64 (1971): 169-187.

Bruce, F. F. "Jesus Is Lord." in *Soli Deo Gloria: New Testament Studies*. Richmond: John Knox Press, 1968.

_____. *Paul: Apostle of the Heart Set Free*. Grand Rapids: Eerdmans, 1986.

_____. *Paul and Jesus*. Grand Rapids: Baker Book House, 1974.

_____. *The Pauline Circle*. Grand Rapids: Eerdmans, 1985.

Brunt, J. C. "Rejected, Ignored or Misunderstood? The Fate of Paul's Approach to the Problem of Food Offered to Idols in Early Christianity." *New Testament Studies* 31 (1985): 113-124.

Bultmann, R. *The History of the Synoptic Tradition.* New York: Scribner & Sons, 1969.

_____. *Theology of the New Testament.* Translated by K. Grobel. 2 vols. London: SCM Press, 1952.

Burkitt, F. C. "The Last Supper and the Paschal Meal." *Journal of TheologicalStudies* 17 (1916-17): 291-297.

Cadbury, H. J. "The Macellum in Corinth." *Journal of Biblical Literature* 53 (1934): 134-141.

_____. "Erastus of Corinth." *Journal of Biblical Literature* 50 (1931): 42-58.

Campbell, R. A. "Does Paul Acquiesce in Divisions at the Lord's Supper?" *New Testament Studies* 33 (1991): 61-70.

Casey, P. M. "The Original Aramaic Form of Jesus' Interpretation of the Cup." *Journal of Theological Studies* 41 (1990): 1-12.

Chapple, A. "Local Leadership in the Pauline Churches: Theological and Social Factors in Its Development." Ph.D. diss., Durham University, 1984.

Charlesworth, J. H., ed. *The Old Testament Pseudepigrapha.* London: Darton, Longman & Todd, 1985.

_____. *The Pseudepigrapha and Modern Research with a Supplement.* Chico: Scholars Press, 1981.

Cheung, Alex T. Idol Food in Corinth: Jewish Background and Pauline Legacy. Sheffield: Sheffield Academic Press, 1999.

Christophersen, Alf, C. Claussen, Jörg Frey. *Paul, Luke and the Graeco-Roman World.* Sheffield Academic Press, 2002.

Chow, J. K. *Patronage and Power.* Sheffield: Sheffield Academic Press, 1992.

Carcopino, Jerome. *Daily Life in Ancient Rome.* New Haven: Yale University, 1940.

Clark, Gillian. "The Social Status of Paul." *Expository Times* 96 (1984-85): 110-111.

Clarke, A. D. *Secular and Christian Leadership in Corinth: A Socio-Historical and Exegetical Study of 1 Corinthians 1-6.* Leiden: J. D. Brill, 1993.

_____. *Serve the Community of the Church: Christian as Leader and Ministers.* Grand Rapids: Eerdmans, 2000.

Cerfaux, L. *The Church in the Theology of Paul.* Translated by G.Webb and A. Walker. New York: Herder and Herder, 1959.

Conzelmann, H. *Acts of the Apostles.* Translated by J. Limburg et al. Philadelphia: Fortress Press, 1987.

Corley, Kathleen E. *Private Women Public Meals.* Peabody: Hendrickson, 1993

Coutsoumpos, P. "The Social Implication of Idolatry in Revelation 2:14: Christ or Caesar? *Biblical Theology Bulletin* 23 (1997): 23-27.

Cullmann, O. *Early Christian Worship.* Translated by A. S. Todd and J. B. Torrance. London: SCM Press, 1952.

_____. *The Christology of The New Testament.* Translated by S.C. Guthrie and C. A. M. Hall. Philadelphia: The Westminster Press, 1963.

_____. "Kyrios as Designation for the Oral Tradition Concerning Jesus." *Scottish Journal of Theology* 3 (1950): 180-197.

Dawes, Gregory. W. "The Danger of Idolatry: First Corinthians 8: 7-13." *Catholic Biblical Quaterly 58 (1996): 82-98.*

De Jonge, Marinus.*Christology in Context.* Philadelphia: The Westminster Press, 1988. .

Deissmann, A. *Light from the Ancient East.* London: Hodder & Stoughton, 1927.

Delcor, M. "Repas cultuels esséniens et thérapeutes. Thiases et Haburoth." *Revue de Qumran* 23 (1968): 401-425.

Delling, D. Gerhard. *Worship in the New Testament.* Translated by P. Scott. London: Darton, Longman & Todd, 1962.

Dentzer, Marie-Jean. "Aux origines de l'iconographie du banquet couché." *Revue d'assyriologie et d'archéologie orientale* (1971): 215-258.

Dupont, Jacques. *Gnosis: La Connaissance Religieuse dans les Epîtres de S. Paul.* Louvain: Nauwelarts, 1960.

Dunn, J. D. G. "The Lord's Supper," in Dunn, *The Theology of Paul and the Apostle.* Grand Rapids: Eerdmans, 1998.

Ehrhardt, Arnold. *The Framework of the New Testament Stories.* Manchester: University Press, 1964.

Ellis, E. Earle. *Pauline Theology: Ministry and Society.* Grand Rapids: Eerdmans, 1989.

_____. "Christ Crucified." in *Reconciliation and Hope.* Ed. Robert Banks.
Exeter: The Paternoster Press, 1974.

Engberg-Pedersen, Troels. "Proclaiming the Lord's Death: 1 Corinthians 11: 17-34 and the Forms of Paul's Theological Argument." *Pauline Theology,* vol 2. Minneapolis: Fortress Press, 1993, 103-132.

Esler, P. F. *The First Christians in Their Social Worlds: Social-Scientific* Approaches to New Testament Interpretation. London: Routledge , 1994.

Fee, Gordon D. "Εἰδωλόθυτα Once Again: An Interpretation of 1 Corinthians 8-10." *Biblica* 61 (1980): 172-197.

Ferguson, E. *Backgrounds of Early Christianity.* Grand Rapids: Eerdmans, 1987.

Filson, Floyd V. "The Significance of the Early House Churches." *Journal of Biblical Literature* 39 (1939): 4-15.

Fisk, Bruce N. "Eating Meat Offered to Idols: Corinthian Behavior and Pauline Response in 1 Corinthians 8-10." *Trinity Journal* 10 (1989): 49-70.

_____. *First Corinthians.* Interpretation Bible Studies. Louisville: Westminster/John Knox, 2000.

Fitzmyer, Joseph A. *A Wandering Aramean.* Missoula: Scholars Press, 1979.

Fotopoulos, John. *Food Offered to Idols in Roman Corinth.* Tübingen: J.C. B. Mohr (Paul Siebeck), 2003.

Fuller, R. H. "The Double Origin of the Eucharist." *Biblical Research* 8 (1963): 60-72.

Furnish, Victor, P. *The Theology of the First Letter to the Corinthians.* Cambridge: University Press, 1999.

_____. *The Moral Teaching of Paul.* 2d edition. Nashville: Abingdon Press, 1985.

Gager, John G. "Shall We Marry Our Enemies? Sociology and the New Testament." *Interpretation* 36 (1982): 256-265.

Garland, David. *1 Corinthians.* Grand Rapids: Baker Academic, 2003.

Garlatti, J. Guillermo. "La Eucaristía como Memoría y Proclamación de la Muerte del Señor." *Revista Biblica* 47 (1985): 1-25.

Garnsey, P. *Non-slave Labour in the Roman world, Non-Slave Labour in the Greco-Roman World.* CPS Supp. 6; CUP, 1980.

Gaventa R. Beverly. "You Proclaim the Lord's Death: 1 Corinthians 11:26: Social Description and Sociological Explanation." *Religious Studies Review* 5 (1979): 10-15.

Goppelt, L.*Theology of the New Testament.* Translated by J. E. Alsup. 2 vols. Grand Rapids: Eerdmans, 1981.

Gooch, Peter W. *Dangerous Food: 1 Corinthians 8-10 in Its Context* Ontario: Wilfred Laurier University Press, 1993.

_____. "Conscience in 1 Corinthians 8 and 10." *New Testament Studies* 33 (1987): 244-254.

Goulder, Michael E. *Paul and the Competing Mission in Corinth,* Peabody: Hendrickson, 2001.

_____. "Σοφία in Corinthians." *New Testament Studies* 37 (1991): 516-34.

Grant, Robert M. *Early Christianity and Society.* London: W. Collins, 1978.

_____. *Paul in the Roman World: The Conflict at Corinth.* Louisville: Westminster John Knox Press, 2001.

_____. *Gods and the One God.* Philadelphia: Westminster Press, 1986.

Gundry, Robert H. *Soma in Biblical Theology.* Cambridge: University Press, 1976. Exploration Fund, 1898-1916.

Harrington, Daniel. J. "Sociological Concepts and the Early Church: A Decade of Research." *Theological Studies* 41 (1980): 181-190.

Hengel, Martin. *Property and Riches in the Early Church.* Translated by J. Bowden. London: SCM Press, 1977.

_____. *The Son of God.* Translated by J. Bowden. London: SCM Press, 1976.

Higgins, A. J. B. *The Lord's Supper in the New Testament.* London: SCM Press, 1964.

Hill, C. S. "The Sociology of the New Testament Church to A.D. 62: An Examination of the Early New Testament Church in Relation to Its Contemporary Social Setting." Unpublished Ph.D. Thesis: Nottingham University, 1972.

Hock, Ronald F. "Paul's Tent-Making and the Problem of His Social Class." *Journal of Biblical Literature* 97 (1978): 555-564.

_____. *The Social Context of Paul's Ministry*. Philadelphia: Fortress Press, 1980.

Hofius, O. "Το σωμα το υπερ υμών1 Kor 11:24," *Zeitschrift für die neutestamentliche Wissenschaft* 80 (1989): 80-88.

Holmberg, Bengt. *Sociology and the New Testament*. Minneapolis: Fortress Press, 1990.

Horsley, Richard A. "Consciousness and Freedom Among the Corinthians: 1 Corinthians 8-10." *Catholic Biblical Quarterly* 40 (1978): 574-589.

_____."Gnosis in Corinth: 1 Corinthians 8: 1-6." *New Testament Studies* 27 (1981): 32-51.

_____. *Sociology and the Jesus Movement*. New York: Crossroad, 1989.

Horrell, D. G. *The Social Ethos of the Corinthian Correspondence*. Edinburg: T. & T. Clark, 1996.

_____. "The Lord's Supper at Corinth and in the Church Today." *Theology* 98 (1995): 196-202.

_____, and Edward Adams. *Christianity at Corinth: The Quest for the Pauline Church*. Louisville: Westminster John Knox Press, 2004.

Hunter, A. M. *Paul and His Predecessors*. London: SCM Press, 1961.

_____. *The Message of the New Testament*. Philadelphia: The Westminster Press, 1945.

Hurd, J. C., Jr. *The Origins of 1 Corinthians*. London: S.P.C.K., 1965.

Jaubert, A. *La date de la Cène. Calendrier biblique el liturgie chrétienne* (EtB), Paris, 1957.

Jeremias, Joachim. *Jerusalem in the Time of Jesus*. Philadelphia: Fortress Press, 1969.

_____. *The Eucharistic Words of Jesus* . Translated by Norman Perrin. London: SCM Press, 1966.

_____. "The Last Supper." *Expository Times*. (1952-3): 91-92.

_____. "Zur Gedankenführung in den Paulinischen Briefen." *Studia Paulina in Honorem J. de Zwaan*, ed. J.N. Sevenster and W. C. van Unnik. Netherlands: Haarlam, 1933.

_____. "This Is My Body," *Expository Times* 83 (1972): 196-203.

Jewett, Robert. *Paul's Anthropological Terms*. Leiden: E. J. Brill, 1971.

Jones, D. "αναμνησις" in the LXX and the Interpretation of 1 Corinthians 11:25." *Journal of Theological Studies* 6 (1955): 183-191.

Judge, E. A. "Early Christians as a Scholastic Community." *Journal of Religious History* 1 (1960-61): 4-15.

_____. *The Social Pattern of the Christian Group in the First Century.* London: The Tyndale Press, 1960.

Käsemann, Ernst. *Essays on New Testament Themes.* Translated by W. J. Montague. Philadelphia: Fortress Press, 1982.

Kee, Howard C. *Christian Origins in Sociological Perspective.* London: SCM Press, 1980.

Kilpatrick, G. D. "The Last Supper." *Expository Times.* 64 (1952-3): 4-8.

Kim, Seyoon. *The Origin of Paul's Gospel.* Grand Rapids: Eerdmans, 1981.

Kircher, Karl. *Die sacrale Bedeutung des Weines.* RVV 9.2 Giessen: A. Töpelmann, 1910.

Klappert, B. "Lord's Supper." *NIDNTT.* 3 vols. Grand Rapids: Zondervan, 1980.

Klauck, Hans-Josef. *Herrenmahl und Hellenistischer Kult.* Münster: Aschendorff Verlagsbuchhandlung Gmb H & Co., 1986.

_____. "Eucharist and Church Community in Paul," *Theology Digest* 35 (1988): 19-24.

Koester, Helmut. *History, Culture and Religion of the Hellenistic Age.* Philadelphia: Fortress Press, 1982.

Kramer, Werner. *Christ, Lord, Son of God.* Translated by B. Hardy. London: SCM Press, 1966.

Kreissig, Heinz. "Zur sozialem Zusammensetzung der frühchristlichen Gemeinden im ersten Jahrhundert u. Z.' *Eirene. Studia Graeca et Latina* 6 (1967).

Kugelman, R. "The First Letter to the Corinthians." *The Jerome Biblical Commentary.* Englewood Cliffs, 1968.

Kuhn, Karl G. *The Lord's Supper and the Communal Meal at Qumran.* Edited by Krister Stendahl. London: SCM Press, 1952.

_____. "Μαρανα θα," *TDNT* 4 (1967): 466-472.

Kümmel, W. G. "Das Urchristentum." *TRu* 50 (1985): 132-164.

Lake, K. *The Earlier Epistles of St. Paul: Their Motive and Origin.* London: Rivington, 1927.

Lampe, Peter, "The Corinthian Eucharistic Dinner Party: Exegesis of a Cultural Context (1 Corinthians 11:17-34)." *Affirmation* 4 (1991): 1-13.

_____. "The Eucharist: Identifying with Christ on the Cross." *Interpretation* 48(1994): 36-49.

Leenhardt, F. J. *Le Sacrement de la Sainte Cène.* Neuchâtel-Paris, 1948.

Léon-Dufour, Xavier. *Sharing the Eucharistic Bread.* Translated by M. J. O'Connell. New York: Paulist Press, 1987.

_____. *Mass and Lord's Supper.* Translated by D. H. G. Reeves. Leiden: E. J. Brill, 1979.

Lohmeyer, E. "Das Abendmahl in der Urgemeinde." *Journal of Biblical Literature* 56 (1937): 217-252.

_____. "Von urchristlichen Abendmahl." *Theologische Rundschau* 9 (1937): 168-227.

Lohse, Eduard. *The New Testament Environment.* Translated by J. Bowden. London: SCM Press, 1976.

MacMullen, R. *Roman Social Relations.* New Haven: Yale University Press, 1974.

Maccoby, H. "Paul and Eucharist." *New Testament Studies* 37 (1991): 247-267.

Malherbe, Abraham J. *Social Aspects of Early Christianity.* Philadelphia: Fortress Press, 1983.

_____. *Paul and the Popular Philosophers.* Minneapolis: Fortress Press, 1989.

Manson, T. W. "The Corinthian Correspondence." *Studies in the Gospels and Epistles.* Edited by Matthew Black. Manchester: Manchester University Press, 1962.

Marshall, I. Howard. *Last Supper and Lord's Supper.* Exeter: The Paternoster Press, 1980.

_____. "Lord's Supper in *Dictionary of Paul and His Letters* eds., R. P. Martin,

G. Hawthorne and D. Reid Downers Grove: InterVarsity Press, 1993.

_____. *The Gospel of Luke.* Exeter: The Paternoster Press, 1977.

Martin, D. B. *The Corinthian Body.* New Haven: Yale University Press, 1995.

Martin, Ralph P. *Eucharistic Teaching in St. Paul's First Letter to the Corinthians.* Unpublished M.A. Thesis, University of Manchester, 1956.

_____. "Communion." in *The Illustrated Bible Dictionary.* Ed.-at-large J. N. Douglas. Wheaton: Tyndale House Publishers, 1980, 307-388.

_____. "Meats Offered to Idols." *The New Bible Dictionary.* London: Inter-Varsity Press, 1972.

_____. *New Testament Foundations.* 2 vols. Exeter: The Paternoster Press, 1978.

_____. *The Spirit and the Congregation: Studies in 1 Corrinthians 12-15.* Grand Rapids: Eerdmans, 1984.

_____. *The Worship of God.* Grand Rapids: Eerdmans, 1982.

_____. *Worship in the Early Church.* Grand Rapids: Eerdmans, 1981.

Marxsen, W. *The Lord's Supper as a Christological Problem.* Translated by A. Achtemeier and L. Nieting. Philadelphia: Fortress Press, 1970.

McDermott, John M. "The Biblical Doctrine of KOINWNIA." *Biblische Zeitschrift* 19 (1975): 219-233.

McKnight, Scot and G. R. Osborne. *The Face of New Testament Studies: A Survey of Recent Research.* Grand Rapids: Baker Academic, 2004.

McDonald, William A. "Archaeology and St. Paul's Journey in Greek Lands, III-Corinth," *Biblical Archeologist* (1942): 39-45.

Meeks, W. A. *The First Urban Christians.* New Haven: Yale University Press, 1983.

_____. *The Moral World of the First Christians.* London: SCM Press, 1987.

_____. "The Social Context of Pauline Theology.' *Interpretation* 37 (1982):   18-24.

Meggitt, J. J. "Meat Consumption and Social Conflict in Corinth." *Journal of Theological Studies* 45 (1994): 138-140.

_____. *Paul, Poverty, and Survival.* Edinburgh: T & T Clark, 1998.

Meyer, W. A. H. *Critical and Exegetical Handbook to the Epistles to the Corinthians* trans. rev. W.P. Dickson, 5th ed. (New York: Funk and Wagnals, 1890), p.266.

Mitchell, Margaret M. "Concerning ΠΕΡΙ ΔΕ in 1 Corinthians." *Novum Testamentum* 31.3 (1989): 229-256.

_____. *Paul and the Rhetoric of Reconciliation: A Exegetical Investigation of the Language and Compositon of 1 Corinthians.* Louisville: Westminster/John Knox Press, 1991.

Moule, C. F. D. *The Origin of Christology.* Cambridge: University Press, 1977.

Munck, J. *Paul and the Salvation of Mankind.* Translated by F. Clarke. London: SCM Press, 1959.

Murphy-O'Connor, J. "Freedom of the Ghetto." *Revue Biblique* (1978): 543-574.

_____. *St. Paul's Corinth.* Wilmington: Michael Glazier, 1987.

_____. "Food and Spiritual Gifts in 1 Cor. 8:8." *Catholic Biblical Quaterly* 41 (1979): 292-298.

_____. *Paul: A Critical Life.* Oxford: Clarendon Press, 1998.

Neuenzeit, P. *Das Herrenmahl: Studien zur paulinischen Eucharistieauffassung.* München: Kösel-Verlag, 1960.

Newton, D. *Deity and Diet: The Dilemma of Sacrificial Food at Corinth.* Sheffield: Sheffield Academic Press, 1998.

Oropeza, B. J. "Laying to Rest the Midrash: Paul's Message on Meat Sacrificed to Idols in Light of the Deuteronomic Tradition." *Biblica* (1998): 57-68.

Osborne, H. "Συνειδησις." *Journal of Theological Studies* 32 (1931): 167-79.

Panikulam, George. *Koinonia in the New Testament: A Dynamic Expression of Christian Life. An Bib* 85. Roma: Biblical Institute Press, 1979.

Patsch, H. *Abendmahl und historischer Jesus.* Stuttgart, 1972.

Passakos, D. C. "Eucharist in First Corinthians: A Sociological Study." *Revue biblique* 192 (1997): 192-210.

Pesch, R. *Das Abendmahl und Jesu Todesverständnis.* Freiburg, 1978.

Pétrement, Simone. *A Separate God: The Christian Origins of Gnosticism.* Translated by Carol Harrison. San Francisco: Harper & Row, 1984.

_____. "Le Colloque de Messine et le problème du gnosticisme." *Revue de Métaphysique et de Morale* 72 (1967): 350-371.

Petuchowski, J. J. "Do This in Remembrance of Me 1 Corinthians 11:24." *Journal Biblical Literature* 76 (1957): 293-298.

Pickett, R. *The Cross in Corinth: The Social Significance of the Death of Jesus.* Sheffield: Sheffield Academic Press, 1997.

Pierce, A. C. *Conscience in the New Testament.* Chicago: Alec R. Allenson, 1955.

Pogoloff, M. Stephen. *Logos and Sophia: The Rhetorical Situation of 1 Corinthians.* Atlanta: Scholars Press, 1992.

Polhill, J. B. "The Wisdom of God and Factionalism: 1 Corinthians 1-4." *Review and Expositor* 80 (1983): 325-339.

Pope, M. H. *Song of Songs.* AB. Garden City: Doubleday, 1977.

Ramsaran, A. Rollin. *Paul's Use of Liberating Rhetorical Maxims in Words 1 Corinthians 1-10.* Valley Forge: Trinity Press International, 1996.

Ramsay, W. *St. Paul the Traveller and Roman Citizen.* New York: Putnam's Sons,1896.

Rawlinson, J. E. A. *The New Testament Doctrine of the Christ.* London: S.P.C.K., 1926.

Rice, David G., and Stambaugh, J. E. *Sources for the Study of Greek Religion.* Chico: Scholars Press, 1979.

Richardson, P. and P. W. Gooch. "Accommodation Ethics." *Tyndale Bulletin* 29 (1978): 89-142.

_____. *Paul's Ethic of Freedom.* Philadelphia: Westminster Press, 1979.

Roebuck, Carl. *Corinth XIV: The Asklepieion and Lerna.* Princeton: The American School of Classical Studies at Athens, 1951.

Robinson, John, A.T. *The Body: A Study in Pauline Theology.* Indiana: Wyndham Hall Press, 1988.

Rosner, Brian. "No Other Gods: The Jealousy of God and Religious Pluralism." eds., B. W. Winter, and A. D. Clarke. *One God, One Lord: Christianity in a World of Religious Pluralism.* Grand Rapids: Baker, 1992.

Sawyer, W. T. "The Problem of Meat Sacrificed to Idols in the Corinthian Church." Th.D. diss. Souhern Baptist Theological Seminary, 1968.

Segal, A. F. *Paul the Convert: The Apostolate and Apostasy of Saul the Pharisee.* New Haven: Yale University Press, 1990.

Sigal, P. "Another Note to 1 Corinthians 10: 16." *New Testament Studies* 29 (1983):134-39.

Schattenmann, J. "Κοινωνία." *NIDNTT.* 3 vols. Grand Rapids: Zondervan, 1971.

Schmithals, W. *Gnosticism in Corinthians.* Translated by J. E. Steely. Nashville: Abingdon Press, 1971.

Schöllgen, Georg. "Was wissen wir über die Sozialstruktur der paulinischen Gemeinden?" *New Testament Studies* 34 (1988): 71-82.

Schweitzer, Albert. *Paul and His Interpreters.* Translated by W. Montgomery. London: Adam and Charles Black, 1912.

_____. *The Mysticism of Paul the Apostle.*Translated by W. Montgomery. New York: The Seabury Press, 1968.

_____. *The Problem of the Lord's Supper*. Translated by A. J. Mattiel, Jr. Macon: Mercer University Press, 1982.

Schweizer, Eduard. *The Lord's Supper According to the New Testament*. Translated by J. M. Davis. Philadelphia: Fortress Press, 1982.

Scroggs, Robin. "The Sociological Interpretation of the New Testament: The Present State of Research." *New Testament Studies* 26 (1980): 164-179.

Smit, Joop. "1 Cor 8:1-6: A Rhetorical Partitio, A Contribution to the Coherence of 1 Cor 8: 1-11:1." in *The Corinthian Correspondence*. Ed by R. Biering. Leuven: Leuven University Press, 1996.

_____. "About the Idol Offering." In *Rhetoric, Social Contest and Theology of Paul's Discourse in First Corinthians 8: 1-11:1*. Leuven: Peeters, 2000.

_____. "Do not Be Idolaters: Paul's Rhetoric in First Corinthians 10: 1-22." *Novum Testamentum* 39 (1997): 40-53.

Smith, D. E. "Social Obligation in the Context of Communal Meals." Th.D. diss., Harvard University, 1980.

_____. "The Historical Jesus at Table." *SBLP* (1989).

_____. In *Many Tables: The Eucharist in the New Testament and Liturgy Today.*Philadelphia: Trinity Press International, 1990.

_____. "Meal Customs." *ABD* Edited by N. D. Freedman et al. New York: Doubleday, 1992), 4.

_____. "Meals and Morality in Paul and His World." SBLSP (1981). 648.685.

_____. *Symposium to Eucharist: The Banquet in the Early Christian World*. Minneapolis: Fortress Press, 2003.

Sparks, H. F. D. *The Apocryphal Old Testament*. Oxford: Clarendon Press, 1984.

Stambaugh, J. E. and Balch, D. L. *The New Testament in Its Social Environment*. Philadelphia: The Westminster Press, 1986.

_____. "The Functions of Roman Temples." *ANRW* 16.1 (1978).

Stegemann, Wolfgang. "War der Apostel Paulus ein römischer Bürger?" *Zeitschrift für die Neutestamentliche Wissenschaft* 78 (1987): 200-229.

Stein, S. "The Influence of Symposia Literature on the Literary Form of the Pesah Haggadah." *Journal of Jewish Studies* 8 (1957): 13-44..

Still, Coye. "Divisions over Leaders and Food Offered to Idols." *Tyndale Bulletin* 55 (2004): 7-41.

Stowers, Stanley, K. "Social Status, Public Speaking and Private Teaching: The Circumstances of Paul's Preaching Activity." *Novum Testamentum* 24 (1984): 59-82.

_____. "Paul on the Use and Abuse of Reason." *Greeks, Romans, and Christians*. eds., D. L. Balch, E. Ferguson, and W. A. Meeks. Minneapolis: Fortress, 1990.

Strack, H. L. and Billerbeck, P. *Kommentar zum Neuen Testament aus Talmud und Midrasch*. 3 vols. Munich: D. H. Beck, 1924-1932.

Talbert, Charles, H. *Reading Corinthians: A Literary and Theological Commentary on 1 and 2 Corinthians.* New York: Crossroad, 1987.

Taylor, V. *The Gospel According to St. Mark.* London: SCM Press, 1953.

_____. *Jesus and His Sacrifice.* London: S.P.C.K., 1937.

_____. *The Names of Jesus.* New York: St. Martin's Press, 1953.

Theissen, Gerd. "Die Tempelweissagung Jesu: Prophetie im Spannungsfeld von Stadt und Land." *Theologische Zeitschrift* 32 (1976): 144-158.

_____. *Sociology of Early Palestinian Christianity.* Translated by J. Bowden. Philadelphia Fortress Press, 1978.

_____. *The Social Setting of Pauline Christianity.* Translated by J. H. Schütz. Edinburgh: T. & T. Clark, 1982.

_____. *Psychology Aspects of Pauline Theology.* Edinburgh: T & T Clark, 1987.

Thiselton, Anthony. C. *The First Epistle to the Corinthians.* Grand Rapids: Eerdmans, 2000.

_____. "Realiazed Eschatology at Corinth," *New Testament Studies* 24 (1978): 510-526.

Thrall, Margaret. "Pauline Use of Syneidesis." *New Testament Studies* 14 (1967) 118-125.

Tidball, Derek. *An Introduction to the Sociology of the New Testament.* Exeter: The Paternoster Press, 1983.

Thiselton, C. Anthony. "Realized Eschatology at Corinth." *New Testament Studies* 24 (1978): 500-519.

Tomson, J. Peter. *Paul and the Jewish Law.* Minneapolis: Fortress Press, 1990.

Troeltsch, Ernst. *Die Soziallehren der Christlichen Kirchen und Gruppen.* In Gesammelte Schriften I: Tübingen, 1912.

Verner, D. C. *The Household of God.* Chico: Scholars Press, 1983.

Von Soden, Hans. "Sakrament und Ethik bei Paulus." In *Marburger Theologische Studien.* Vol. 1 (1931): 31-40.

Vos de, C. S. *Church and Community Conflicts: The Relationships of the Thessalonian, Corinthian, and Philippian Churches with Their Wider Civic Communities.* Atlanta: Scholars Press, 1999.

Wainwright, Geoffrey. *Eucharist and Eschatology.* London: Epworth Press, 1978.

Watson Duane F. "1 Corinthians 10:23-11:1 in the Light of Greco-Roman Rhetoric: The Role of Rhetorical Questions." *Journal of Biblical Literature* 108 (1989): 301-318.

Wedderburn, A. J. M. *Baptism and Resurrection.* Tübingen: J. C. B. Mohr (Paul Siebeck), 1987.

_____. "The Problem of the Denial of the Resurrection in 1 Corinthians XV." *Novum Testamentum* 23 (1981): 85-98.

Weiss, Johannes. *Der erste Korintherbrief.* 9th ed. *KEK.* Göttingen: Vandenhoeck & Ruprecht, 1910.

Welborn, L. L. *Politics and Rhetoric in the Corinthian Epistles.* Maco: Mercer University Press, 1997.

Willis, W. L. *Idol Meat in Corinth.* Chico: Scholars Press, 1985.

Wilson, Mcl. R. "Gnosis at Corinth." in *Paul and Paulinism* edited by M. D. Hooker and S. G.Wilson. London: S.P.C.K., 1982.

_____. "How Gnostic Were the Corinthians?" *New Testament Studies* 19 (1972-73): 65-74.

Winter, Bruce. W. "Secular and Christian Responses to Corinthian Famines." *TyndaleBulletin* 40 (1989): 86-106.

_____. *After Paul left Corinth: The Influence of Secular Ethics and Social Change.* Grand Rapids: Eerdmans, 2001.

_____. "Acts and Roman Religion: The Imperial Cult." In *The Book of Acts in Its First Century Setting.* edited by D. W. J. Gill and Corand Gempf. Grand Rapids:Eerdmans, 1994.

_____. *Seek the Welfare of the City: Christians as Benefactors and Citizens.* Grand Rapids: Eerdmans, 1984.

_____. "The Achaean Federal Imperial Cult II: The Corinthian Church." *Tyndale Bulletin* 46.1 (1995): 169-178.

Witherington, Ben. *Conflict & Community in Corinth: A Socio-RhetoricalCommentary on 1 and 2 Corinthians.* Grand Rapids: Eerdmans, 1995.

_____."Not So Idle Thoughts about Eidolothuton." *Tyndale Bulletin* 44 (1993): 237-254.

Wuellner, W. H. "The Sociological Implications of 1 Corinthians 1:26-28 Reconsidered." *Studia Evangelica* 43 (1973): 1-26.

Yeo, Khiok-Khng. *Rhetorical Interaction in 1 Corinthians 8 and 10: A Formal Analysis with Preliminary Suggestions for a Chinese Cross Cultural, Hermeneutic.* Leiden: E. J. Brill, 1995.

Zerwick, Max. *A Grammatical Analysis of the Greek New Testament.* 2 vols. Translated by M. Grosvenor. Rome: Biblical Institute Press, 1979.

Index of Subjects and Authors

F

Familia Caesaris, 47
Fee, Gordon, D., 6, 7, 14, 15, 16,
    20, 30, 51, 67, 72, 81, 82, 86-
    88, 90, 91, 95, 96, 98, 99, 100,
    101, 112, 114, 115, 120, 121,
    124, 133, 135, 137-139
Fellowship meals (see table
    fellowship), 13, 15, 51, 53, 66,
    77, 79, 81, 82, 106, 114, 115,
    123, 136
Ferguson, E., 70, 93,
Ferguson, W. S. 26
Freedmen, 39,
Filson, F. V., 36, 47, 59, 61-63, 71,
    72, 73
Fisk, B. N., 91, 93, 98,
Food-basket, 2,
Fotopoulos, J. 5.

G

Gager, J. G., 57, 58, 34, 37, 60, 62,
    63
Gardner, P., 70, 84, 92,
Garlatti, G. J. 128, 141
Gamaliel, 118
Garnsey, P., 111, 114, 134
Gaventa, B. R., 125, 128, 141
Gaius, 53
Grant, R. M., 59, 140
Gentile Christians at Roman
    Corinth (church), 2, 3, 5, 15,
    20, 25, 53, 61, 66, 74, 77, 78,
    88, 90, 91, 92, 107, 108, 109,
    111,
Gentile community, 84
Grant, R. M., 36, 37, 62, 126,

Greco-Roman (clubs, household,
    society, religion and world,
    meal custom), 2, 3, 5, 7, 9, 10,
    11, 12, 14, 15, 20, 23, 31, 34,
    35, 39, 40, 45, 46, 47, 50, 51,
    53, 54, 65, 70, 71, 75, 78, 81,
    89, 105, 107, 123, 129, 132,
    133, 136, 143, 148
Greek belief, influence, philosophy,
    and religion, 10, 40, 70, 126
Greek *eranos,* 3, 15, 25,
Greek Religion, 8
Greek-speaking Jews (language
    and culture), 40, 46, 65, 70,
    117, 118, 120
God-fearers, 45, 61, 70,
Goppelt, L., 84, 96, 97, 99, 100,
    101,
Guenther, H. O., 96
Goulder, Michael, 5
Guthrie, W. K., 17, 18
Gluttony, 1, 3, 15, 17, 48, 73, 145
Gnosis, 51, 66, 75, 76, 80, 81, 90,
    91, 92, 94, 95, 96,
Gnosticism, gnostic (*in status
    nascendi,* Christian), 51-53,
    75, 76, 78, 90 126, 131, 143

H

Haggadistic Addition, 119
Halakah, 84,
Harrington, D. J., 56, 58,
Haustafeln, 47,
Hebrew-speaking Jews (language),
    46, 70
Hellenistic Cults, 78
Hellenistic Custom, 120